Everyday Holiness

Everyday
Holiness

The Jewish Spiritual Path of
Mussar

Alan Morinis

Trumpeter
Boston & London
2007

Trumpeter Books
An imprint of Shambhala Publications, Inc.
Horticultural Hall
300 Massachusetts Avenue
Boston, Massachusetts 02115
www.shambhala.com

Excerpts from "The Sources of My Being" and "If Fear Is Like a Rock," from
Jewish Poets of Spain, copyright © David Goldstein. Reprinted with permission.

Excerpt from "Thanks" by W. S. Merwin from the March 14, 1987 edition of
The Nation. Reprinted with permission.

9 8 7 6 5 4 3 2

Printed in the United States of America

⊗ This edition is printed on acid-free paper that meets the American
National Standards Institute z39.48 Standard.

Distributed in the United States by Random House, Inc., and in Canada by
Random House of Canada Ltd

Interior design and composition: Greta D. Sibley & Associates

Library of Congress Cataloging-in-Publication Data
Morinis, E. Alan.
Everyday holiness: the Jewish spiritual path of mussar / Alan Morinis.—1st ed.
  p.   cm.
ISBN 978-1-59030-368-9 (alk. paper)
1. Spiritual life—Judaism. 2. Jewish ethics. 3. Musar movement. 4. Self-actualization
(Psychology)—Religious aspects—Judaism. I. Title.
BM723.M68 2007
296.7—dc22
2007006503

To my teachers,
Rabbi Yechiel Yitzchok Perr and
Rebbetzin Shoshana Perr:
may they be granted long, healthy,
and productive lives

Contents

Preface

Spiritual truths are not so much learned as recalled. Some ideas that we encounter, even if for the first time, don't strike us as new information but more like memories being reawakened within us. It is as if our hearts innately possess these truths and so we don't need lessons, only reminders of wisdom that we already know. These reminders awaken us, and then we see life more clearly and we know what we must do.

This book will serve its purpose if it awakens you to truths you will feel are already ingrained in your bones. In doing so, it will take its place in a long line of Jewish guides for living a meaningful, well-directed life. That lineage is the Mussar tradition, which offers you centuries of accumulated lessons to help you live your life right and truly, as life is meant to be lived. Even the idea that I am coming only to remind you of what you already know has a history, being part of the introduction to the Mussar classic, *The Path of the Just,* written by Rabbi Moshe Chaim Luzzatto in 1740.

Those who lived in the eighteenth century needed the same reminders as we do today. So much has changed in our world, but not human nature. In ways that really matter, you and I are little different from our ancestors. And so we are very fortunate that they recorded their lessons for living, so we can learn from their experience as we seek to find meaning and direction in our own lives. My intention is that this book will serve you by making available the teachings and wisdom of Mussar that have had such an enormous impact in my own life.

I could never have written this book, nor gotten as much from the Mussar tradition as I have, without the help of some key people. I want to thank my agent, Jim Levine, who knew what I would write about before I did, and supported it all the way; and Eden Steinberg, my editor, whose qualities of soul are exemplary, especially her equanimity and faith—which were indeed tested.

I continue to be blessed with the guidance of my loving and wise primary Mussar teachers who awaken me with every contact, Rabbi Yechiel Yitzchok Perr and Mrs. Shoshana Perr, may they and their family live long and healthy lives.

Though a small group of Mussar teachers meets only once a year at the annual Mussar Kallah, these people have influenced me greatly, becoming beloved colleagues and friends. Among these great souls, I want especially to acknowledge Rabbi Ephraim Becker, Rabbi Micha Berger, Rabbi Eytan Kobre, Rabbi Elyakim Krumbein, Rabbi Zvi Miller, and Rabbi Ira Stone for all they have taught me and for the joy of having others with whom to traverse this road.

Words are too puny to capture the gratitude I feel for the forbearance and generosity shown me by the partners with whom I have shared learning. Mr. Shlomo Jakabovits, Dr. Seymour Boorstein, Rabbi Dovid Davidowitz, Rabbi David Mivasair, Rabbi Charles Feinberg, Rabbi Barry Leff, and Dr. Cheri Forrester have been my partners in the exploration of Mussar and other Jewish texts, often on a weekly basis. They have added so much to my life, and through my life to this book (though all that is faulty here is surely my own).

Interest in Mussar has grown to the extent that it has been necessary and desirable to create an institute to house this work, so that it can be made more widely available in an effective way. I am so grateful to the generous and hardworking members of the board of directors of the Mussar Institute: Jeff Agron, Dr. Sam Axelrad, Rabbi Micha Berger, David Goldis, Rabbi Eytan Kobre, Roger Low, Martha Rans, Carol Robinson, Gary Shaffer, Modya Silver, Dr. Bev Spring, and Suzanne Stier. Dr. Shirah Bell in particular has become a very special colleague, coteacher, sponsor, collaborator, and friend. May the merit of their gifts redound to them.

In the Talmud, Rabbi Yehuda states "I have learned much from my teachers, more from my colleagues, and most of all from my students" (*Makkot* 10a). When *Climbing Jacob's Ladder* was published, I asked Rabbi Perr for his permission to begin to teach and he answered, "Go ahead. You'll learn so much." I have had hundreds of students since then who have taught me so much, just as he said they would, and I express my gratitude to each one.

There are three people who are closer to me than my life itself and whose hearts beat in mine: my wife Bev and daughters Julia and Leora. You are my spirit and my muse, and define all that I know of love.

The final bow goes to the first cause. May HaShem remember us and bless us to live in ways that bring true holiness into our lives and, through us, into our world, as is our purpose.

PART ONE

The Inner World of the Soul

1

Introduction

Life Is a Curriculum

Every one of us is assigned to master something in our lives. You have already been given your assignment and you have already encountered it, though you may not be aware that what faces you is a curriculum, nor that this is the central task of your life. My purpose in this book is to help you wake up to your personal curriculum and to guide your steps toward mastering it.

What I am calling your curriculum shows up most clearly in issues that repeatedly challenge you. I'm talking about the behaviors that dunk you in the same soup, time and time again. You probably can identify one or two of these patterns without much effort, in a string of soured or even broken relationships, in financial dreams that are never realized, in fulfillment that is forever elusive. But despite your experience, you may not have realized that there is a curriculum lying embedded within this personal history. The sooner you become familiar with your curriculum and get on with mastering it, the faster you'll get free of these habitual patterns. Then you will suffer less. Then you will cause less suffering for others. Then you will make the contribution to the world that is your unique and highest potential.

Will this help you to accomplish all your dreams? No, not at all. I'm referring not to dreams but to reality. It is a fact that your life embodies a curriculum. Why? Because life is set up so you will be challenged, and through the experiences you have dealing with the challenges, you will grow as a person. You are likely to find, then, that new dreams have grown up, too.

As for growing, none of us has a choice about that. Life makes us grow. You do have a choice, however, of whether you just let your curriculum play out in any way it will, without preparing yourself through study and

3

with guidance, or whether you will seek to uncover pathways for living and growing that prior generations already marked and illuminated to help you engage with your curriculum and grow in a conscious, directed way. That important choice is in your hands.

Because this book tracks a Jewish spiritual path, it is useful to see that the Torah acknowledges this primary choice that confronts us. In the book of Deuteronomy we are told: "You shall circumcise the foreskin of your heart."[1] That enigmatic image occurs only one other time in the Torah,[2] in the variant: "And the Lord your God will circumcise your heart."[3] I understand *circumcision* here to be a metaphor for spiritual initiation—removing the obstacles to having an open, sensitive, initiated inner life. In the first quote, we are offered the option of initiating ourselves. The second quote tells us that God will do it. The second verse begins with the Hebrew letter *vav,* which can be translated "or." Initiate yourself, or God will initiate you. The Torah gives no third option.

Unguided in how to initiate themselves, too often people go after the wrong things, or, if they get it right, go about it in the wrong way. They stumble after false answers to the questions on their curriculum: "If only I were rich." "Nip and tuck by the plastic surgeon might do it." "Defeat that enemy." "Support that cause." "Join that club." Recourse to those sorts of answers to your inner challenges is equivalent to turning yourself over to God to be wisened up, which unfortunately usually happens through bitter experiences of loss, failure, and brokenness. Those experiences do cause us to grow, with certainty. It seems a pity, though, that entire lives are spent fumbling blindly, in personal suffering and at the cost of an increase of evil— yes, evil—in the world, when each of us has another choice as to how we can grow. The Torah states very clearly that you have the option to take steps to initiate your own heart.

Your Guide to the Way of Mussar

This book introduces a practical way to tackle this universal situation of how to initiate our hearts to better ourselves and the world, drawing on a body of ancient teachings developed just for this purpose. These guidelines, known as Mussar, have been compiled over the past thousand years by great Jewish thinkers and spiritual seekers.

In offering my own lessons in Mussar, I do so as a student of this tradition, not an accomplished master. My journey of seeking is not over, and what I offer here is a description of the path I am walking right now. I write as one student addressing another, sharing the gifts of this tradition just as I have received them.

There are others who know Mussar far better than I do, people who grew up in a world where Mussar was integral, as I did not. Yet that very history turns out to be the chief reason that this project has become my personal task, for I see and appreciate Mussar differently from one to whom it is just a constituent part of their world. Though I open myself to criticisms of all sorts, I am inspired to take the risk by the words of Rabbi Bachya ibn Pakuda, whose classic work of Mussar was published in the year 1070, and who seems to have faced similar doubts to my own:

> I knew many good ideas were rejected because of fear, that dread causes a lot of damage, and I recalled the expression, "Be careful not to be too careful!" I realized that if everyone who ever resolved to do something good or to instruct others in the path of righteousness kept still until he himself could accomplish everything he set out to, that nothing would have been said since the days of the prophets.

I can, however, speak with real authority about the potholes that exist on the road of life, because I have fallen into so many myself. I am committed to sharing the lessons of Mussar because in hindsight I see how I could have avoided the jolting pain of having hit them square on. I am sharing what I have learned in the hope that it will smooth and straighten your way.

I don't want to give the impression that my life has been a disaster. It hasn't. I am healthy and come from a loving and stable family. I was awarded a Rhodes Scholarship that took me to Oxford University, where I got my doctorate, and my dissertation was published by Oxford University Press. Three other books followed. I had no trouble getting a university job, and later on, when I reached for more fruit from the tree of life, I started a film production company that eventually went public, with me as the CEO. My films won awards and I made money. I have been married to the same dear woman for over thirty years, and we have two wonderful and accomplished children. We have a nice house in the nice part of town.

At this point the story usually goes: and then it all fell apart. But that's not how it went for me. Only one thing fell apart, and that was my work life. The collapse of my company was a crisis, but it also turned out to conceal a gift, because that's what brought me to discover Mussar. My company had collapsed because I had acted badly. I was disgusted with myself, and my pained heart was cut open. I felt compelled to change my life, from the inside. That's what sent me searching, and Mussar is what I found.

I have already told the story of my discovery and early steps in the learning of Mussar in my earlier book, *Climbing Jacob's Ladder*. There I describe how I encountered Mussar, and the extraordinary, deep teachers I met in that way: Rabbi Yechiel Yitzchok Perr, of the Yeshiva of Far Rockaway, on Long Island, New York, and his wife, Rebbetzin Shoshana Perr, who continue to be my guides. This book takes that story further, though now the story isn't so much about me as it is about you. I have learned so much that I want to share in the hope that my experience will be of value to you. I especially hope that sharing the many lessons I have learned (some the hard way, some through imbibing Mussar) will spare you from having to stumble through similar experiences yourself. Mussar has helped me and others I know to become better at guiding our own lives. I am convinced it can do that for you, too.

How to Use This Book

This book is meant to provide you with what you need to understand Mussar, to garner its insights and, if you choose, to guide you into a Mussar practice of your own, so you can engage with and master your own personal spiritual curriculum.

Part 1 provides an overview of Mussar as it has evolved in the centuries that the masters of the tradition have been observing and experimenting with it. Part 2 is made up of eighteen chapters, each of which focuses on an inner trait the Mussar masters tell us is important to our lives. (The masters have identified and illuminated many more traits than these eighteen, many of which are listed in the appendix: A Soul-Trait Inventory.)

All the traits examined in part 2 have names you will recognize and think you understand—common names like *humility, generosity,* and *truth.* Unless you are already familiar with the Mussar teachings, however, you will not likely define these terms as the Mussar teachers do. Each of the chapters in this section draws on their observations and profound insights, so that you will come to a new understanding of how each of these inner qualities plays out in your life. Through this learning, you will be guided to identify where to focus your own practice, since each individual's spiritual curriculum is different.

Learning Mussar often starts with the study of a passage of Talmudic thought that, when penetrated deeply and allowed to penetrate you deeply, yields surprise, insight, and enlightenment. I make modified use of this technique, often citing the sages of the Talmud but drawing on other sources of philosophical insight as well. Don't read these explorations passively and intellectually. You're meant to chew on them, argue with them, compare them to other ideas, try them out on your friends. Let them challenge you and stir you up, because that stimulation is itself a basic ingredient of the transformative potential of Mussar. Find something in every chapter to grab onto in order to stimulate new thought and understanding. You will come to know yourself in new and surprising ways, and you will already have started to change.

This brings us to the third section of the book, which provides the guidance, practices, and exercises that will help you take small but sure steps toward bringing the ideals and virtues that have not yet found a place in your life into your heart as your own living truth. Here you will find simple steps to creating a daily and a weekly routine of Mussar practice.

None of the Mussar methods takes much time, but the regular daily routine gives rise to a sharpened sense of awareness of your life and the factors that shape it, and ultimately to transformation in those areas where change is called for. You will come away equipped with new tools that add possibilities to your repertoire of living, that become fixed in your heart as an integral part of who you are. Followed faithfully, Mussar practice can bring about an inner reworking that is deep and lasting. The Mussar masters attest to this. I have seen it in my own life, as well as in the lives of hundreds of other people.

So to use this book well, read it through from beginning to end. Then, when you are ready to put its teachings to work in your own life, you will return to selected sections as this book grows into a handbook of practice and transformation in your life.

2

What Is Mussar?

PERHAPS YOU ALREADY HAVE a good idea of what Mussar is. If you have not yet encountered it, Mussar refers to a spiritual perspective and also to a discipline of transformative practices. It also names a popular movement that developed primarily in Lithuania in the second half of the nineteenth century, under the leadership of Rabbi Yisrael Lipkin Salanter. The word *mussar* itself means "correction" or "instruction"[1] and also serves as the simple modern Hebrew word for "ethics." But Mussar is most accurately described as a way of life. It shines light on the causes of suffering and shows us how to realize our highest spiritual potential, including an everyday experience infused with happiness, trust, and love.

The wellsprings of modern Mussar can be traced back to tenth-century Babylonia, when the sage Sa'adia Ga'on published his *Book of Beliefs and Opinions*. There is a chapter in that book entitled "How a Person Ought to Behave in the World," which set in motion an inquiry into human nature that has been going on in the Jewish world for over a full millennium now. In every succeeding generation right up to the present, insightful, discerning, and compassionate rabbis have been adding their own reflections and prescriptions to the accumulating tradition. Each book they have written builds on the insights of those who came before, as they have tried out and expanded on earlier developments.

Until the nineteenth century, Mussar was solely an introspective practice undertaken by an individual seeker. In the mid-1800s, however, Rabbi Yisrael Salanter perceived that Mussar could be an answer to the diverse social tensions that were tearing at the Jewish community and its members in Europe at that time. The oppression of the Czar, the magnetic attraction of the new social ideologies of communism and socialism, the passionate call of the Zionist movement, the secularizing thrust of the so-called Enlightenment, and the fact that the Chassidic movement had lost some of its earlier spiritual authenticity each contributed to the strain the Jewish community was feeling. Rabbi Salanter's response was to call on people to learn and practice Mussar as a means to strengthen the final and most important bulwark for the defense of spiritual life: the solitary human heart.

Rabbi Salanter himself taught and inspired but did not institutionalize his efforts. That task fell to one of his primary disciples, Rabbi Simcha Zissel Ziv,[2] who founded a yeshiva in the Lithuanian town of Kelm that became the seat of the Kelm stream of Mussar. Two other disciples, Rabbi Noson Tzvi Finkel of Slabodka[3] and Rabbi Yosef Yozel Hurwitz of Novarodok,[4] also founded yeshivas and articulated their own versions of Mussar teaching. All shared a profound commitment to guiding the individual in the cultivation of personal inner traits, as Mussar has always aimed to do. Where they differed is largely in emphasis and style.

Kelm Mussar is highly introspective, emphasizing the powers of mind. The motto of Rabbi Simcha Zissel, the Alter (Elder) of Kelm, was "Take time, be exact, unclutter the mind."

Slabodka Mussar has been more behavioral, asking its students to internalize and then conduct themselves with the deportment of people who really believe that we are made in the image of God. The Slabodka approach is summed up in its slogan, "the majesty of man."[5]

Novarodok Mussar has been the more radical school, adopting a more aggressive methodology for inner change. The Alter of Novarodok taught that it was not enough to try to influence the soul; what is needed is to "storm the soul."

Nowadays, the differences between the three schools have become largely obsolete, as contemporary Mussar teachers draw on all three as well as other sources to inform their teaching.

The teachings of Mussar are as applicable to our lives today as they have been to generations gone by. While the circumstances of our current lives are surely very different from those of centuries past, the passage of time has not altered human nature. As a result, the Mussar teachers' insights into the makeup and dynamics of our inner life hold as true for our lives now as they did for people living in those earlier ages. We've changed in so many ways through the centuries, yet at our deepest core, we've really not changed at all.

A Spiritual Legacy

Because human nature has not changed, Mussar's precious and time-tested legacy is available to help guide our own footsteps through life. To think that we have to invent how we live all on our own, or in completely novel ways because our ancestors did not know cars or dishwashers or computers, is a curse, because it means we have to relearn all the lessons in living that have already been learned. Why deprive ourselves of the cumulative experiences and conclusions drawn by dozens of generations who passed this way before? We must be grateful to our forebears who had the foresight and compassion to record their insights and guidance and pass these down to us.

In this retelling of the Mussar tradition, I endeavor to stay true to the insights and ideas of the classic sources, but to express them in a way that is more congenial and accessible to a modern person. The practical guidance that the rabbis wrote in Arabic in eleventh-century Spain or in Hebrew in nineteenth-century Lithuania would otherwise be unavailable to the vast majority today, including most Jews, not only because of the obvious barriers of language but perhaps even more so because the gems they contain are often obscured behind cultural garbing that can feel very alien to a seeker. In offering a handbook of Mussar for people of this generation, I am not trying to innovate on the authentic tradition, but rather to rearticulate the perennial truths in a more contemporary form. History shows that this is exactly what the teachers of Mussar have always done, as its sages retold timeless lessons in language and in styles intended to meet up with the unique circumstance of their generation.[6] In that way, too, I strive to stay true to tradition.

The spiritual heritage of Mussar was almost lost when so many of its practitioners and students were killed in the Holocaust. Even before that catastrophe, in the late nineteenth and early twentieth centuries, Mussar had already been put on a path that led away from the main currents of Jewish community life when its leaders decided to focus their efforts primarily on instilling values and good behavior in the teenagers who populated their yeshivas. But Mussar did not die, and in the twentieth century produced recent masters like Rabbi Elyah Lopian, Rabbi Eliyahu Dessler, and Rabbi Shlomo Wolbe, among others. Today, Mussar is undergoing a revival, its spiritual treasury being opened once again.

Though developed in the Jewish world, and with roots that are insep-
arable from the laws, commandments, and traditions of the most traditional segment of the Jewish community, Mussar's ancient vault contains
universal spiritual wisdom. Because Mussar's purpose is to provide guidance on how to live, and because it addresses the fundamental ways human
beings are put together and function, its teachings have universal applica-
tion. The fact is that you don't have to be Jewish to benefit from Mussar. Its
acutely accurate and insightful teachings are applicable to all souls—men
and women,[7] young and old, Jew and non-Jew—without exception.

A Person's Purpose in the World

Before you can appreciate the chapters that follow, and especially before
you will want to put them to work in your life, you need to know more
about what Mussar is and how it can serve you.

The starting point for understanding Mussar is the verse in the Torah
that tells us: "You shall be holy."[8] The Torah here reveals in no uncertain
terms what a human being's job description is. In essence, we are here on
earth for no other purpose than to grow and blossom spiritually—to become holy. Our potential and therefore our goal should be to become as
spiritually refined and elevated as is possible.

It is interesting that when the rabbis combed through the Torah to seek
out the commandments that are the backbone for living a Jewish life, none
of the major codifiers seized on "You shall be holy" as a commandment
they told us we must follow. This omission is classically explained by saying that our spiritual pursuits are the overarching and all-encompassing
goal of our lives, and so this injunction can't be brought down to the level
of an ordinance on par with the other 613 commandments the rabbis identified in the Torah.[9]

That seems true to me, and yet I want to offer another possibility as
well. My thought here is based on an analysis of another piece of the
Torah, the famous story of Adam and Eve eating from the Tree of Knowl-
edge. There, too, we read what sounds like an explicit commandment, as
God tells them, "Of the Tree of Knowledge of Good and Evil, do not eat."[10]
Rabbi Yosef Yozel Hurwitz, who founded and led the Novarodok school of
Mussar in the late nineteenth and early twentieth centuries, writes about

this episode,[11] saying that this directive was not a commandment to Adam and Eve. Rather, it was God's good advice to them.

The same can be said about the Torah's bidding, "You shall be holy." Not just an injunction, this too is advice that helps us understand and act on an impulse we all already feel within ourselves, which is the inner drive to improve and to make something better of our lives. How many hours every day go into fixing, cleaning, upgrading, improving, reconfiguring, and maintaining the things and aspects of your life? You commit so much time, thought, and effort because you are born with an impulse to improve. Since we live in a time and place that emphasizes the material, we commonly give rein to that impulse in material ways. We change the color of our hair, straighten our teeth, replace the car, get a new roof, do the laundry, upgrade the computer, and spend innumerable hours and dollars in answering the call to improve. It's against this picture of our lives that the Torah offers its advice, calling our attention to that inner urge we already feel and warning us not to mistake it for a drive for material improvement. The Torah's advice is to recognize that, at heart and in reality, the inner impulse to improve that you feel is a spiritual urge, an innate drive toward spiritual refinement that is squandered when it is spent on your clothes or your car. It is a sad mistake to put it to any use other than becoming the holy being you have the potential to be, the Torah advises.

The Torah's counsel is aimed directly to the soul. The word translated as *holy* in the phrase "You shall be holy" is given in the Torah in the plural.[12] Becoming holy is thus the task of every individual, and the Torah's advice is meant to be taken to heart by each of us.

An Extraordinary Ordinary Life

While the goal of holiness is the same for everyone, the path each of us has to follow in pursuit of that goal is unique, as each of us is unique. In crafting the Mussar movement, Rabbi Salanter acknowledged the reality of our individuality:

> We see that the affairs of man constantly vary, each person clinging
> to different transgressions. There are those whose transgressions
> are more inclined towards neglect of Torah study than unfaithful

business practices and not giving charity, and there are those who are more inclined towards unfaithful business practices and not giving charity than neglect of Torah study. No person is like another when it comes to transgression.[13]

Though he writes here only of transgression, his thought reflects the reality that each of us has our own personal strengths and weaknesses. This means that you have a unique spiritual curriculum to master on the journey toward holiness.

Generation after generation, thoughtful Mussar teachers have faithfully asked themselves, "How are we to become holy?" They take as a given that the Torah and its commandments will be our guides, but an argument that took place over the very verse we have been discussing—"You shall be holy"—highlights the need for a spiritual discipline that offers something more than the commandments.

The medieval commentator Rashi[14] says that becoming holy means withdrawing and separating from that which is impure and improper. He presents holiness as if it is our default position, if only we keep away from defilements.

The Ramban,[15] who followed Rashi by a full century and a half, argues back that this sort of avoidance can't possibly be enough to bring forth the light of holiness in our lives. He points out that there are many ways to live within the letter of the law and yet still behave like a complete rascal—for example, eating kosher food to gluttonous extremes or indulging excessively in permitted sexual relations. He said famously that a person could be a "scoundrel with the license of the Torah," and it is to forestall that possibility that the Torah gives us the general guidance to elevate our inner lives in ways that can't be defined in law and for which there can be no uniform standards.[16]

The Mussar tradition is an answer to this need for inner cultivation. Rabbi Yechezkel Levenstein, the Mussar supervisor[17] of the famous yeshivas of Mir and Ponevezh in the twentieth century, tells us that "a person's primary mission in this world is to purify and elevate his soul." To do that, we must walk the way of the soul, and Mussar has been developed to guide our footsteps.

Lest the goals that Mussar sets for us of holiness, purity, transformation, and elevation seem more for saints than the likes of you and me, the

Mussar teachers describe the goals they guide us toward in two other much more homely ways.

Sometimes they say that the purpose of Mussar practice is to help us move in the direction of *sh'lemut* (or *sh'lemus*), which translates literally as "wholeness."[18] The great Mussar teacher Rabbi Moshe Chaim Luzzatto discusses this notion in his book *Da'at Tevunot* (Discerning Knowledge):[19] "The one stone on which the entire building rests is the concept that God wants each person to *complete* himself body and soul. . . ." He is telling us that we are created incomplete so that we can complete the work of our own creation. He continues:

> God is certainly capable of making people, and all of Creation, absolutely complete. Furthermore, it would have made much more sense for Him to have done so, because insofar as He himself is perfect in every way, it is fitting that His works should also be totally perfect. But in His great wisdom he ruled it better to leave to people the completion of their own creation. So He cut short His own trait of perfection, and out of His greatness and goodness withheld Himself from His greatness in these creations, and made these creations incomplete. This was the way He wanted them made, according to His sublime plan.

From this perspective, all our weaknesses, failings, and shortcomings are there for a reason, and it is left to us to bring them to wholeness. In English the relationship between wholeness and holiness is evident, even in the words themselves. Achieving our potential for wholeness—*sh'lemut*—is not so much a reward as it is the fulfillment of the purpose of our lives. Rabbi Yisrael Salanter, who did so much to mark the way of the soul, speaks to the same issue:

> The Midrash teaches (*Bereishis Rabbah* 11:6), "Everything that came into being during the six days of Creation requires improvement— for example, the mustard seed needs to be sweetened . . . also man needs rectification." Our world is a world of transformation. When we are improving and refining ourselves, we are in concert with the Divine plan—fulfilling our purpose for existing in this world. . . . Not only is the human being created for this purpose, but he is also given the ability and capacity to attain this supreme goal.[20]

There is one other way the Mussar teachers describe the goal. When all is said and done, holiness and wholeness and any other elevated idea of the spiritual goal come down to a simple Yiddish notion: you are supposed to be a *mensch*, which means "a decent human being." That one Yiddish word conveys the full measure of the integrity, honor, and respect that a person can hope for in this life. In the words of the Chassidic teacher, known as the Kotzker, "Fine," he says, "be holy. But remember first one has to be a *mensch*." [21]

Rabbi Yisrael Salanter articulates this down-to-earth goal of Mussar when he speaks in one place about a *golem*, a supernatural creature of Jewish folklore: "The Maharal of Prague [22] created a *golem*, and this was a great wonder. But how much more wonderful is it to transform a corporeal human being into a *mensch*."

I found another way of stating the goal of Mussar in an unlikely place. When Chuck Cadman, a respected member of the Canadian parliament, died, a member of the federal cabinet came to pay his respects to his widow. When the minister praised the late member lavishly, his widow said that Chuck saw himself as just an ordinary person. "Yes," responded the minister, "but he was an extraordinary ordinary person." This is just what Mussar helps us become.

Not Just for You

Mussar is a path of spiritual self-development. It means working on yourself, but not for the sake of your self. By refining and elevating your inner life and nourishing the soul, you clarify your inner light and thus become a lamp shedding light into the world. This is why Mussar is not self-help. Its purpose is not that you will gratify all your desires but that you will become the master of your desires, so that you can fulfill the potential of your higher nature.

Dedication to be of service and to hold the needs of the other in your heart even as you work on yourself is a central tenet of Mussar. How it works is conveyed in a story attributed to many people, but most commonly to the Chafetz Chaim.

When asked how he had had such an impact as a great sage and leader in the twentieth-century Jewish world, the Chafetz Chaim answered, "I set out to try to change the world, but I failed. So I decided to scale back my efforts and only try to influence the Jewish community of Poland, but I failed there, too. So I targeted the community in my hometown of Radin, but achieved no greater success. Then I gave all my effort to changing my own family, and failed at that as well. Finally, I decided to change myself, and that's how I had such an impact on the Jewish world."

Rabbi Meir Chodosh had a way of describing the role of an educator that holds for how all students of Mussar influence their world by working on themselves. The task is to fill yourself up with wisdom and knowledge until you brim over, and the overflow spills out of you and into the adjacent vessels, who are other people.[23]

3

A Map of the Inner Life

THE ESSENTIAL FEATURES of Mussar can be summarized under two headings: (1) it offers us a "map" of the inner life and (2) it offers us a body of practices we can employ to transform our inner ways.

All disciplines that are concerned with the interior life, be they religious or spiritual traditions or one of the many schools of psychology or neuroscience, start by laying out a map of the inner territory. Through the centuries, the Mussar masters have evolved an accurate, insightful map that revolves around seeing our lives in terms of soul.

The Mussar blueprint of the inner life considers soul not as an organ or a separate spirit but as the essence of who you are. In common usage, if we speak of soul, we are likely to slip into using the possessive—"my soul" or "your soul"—but that way of describing our inner life conveys the implicit message that the soul is somehow a possession or offshoot of our identity. In the words of Rabbi Yechezkel Levenstein, "Today, when a person says 'I,' he is typically not referring to his soul, but to his materialistic self."[1] Mussar urges us to see ourselves differently. The deeper reality is not that you have a soul but that in your essential nature, you are a soul.

The ego claims to be king, but its true role is better described as that of valet. When it is put firmly in that role, because the soul is master, our lives become aligned in a deep way we could hardly imagine previously. You and I are souls. That's who we are.

With only limited exceptions, everything we encounter in our inner world is an aspect of soul. This includes features of personality, emotions, talents, desires, conscience, wisdom, and so on. Even the faculties we ordinarily allot to the "mind," like thought, logic, memory, and forgetting, are assigned to the soul. In addition, well before Freud introduced the notion of the unconscious, the Mussar teachers were working with an understanding that there is a dark inner region that is the source of much that appears in the daylight of our lives.[2] The soul encompasses all of our psychological dimensions as well as all that is ethereal, mystical, and spiritual within us.

The Mussar masters developed their insights into the soul from observation and experimentation. The fact that Mussar has had ten centuries in which to experiment and test its insights is one of its strongest recommendations. Rabbi Yaakov Kamenetsky, who was a student of the Alter of Slabodka, was once asked, "Do you mean to say that the Alter understood a student like Freud understood people?" Rabbi Kamenetsky replied, "Aaachh, there is no comparison. The Alter understood a person much better."[3]

Realms of Soul

There are three primary aspects of the soul, though the Mussar teachers insist that this is just a way of talking so we can understand the subject. In reality, the soul is an undivided whole. The teachers' template, then, is holistic and sees no divide between heart and mind, emotions and intellect. All are faculties of the soul.

At the core of the soul is the inner dimension called *neshama*, which is inherently holy and pure. This stainless marrow is the seat of the "image and likeness" in which we are created; it cannot be tainted, even by evil deeds. The Jewish poet Moshe ibn Ezra, who lived in the eleventh and twelfth centuries, writes beautifully of the *neshama:*

> In my body He has kindled a lamp from His glory;
> It tells me of the paths of the wise.
> It is the light which shines in the days
> Of youth, and grows brighter in old age.
> Were it not derived from the mystery of His light
> It would fail with my strength and my years.
> With it I search out the chamber of wisdom,
> And I climb with no ladder to the garden of delights.

And the morning prayers of the traditional liturgy say: "God, the soul [*neshama*] you have given me is pure." Some say the *neshama* is divine; others say it is intimately connected to the divine.[4]

The next dimension of the soul is called *ruach*, that aspect of the soul that is the source of animation and vigor—no more, and no less, than the "spirit of life." It helps to understand the *ruach* to realize that many familiar conditions are ailments of the *ruach*, such as depression, attention deficit disorder, and other ways of being in which the issues revolve around energy and consciousness.

Nefesh, the third aspect of the soul, is the one that is most visible and accessible to us. Here we find all the familiar human traits like anger and love, trust and worry, generosity and stinginess, pride and humility, responsibility and laziness, loving-kindness and judgment, and so on. The Rambam calls these the "moral virtues," but also includes as facets of the *nefesh*-soul "rational virtues" like logic and memory.[5] While the *neshama* is ever and always stainless, the *nefesh* dimension of soul registers the good and the bad we do in our lives and can be cleansed or stained by our actions.[6]

In Hebrew, the collective word for all the traits of the *nefesh*-soul is *middot*. While that plural term is almost always translated into the useful English notion of "traits of character," the Hebrew word (singular *middah*) literally means "measures." We can find in this root a Mussar insight. The message is that each of us is endowed at birth with every one of the full range of the human traits, and that what sets one person apart from another is not whether we have certain traits while someone else has different ones, but rather the degree, or measure, of the traits that live in each of our souls. The angriest person, for example, has an excess of the anger trait, but Mussar insists that there must be at least some degree of calm within that raging soul. So must there also be a touch of anger in even the calmest individual. The stingiest person still has at least a grain of generosity, and so on with all the traits. It's not whether we have the traits—all of us have them all—but rather what gives us our distinctive way of being in the world is where our traits are measured on the continuum. Nor should we aspire to rid ourselves of certain traits. Each has its role, though certain traits will exist in us in too high or too low a measure. That's what sets our spiritual curriculum for us.

Very salient within this Mussar perspective is the affirmation that, at its core, the soul you are is already holy and pure. How could it be otherwise, since we are told in no uncertain terms in the Torah that we are made "in the image" and "likeness" of God?[7] Yet in the reality of our lives, that radiant inner being is often hidden. The holy light of the *neshama* would shine constantly in our lives, and through us into the world, were it not for the fact that the condition of certain inner qualities, which are framed for us as our soul-traits at the level of *nefesh*-soul, obstruct the radiance.

Unbalanced soul-traits act as "veils"[8] that block the inner light. The issue is never the inner qualities themselves—Mussar tells us that all human qualities, even anger, jealousy, and desire, are not intrinsically "bad." These traits that we might call vices have their positive role to play in our lives, in the way that anger is an important signal to action in the face of injustice, or jealousy can be a very motivating inner force to do good. But when a soul-trait persists within us in an extreme of either excess or deficiency, then our innate holiness will be obscured. A trait that tends toward the extreme at either end of the spectrum drops down a veil that blocks the inner light of the *neshama*.

An analogy may help clarify the picture. If you think of the holy essence of your inner life (the *neshama*) as the sun, then the many inner traits of your *nefesh*-soul are like the weather. Each trait that is tending toward the outer edge of the range—because you are too angry or too passive, too greedy or too generous, too proud or too humble—is a cloud in the sky. Though the sun shines on, its light is obstructed according to the degree and thickness of the "clouds" that hang over your inner landscape.

The traits and the veils can be graphed, as in the following chart that illustrates a group of related soul-traits:

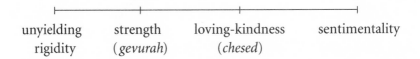

| unyielding | strength | loving-kindness | sentimentality |
| rigidity | (*gevurah*) | (*chesed*) | |

"Strength" and "loving-kindness" are both positive traits. Yet take either of them to the extreme (which I've characterized as "unyielding rigidity" in the case of strength, or "sentimentality" in relation to loving-kindness) and you find a quality that has dropped a veil over the *neshama,* occluding its radiance. The degree to which the trait tends toward the extreme defines the thickness of the veil.

Fulfilling the Torah's injunction to become holy doesn't mean running here or there to acquire this or that. Instead, what is needed is that you make an effort to uncover the holy purity that is innate within you. Through introspection and self-examination you can identify the traits that are hindrances in your life, either because you have too much or too little of them. Awareness of your inner imbalances pinpoints the work you can do to transform those challenging inner qualities.

This map of the inner life is very helpful for making sense of why you have the problems, habits, strengths, and weaknesses that you do. From this mapping emerges another way of defining Mussar: *tikkun middot ha'nefesh*[9]—literally, rectifying the tunings of the soul. Here is your spiritual curriculum. Here is the way of the soul.

4

The Inner Adversary

THERE IS ONE OTHER IMPORTANT FACTOR of the inner life that the Mussar masters identify that not only explains how you got to where you are in your life but also prepares you to engage with your soul curriculum: embedded within each of us is an inner adversary.

Even if you know what is good, right, and desirable, it isn't so simple just to act that way. No sooner does a notion to do something good come into your mind or heart than up pops an objection. It might be a contrary thought, or a feeling, or a desire pulling you in the opposite direction. In whatever form it will arise, when you try to improve the soul-traits that are on your spiritual curriculum you can expect to face a challenge to doing the better thing.

The Jewish sages give a name to this negative impulse. They call it the *yetzer ha'ra,* the inclination to evil. We all have this inclination and it challenges us, which is why it exists. We are born with free will and can choose to do good or bad, but whenever we try to do something that stretches us in the direction of good, we need to expect to encounter this inner resistance arising from the shadows. We have an inner inclination to elevate and purify ourselves—that's the *yetzer ha'tov,* the impulse to do good—and what stands in our way is the built-in adversary, the *yetzer ha'ra.*

Rabbi Eliyahu Dessler has given us a very helpful concept to help us understand this give-and-take, this push and pull that we experience whenever we try to do something that reflects our ambition to elevate ourselves. He identifies what he calls the *bechirah*-points in each of us.[1] The word *bechirah* means "choice" in Hebrew, and refers to our free will. There is, Rabbi Dessler says, an inner battle line that is drawn right at those places where choice is very alive for you, where you really could go either way with a decision. He illustrates what he means by referring to a real battle:

When two armies are locked in battle, fighting takes place only at the battlefront. Territory behind the lines of one army is under that army's control and little or no resistance need be expected there. A similar situation prevails in respect of territory behind the lines of the other army. If one side gains a victory at the front and pushes the enemy back, the position of the battlefront will have changed. In fact, therefore, fighting takes place only at one location.

This image describes the situation we ourselves regularly face whenever we try to do anything that involves an exercise of choice. If it is an easy choice where our values and appetites are well established, we don't experience any struggle at all. Nor is it any harder when the choice is so far outside our interests or potential; then we aren't even tempted. Rabbi Dessler zeroes in: "Free will is exercised and a valid choice made only on the borderline between the forces of good and the forces of evil within that person."

To illustrate, he gives the example of two people who are very confirmed in their relationship to material goods. One is a professional thief raised among thieves and robbers. This person has absolutely no inner struggle over whether or not to steal because that's his established way of life: "For him, whether or not to steal does not present any *behira* [*bechirah*] at all," says Rabbi Dessler. But still, this person retains the potential to ascend spiritually, and so somewhere within him free will is alive and choices are real. Rabbi Dessler wonders, if this thief were to be discovered in the midst of a robbery, would he shoot his way out of the jam and run the risk of killing someone? If that question would be a real struggle for him, and the outcome uncertain, then this would define one of his *bechirah*-points, "where for him the forces of good and evil, truth and untruth, are evenly balanced."

The other person Rabbi Dessler cites is someone brought up in a good home with strong moral values. This person would not have the slightest temptation to steal a penny. Does that mean that he or she has no *bechirah*-point where the tests of spiritual ascent are going to be faced? No, this person must have challenges, too, through which he or she can elevate spiritually. While theft is not a real possibility here, in this case the *bechirah*-point might refer to another aspect of relationship to property, like how much charity he or she gives, and whether giving is done generously and with a pleasant demeanor.

So we all have *bechirah*-points where we find choices to be challenging, and the reality is that we could go either way. Your *bechirah*-points define the front line in your spiritual struggle. On one side is the territory of the *yetzer ha'tov* (good inclination) and on the other that of the *yetzer ha'ra* (evil inclination).

Rabbi Dessler concludes his discussion by advising us that this *bechirah*-point does not remain static:

> With each good choice successfully carried out, the person rises higher in spiritual level; that is, things that were previously in the line of battle are now in the area controlled by the *yetzer ha'tov* and actions done in that area can be undertaken without struggle and without *behira* [*bechirah*]. And so in the other direction. Giving in to the *yetzer ha'ra* pushes back the frontier of the good, and an act which previously cost one a struggle with one's conscience will now be done without *behira* at all.

So just as your spiritual curriculum is composed of a set of soul-traits that are particularly relevant to you as an individual, so too do you have a distinctive set of *bechirah*-points. Think of those choices that often confront you, when you really do experience the possibility of going either way. Do you waver over the second piece of dessert? Is reaching into your purse or wallet to give charity a struggle with an uncertain outcome? Do you know you should call or visit a sick friend, and yet you hesitate and vacillate over actually doing it? Do you look at the sink full of dishes and lean this way and that way and back again and go all around over whether the responsibility is yours?

You may see yourself reflected in some of these examples, or you may be able to name your own. Wherever your *bechirah*-points may be, rest assured that you have them. They represent not only places of uncertainty in your behavior but also openings where you have the greatest potential to ascend spiritually. It is important to recognize that each choice you make can be a rung on the ladder of your spiritual ascent (or, unfortunately, the opposite).

Just as your spiritual curriculum and set of *bechirah*-points are distinctive to you, so does your inner adversary, your *yetzer ha'ra,* come at you with challenges that are uniquely tailored just to you. You're only going to be tempted or pushed in regard to traits and choices that are personally challenging for you. Perhaps you know you should be more patient with your spouse or children, and you want to be, but as soon as you set that resolution, whose inner voice is it that points out to you how outrageous it is that they are so slow or late? You want to open your hand in charity, but as soon as you make the first move to reach into your pocket, where does the thought originate that wonders whether you will have enough for yourself? You decide to lose a few pounds, so who is it who tells you that having only one more won't matter?

Although our spiritual ancestors named this inner adversary as the inclination to evil, their descriptions tell us that this impulse isn't exactly "evil" as we ordinarily understand that term. What they are alerting us to is made clearer by some of the lessons they passed down to us.

In a famous story, the rabbis once captured the *yetzer ha'ra* and confined it in a big pot.[2] They prepared to kill it, but then they noticed that throughout the kingdom, no one went to work, and even the chickens had stopped laying eggs. The rabbis had to let it go.

In another source text, the lesson concludes, "If not for the evil impulse no one would build a house, marry, have children, or engage in trade."[3]

These references tell us that despite the literal translation of its name, the *yetzer ha'ra* isn't an impulse to do harm that dooms us all. Rather, they are pointing to the inner drives that arise from our lower selves. The drives themselves are certainly not appraised as bad; in fact, they are necessary and useful for human life. But whenever you try to control or overrule those drives because of an intention of your higher nature, or when one of those drives becomes exaggerated, you will have a struggle on your hands. The *yetzer ha'ra* will do everything in its power to subvert your higher self and to influence you to indulge your desires. Hence the goal is not to try to destroy the *yetzer ha'ra* but to control it and apply it for good. Ben Zoma asked, "Who is strong?" His answer is: "Whoever controls their evil inclination."[4]

In our uniqueness, you and I have desires that have their own distinctive weave and coloration. And your *yetzer ha'ra* is matched up to your desires, inch for inch, stitch for stitch. Your *yetzer ha'ra* is perfectly contoured to provide exactly the challenges you must overcome in order to grow spiritually. And just as there is an infinite range of human personalities, the *yetzer ha'ra* comes in an infinite number of variations. In every

case, though, the *yetzer ha'ra* will perfectly match a person's spiritual curriculum. Like the settings of your soul-traits, your *yetzer ha'ra* is an inevitable companion on the way of the soul. You are well advised to get to
know yours.

Do you? Are you familiar with the inner impulses that push you to do
what you know you shouldn't, or keep you from doing what you should?
Take a moment to consider for yourself.

Your *yetzer ha'ra* may push you to do things you really shouldn't. "Go
ahead," it says. "Who's counting? Who will see? How could one hurt? You
deserve it." It will flatter, cajole, seduce, or come up with whatever it takes
to induce you to step over the line.

Or your *yetzer ha'ra* will be the voice that tells you not to do what you
know you should. "Don't bother," it will counsel. "What's in it for you?
Surely it's somebody else's turn." Or even more negatively, "You don't deserve it, so don't even try. You're bound to fail, so don't even start."

Rabbi Elijah of Vilna, known as the Vilna Ga'on,[5] writes that the *yetzer
ha'ra* does not try to seduce you to do something that is outright sinful
because in that case, you'd never take the bait. Rather, the *yetzer ha'ra* tries
to get you to take only one small step down a wrong road, which it can
do by convincing you that this first step is actually a good and righteous
thing. For example, the *yetzer ha'ra* won't try to entice a person who keeps
kosher to outright eat pork, because that is not likely a point of vulnera-
bility. Instead, it would try to entice that person to eat roasted kosher meat
on Passover, which is not to be done, and it would whisper convincingly,
"You'll really enjoy the festive meal so much more." Once the *yetzer ha'ra*
has succeeded in that small measure, it will continue enticing the person
farther and farther down the path of transgression.[6]

Rabbi Yosef Yozel Hurwitz of Novarodok alerts us to the way the *yetzer
ha'ra* works by exploiting what he calls "a righteous opening."[7] His example is Cain, who ultimately killed his brother, Abel. His first step toward
that terrible act came with his reaction to God's acceptance of Abel's sacrifice but not his. Cain wanted his sacrifice to be accepted, too, which was
a positive and righteous kind of jealousy. But it was still jealousy, and that's
what created a righteous opening for the *yetzer ha'ra*. He was led along
until he committed the first recorded fratricide.

Some Mussar teachers talk about overcoming your *yetzer ha'ra*. Others
speak of befriending it or redirecting its energy. However it is approached,

the task of taming the adversary is not to be underestimated. Be fore-warned that the foe is wily, unruly, deceptive. It doesn't play by our rules. And the better we get at dealing with it, the more subtle does it render its resistance. It is the proverbial trickster.

The *yetzer ha'ra* makes sure it is hard to overcome. When he was a child, the future Chassidic master Eliezer of Dzikov was scolded by his father for some misdeed. "But what can I do if my *yetzer ha'ra* tempts me?" the child asked.

"Learn from your *yetzer ha'ra*," his father said. "Look how diligent he is."

"Yes," said Eliezer, "but my *yetzer ha'ra* has no *yetzer ha'ra* to distract him!"

The Mussar masters want you to be very alert to the nature of your *yetzer ha'ra* and particularly to how it operates in your life. They want you to be aware that it can pop up at any moment and that the struggle to over-come its influence goes on for a lifetime. They want each of us to learn to be skillful in dealing with our own *yetzer ha'ra.*

And they warn us that despite our best efforts—and never has a civiliza-tion been more inventive and effective at this than ours—our lower self, with its bundle of self-preserving and other urges, is not susceptible to being anesthetized. Nor will it succumb to bludgeoning. Those efforts only tem-porarily send this stealthy psycho-terrorist back to its cave, where it gorges on our foolishness and plots its survival and our downfall. With every blow we deliver, its subterranean force expands, until one day it reemerges, ei-ther as a stomping monster or as an equally deadly foul gas, seeping through the cracks in who we'd like to think we are.

That you can expect never to be freed of the inner adversary is con-veyed in a story about the eighteenth-century Vilna Ga'on. One day, his students told him, "Rebbe, we wish we could have your *yetzer ha'ra.*" He answered them, "Oh no you don't." And he cited as proof the saying in the Talmud, "The greater the person, the greater the *yetzer ha'ra.*"[8] If we are wise, we should not even want to be freed of this inclination. As you ad-vance spiritually, your *yetzer ha'ra* continues to offer its challenges. That's so you can continue to grow.

5

Navigating the Way

THE MUSSAR MASTERS mapped the inner territory not out of curiosity but as the basis for prescribing practical techniques that will help us rework our inner qualities. For centuries they have told us that we can elevate our inner selves, but only through a discipline of practice, as we can see from the following passage from *Path of the Just*,[1] which was published by Rabbi Moshe Chaim Luzzatto in Amsterdam in 1740:

> Matters of piety, God-reverence and love, and purity of heart are not so ingrained in your heart that you would not have to find the means of acquiring them. They are not just come upon nonchalantly like natural processes such as sleep and wakefulness, hunger and satiety, and so forth. In truth, you have to foster means and devices to acquire them. And there is no lack for things to keep them back from you (just as there is no lack for ways to hold back the deterrents).

Through the generations Mussar masters have experimented with and innovated a range of practices aimed at bringing about lasting inner refinement. They have sought methods that would instill change so deeply that a person's intuitive responses to situations would be altered and brought more in line with their values. In other words, they were looking for ways to bring about change that would be so profound that our second nature would be altered. They asked, what would it take to convert a miser into someone whose hand will reach spontaneously to give? By what means could a person whose habit was anger become someone whose intuitive response was kindness?

There is a story that describes well what they were after. One morning, a man came to a rabbi to ask for help. "I'm sick and can't work," the man said. "My wife is unwell, too, and she can't even take in laundry to make a little. Even our children are ill. I don't know what to do. Could you possibly give us a little help, just to tide us over?"

The rabbi reached into his desk drawer, pulled out some money, and handed it to the hapless man.

That afternoon, someone came running to the rabbi and said, "Rabbi, you know that man who came to you this morning with that story about him being sick and his wife being sick and his children, too? Well, it's not true. None of them is sick!"

To this the rabbi responded heartily, "Thank God they're healthy!"

Now if you had been in the rabbi's position, would that have been your immediate response? Or would you have felt cheated and said so? Yet if I were to ask you what is more important, $100 or the health of a family, I'm sure your values would cause you to answer, the health of a family. The challenge the Mussar masters took on was to develop methods that would cause your second nature to align with your values.

Text Study

Intensive study of the texts that the Mussar masters have written through the centuries is a primary form of Mussar practice. Many of these several dozen books have been translated into English, and two are generally considered to be pillars of the Mussar tradition: *Duties of the Heart* by Rabbi Bachya ibn Pakuda,[2] and *Path of the Just* by Rabbi Moshe Chaim Luzzatto,[3] though others are held in very high esteem as well.

There is a particular way to read a Mussar book, which is slowly, in little segments, so the material can be thoroughly absorbed and digested. Text study is often done with a partner (*chevruta*) or in a group (*va'ad*).

Studying the classic wisdom of the texts helps set our agenda for change and firm our understanding and commitment. But learning of any kind is predominantly an intellectual activity, and the Mussar masters recognized from experience that the intellect is a valuable but incomplete tool for transformation. Just because we have a clear idea of some ideal doesn't mean we are any closer to living it, as we saw in the story of the rabbi and the sick man. Just as it isn't enough to know the ideal level for our blood pressure or cholesterol, we have to take the next step of getting up off the couch and becoming active to make those numbers real in our lives.

A twentieth-century Mussar master, Rabbi Eliyahu Lopian,[4] takes this as the core of his understanding of Mussar. He defined Mussar as "making the heart feel what the intellect understands." He continues: "Even when the intellect sees and understands, the heart, the seat of emotions, remains distant and cold."

We know this to be true. Even if we have the right ideas in our minds, these good thoughts do not become part of our lives until they are somehow internalized, as if woven into the flesh of our hearts. For that to happen, something beyond intellectual learning is needed.

Mussar's transformative practices fall into two categories. One group of techniques is designed to bring to conscious awareness material that resides in the darkness of the unconscious, while the other works in the opposite direction, using various techniques to send messages down to the roots of being, beyond the reach of the conscious mind. The intention in both sorts of practical procedures is to bring about transformation at the deep level of soul. These are the prescriptions.

Dredging the Unconscious

Among the practices that seek to reveal to the conscious mind the substance of what lies beneath the surface, Mussar offers:

- meditation (*hitbonenut*)
- silence and retreat (*hitbodedut*)
- diary practices (*cheshbon ha'nefesh*)

Rabbi Yitzchok Isaac Sher notes that a person "cannot undertake to follow the *mussar* way of life until he fully understands the processes of thought formation and the modes of thought development."[5] Reflecting understanding of the deep roots of our thoughts, words, and deeds, all Mussar introspective practices endeavor to reach beyond our conscious minds. It takes special techniques to dig down to bring those inner factors that shape our lives into the light of awareness. Just the act of transferring these inner materials from the unconscious to the conscious level is itself transformative.

A story from the book *Cheshbon ha'Nefesh*, written by Rabbi Menachem Mendel Leffin and published in Lvov in the Ukraine in 1812, provides a good example of one of Mussar's meditative practices. It tells of two young men who "took it upon themselves to pray with devotion, concentrating their attention on the meaning of the text." In the end, one man completely lost his way in life while the other became a famous scholar, a fine human being, and a great devotee of God. "When asked how he had merited reaching this level, he replied: 'For many years I took it upon myself to focus my mind on a single thought—either Torah or prayer—for a specific period of time. By doing so, I eventually trained myself to be able to concentrate for an hour or even more.'"[6]

The meditation practice revealed in this story is both simple and classic. Concentrating on an object—in this case a single word or phrase—is a good general definition of meditation. The power of meditation comes from the mental exercise, as we can learn from the fact that the story doesn't tell us if there was a particular word or phrase he used. Note, too, the case the author makes for the transformative and purifying results of this practice.

Hitbodedut names the practice of secluded meditation and prayer that is done in search of self-transcendence and communion with God. It is, by definition, a practice of solitude, as the root of the Hebrew word is *boded*, meaning "alone." When the Alter of Novarodok overthrew his worldly life after coming in contact with Rabbi Salanter, he had himself closed into a small room where he practiced *hitbodedut*. He lived in that single room for two years to cleanse himself and to refocus his life. While few Mussar teachers would actually advocate that level of withdrawal, there is great spiritual benefit to spending periods of time in seclusion and reflection. Absent the activities that ordinarily keep us engaged and distracted, deep matters of soul rise to the surface, undeniably.

Rabbi Shlomo Wolbe[7] comments on the benefits of practicing retreat:

> You can only get a feeling for your internal life when you are alone. With a half hour of being alone you can come to feel things you never knew about yourself and see what you are lacking in spirituality. You will set new goals to reach. This can only be done if you spend time alone in seclusion [hitbodedut] for a half hour. In this way you can start to build your internal, spiritual world.

The final of the three principal practices of introspection and self-reflection is keeping a Mussar diary. This is a core practice that will be described and discussed at length in part 3 of this book.

Leaving Traces on the Soul

Turning to the second category of Mussar practices, here we find methods that are all meant to work, in a sense, in the opposite direction. Instead of dredging up material from the unconscious, these techniques bypass the intellect and the ego's defenses to send messages and images directly to the deeper reaches of the soul, there to leave a lasting imprint. These sorts of practices include:

- chanting (*hitpa'alut*)
- contemplations
- visualizations (*kibbutz roshmim*)

In his history of the nineteenth-century Mussar movement,[8] Rabbi Dov Katz writes, "Of all the methods introduced by the movement, the most radical and effective was found to be the repetitive, moral recitation," which is how he described Mussar chanting.[9]

The Hebrew term used for Mussar chanting means "with emotion," and, in fact, Mussar chanting is always emotional. Rabbi Salanter emphasized that the soul is directly influenced by the language of emotion, which it understands very well, and so he taught that chanting be done "with lips aflame." It also calls for melody, as a phrase is repeated in a singsong way. Rabbi Salanter recognized that melody is another modality that penetrates to the core of being where conscious thought can't reach.

The choice of phrase to be chanted is important. Drawing on the Mussar view that the inner life is composed of soul-traits that we can alter by means of spiritual practice, the phrase that you choose is one that carries an important message about a trait that currently figures in your spiritual curriculum. If, for example, you were endeavoring to cultivate humility, you might take a phrase like Abraham's statement recorded in the Torah, "I am dust and ashes." Or if honor was your focus, you might choose the liturgical phrase "The soul is pure." Phrases from the Bible, the Talmud, or rabbinical writings, or even a phrase you make up, can all serve the purpose of deepening your spiritual practice with chanting.

The practice of visualizations and contemplations follow similar logic. Holding vivid mental images in mind enlists the power of imagination to etch chosen messages directly to the soul. Strong mental impressions leave a trace that influences one's inner qualities, emotions, perceptions, judgment, and behaviors. The intellect is not the most profound of the aspects of soul—it is not the root—but impressions (wholesome and unwholesome) gathered in the mind do pass down to the root and color and shape the soul-traits.

This ability to visualize is so important to Mussar practice that when Rabbi Yechezkel Levenstein asks the question "What is the difference between a righteous person and sinner?" he brings what he himself calls "a surprising answer" from the Alter of Kelm: "It is the ability to picture things in one's mind as if they were real." [10]

Here is an example of a Mussar visualization. Rabbi Eliyahu Dessler has left us a visualization that we can follow word by word, with no need for any modern elaboration or revision. Here he explores the notion of eternity and leads us step-by-step into a mind-state of awe. [11]

As you follow this visualization, your job is to let go of any alien or analyzing thoughts, so that you open yourself to experience the awe that arises from images of the vastness of time itself.

Imagine an enormous mountain of sand situated next to the sea. Every thousand years a great bird wings its way to the top of the mountain, takes one grain of sand in its beak and drops it into the sea. Another thousand years must go by until the next grain is removed. The exercise is to attempt to visualize, or experience in imagination, the lapse of a thousand years.... One begins by imagining the events of one day, then two days, a week, a month, two months, a year, etc., recapitulating each time, as far as possible the temporal "feel" of a day or a week, and resisting the temptation to lapse into conceptualization by saying "and so on" or "as we said before." When one has "felt" a year in this manner, one multiplies this progressively until one reaches a lifetime, a century, two centuries, three centuries . . . until one arrives at a thousand years. Then—the bird comes and takes another grain of sand from the mound. But the whole mound is still there. One has to start the whole process over again for the third grain, and for the fourth, and so on and so on. . . . And even when that unimaginably distant moment is reached and the *last* grain of sand disappears into the ocean—*eternity* has still hardly begun.

Rabbi Dessler concludes by saying: "If one allocates, say, ten minutes a day to this mental exercise, the empty words 'eternal life' will soon have acquired a 'felt' meaning which they certainly did not have before."

Contemplations are similar to visualizations, except in place of vivid images the mind is set to work having an intense experience of a concept. For example, in *Duties of the Heart,* Rabbi Bachya ibn Pakuda provides several contemplations that he says will stimulate humility. One of these is to contemplate the inevitability of death and the ensuing decay of the flesh. If you think about and deeply contemplate the reality of your own mortality, any tendency to arrogance will be deflated.

Chanting, visualization, and contemplation imprint notions so deeply within as to be written on our hearts, becoming part of our very flesh. Even things we learn intellectually require this sort of additional process if they are to really become integrally woven into our natures. The Torah alludes to this two-step process when it instructs us, with respect to God's commandments, to "lay up these My words in your heart and in your soul."[12]

The Alter of Novarodok reflects on this need for "sensory learning" to bring about real change and says that if a person toils only with his mind, then he will not really have fostered change, as will surely become apparent when he encounters a challenging real-life situation:

> If he knows . . . only with his mind and not with his senses, he will find that his mental effort yields only a mental [i.e., abstract] result, not a sensory [i.e., actual] one. . . . At the moment of trial, he is like a blind man who never saw the light, because then the cloud covers the sun and he can see nothing. All his exalted knowledge exists either before the fact or after the fact, but when the [trying] situation is at hand, the distraction of the trial makes him like a different man. In retrospect, he will say, "At the time of the trial, I wasn't the same man that I am now, after the trial."[13]

Rabbi Dessler alludes to the same notion of sensory learning by concluding his visualization with his promise that if you did this practice, "the empty words 'eternal life' will soon have acquired a 'felt' meaning." Learning in such a deep way, beyond intellectual ideas, is where growth and healing take place, and this is where Mussar focuses.

Bearing the Burden of the Other

One further practice needs to be noted, which is very characteristic of Mussar. This is action done on behalf of another person. "Bearing the burden of the other," as the Alter of Kelm put it, translates into acts of generosity, loving-kindness, compassion, and care undertaken for the benefit of another. The Mussar teachers encourage us to pay attention to and respond to the needs of others because they recognize that this stance and the ensuing action have the effect of diminishing the focus on self that is a primary spiritual impediment. I have even heard *holiness* defined as the absence of self-interest.[14] It's true as well that in endeavoring to help others, we will surely encounter our own personal spiritual curriculum, which provides us with an ideal opportunity to grapple with our own soul-traits and to grow spiritually.

Practices of this sort are responsible for Mussar having developed its reputation as an "ethical philosophy." It is that, but it is also much more. It certainly tells us to do good and not evil, and it lays the highest priority on the deeds we do and the steps we take as we move through this world. So the good it points to is indeed moral, but it is also more than moral. The ultimate issue is your spiritual potential, which can be explored and developed through the exercise of ethical action.

Rabbi Salanter set the standard here, as in the story that is told about his efforts to get the elders of a town to repair the roof on the poorhouse. When they dragged their feet, Rabbi Salanter went to sleep with the beggars under the dilapidated roof until the city fathers undertook to fund the needed repairs. He summed up the way in which caring for the needs of others can be undertaken as a spiritual practice, saying: "A pious Jew is not one who worries about his fellow man's soul and his own stomach; a pious Jew worries about his own soul and his fellow man's stomach."

We'll return to the Mussar practices in part 3 of this book. I'll close this introduction here with a story that I think captures the general approach of the Mussar teachers to the diverse practices they have taught.

A group of students of Novarodok Mussar had obtained a dead fish, and they had tied a string around its tail and suspended it from the ceiling of their room. Now they were sitting around and observing it as it decayed. This was a contemplation meant to impress upon them the reality of death and the way of all flesh. A group of Slabodka students found out what the Novarodokers were doing and ran to tell their teacher, expecting that he would say something that would affirm their own style of dignified, decorous practice over those of the radical Novarodokers. When they had finished pouring out their tale, their teacher asked them simply, "Does it work?"[15] Such is the underlying pragmatism and flexibility with which the Mussar teachers have approached the issue of practice—the ultimate test is, does it work to bring about inner change?

The Nature of Inner Change

Change brought about through these sorts of spiritual practices does not happen instantaneously or even quickly. The Mussar masters advocate a path of very gradual change involving routine and regular step-by-step practice. Mussar isn't about zooming to the top of the mountain in search of some sort of "instant enlightenment." It advises small steps, repeated regularly, since what changes quickly in one direction can just as easily change back again.

Walking this way requires patience, as the Alter of Novarodok noted caustically. "The problem with people," he said, "is that they want to change overnight—and have a good night's sleep that night, too." Or as Rabbi Salanter[16] cautions:

> Let a person's heart not despair if he studies Mussar and is not awakened, or if he feels no impression on his soul motivating him to change his path. Through an abundance of [Mussar] study over an extended period of time, the impressions will accumulate, and he will be transformed into a different person. His desires will be reined in, without excessive indulgence, and some [desires] will even be completely neutralized. Experience testifies [even] through a cursory observation, that Mussar study—whether a lot or a little—elevates a person above his peers, both in thought and conduct.

Neurobiologists have a way of describing what the Mussar teachers seem to have recognized. They say that "neurons that fire together wire together." This means that repeating an experience over a long period of time results in repeated stimulation of the same neural pathways in the brain, and that's how the brain develops its wiring that defines our thinking and behavior. By the same token, pathways that are neglected soon atrophy, and the wiring uncouples.

Though they didn't have the anatomical evidence or the language, the Mussar teachers observed and appreciated these mechanisms centuries ago and created practices that utilize these principles to bring about inner change that is deep and lasting.

Another thing that the Mussar tradition and the neurobiologists agree on is that change is possible. With the right guidance and effort, inner traits can be changed in ways that you direct.

In Mussar, the sort of change that is emphasized is described as growth. "The greatest sound in the cosmos," notes Rabbi Salanter, "is that of someone changing himself and growing from it." Rabbi Elyakim Krumbein puts it, "To fulfill the Torah means to grow as a person, and to grow truly as a person is tantamount to the fulfillment of Torah."[17] And in the following story told by Rabbi Mordechai Rogov[18] about the Mussar supervisor (*mashgiach*) in the prewar Mir Yeshiva, we see not only an affirmation of our ability to change, but the actual obligation we hold to do so:

> When I was a student in the Mir Yeshivah, I enjoyed a close relationship with the *mashgiach* Rabbi Yerucham Levovitz. One beautiful spring day, when a group of boys gathered in his house to study mussar, the *mashgiach* rushed into the room and had a very agitated look on his face. The *mashgiach* then cried out, "I just came from the street, and I saw that all around me everything was growing. Why are you not growing?" Ever since that day, whenever I get warm and comfortable, I can hear the *mashgiach*'s voice roaring at me, "Why aren't you growing?"[19]

Mussar Practice to Prepare for Mussar Work

As important as practice is to Mussar, it is only preparation. The real focus is Mussar work. What's the difference? By practice I refer to the exercises and methods we do in retreat, in the quiet of private meditation, in our daily disciplines. Mussar work, in contrast, is what comes to us when we deal with the real-life situations for which our spiritual practice is preparation. Mussar has always made a point of stressing both—you need to prepare, but don't think you leave your spiritual curriculum behind when you step out of the synagogue or yeshiva or your own quiet space at home.

Mussar teachers have never counseled withdrawal from the messy currents of life, as if to beach yourself on some sandy, palm-fringed shore where life will not disturb your peace of mind. Practice is meant to ready you to stay upright and awake right within the torrent, so you can see it just as it is and choose your course.

Strengthening your ability to choose expands your capacity to exercise free will, which the Jewish tradition sees as a defining feature of being human. The Mussar teachers encourage us to attune to the pure and holy soul and to free ourselves from the influences of what they call the animal spirit.[20] Our struggle is to lift ourselves up so that our higher self guides our life. This, too, can be expressed in terms of modern science. The most primitive part of our nervous system—the limbic brain—functions only from the emotions and is guided entirely by the instinct to survive. It's the limbic brain that has us act out with aggression when we are threatened, even if it perceives a threat in an innocent gesture. The limbic brain is always primed and ready to pull us into instinctive action, and so all attempts to live to the high standards of the Torah, with generosity, kindness, and self-sacrifice, involve struggling with and overcoming the limbic brain.

When we are in the grip of the deep and ancient limbic system, our lives are governed by fear and instinct, whereas the processes centered in the cerebral cortex allow us to verify or override the evaluations of the limbic system, to exercise choice, and to foresee the consequences of our actions.

This fundamental dichotomous human reality is related in the Torah, in the two stories it tells of how humans were created. In Genesis 1:27–28 we read:

> So God created man in His image. In the image of God, He created him, male and female He created them. And God blessed them. God said to them, "Be fruitful and multiply, and fill the earth and subdue it, and have dominion over the fish of the sea, the birds of the sky, and over the beasts, and over all the earth."

Soon after, Genesis 2:7–8 tells a different story:

> God formed man out of dust of the ground, and breathed into his nostrils a living soul. Man [thus] became a living creature. God planted a garden in Eden to the east. There He placed the man that He had formed.

Rabbi Joseph Ber Soloveitchik names these two creatures "Adam the first" and "Adam the second" and gives us a picture of the difference between them. The Adam of the first creation story was given the mandate of living in the world and subduing it, while the second Adam had a living soul breathed into a body and was told to cultivate and protect a garden:

While Adam the first is dynamic and creative, transforming sensory data into thought constructs, Adam the second is receptive and beholds the world in its original dimensions. He looks for the image of God not in the mathematical formula or the natural relational law but in every beam of light, in every bud and blossom, in the morning breeze and the stillness of a starlit evening.[21]

These two Adams are not meant to be understood as different types of people but rather as two dimensions that live within—and often struggle within—each of us.

Scientists, the Mussar masters, and the Torah agree. The challenge that you and I face in our lives is nothing less than the developmental story of our species, which means doing what we can to free ourselves from the dictates of our primitive natures and establish the governance of our higher self, the soul. "A man should always incite his good inclination against the evil impulse,"[22] is how the rabbis of the Talmud put it. Every day, many times a day, each of us engages in this struggle. It takes place on the world stage, in major events that pit the good in humanity against that which is base and self-serving. But the struggle strikes much closer to home as well. Rabbi Moshe Chaim Luzzatto tells us that as humans we are all "placed between wholeness and deficiency, with the power to earn wholeness. Man must earn this wholeness, however, through his own free will. . . . Man's inclinations are therefore balanced between good and evil, and he is not compelled toward either of them. He has the power of choice and is able to choose either side knowingly and willingly."[23]

In every decision and choice you make, there will be an option that represents the way of the higher self, and another that answers the call of the lower self. What you eat, whom you speak to, how much you sleep, what you read, how you do your hair, and a hundred other daily decisions are the battleground between higher and lower self, in you. It is to help us walk this way of the soul that for one thousand years the Mussar masters have been developing, recording, and passing on their techniques. Rabbi Simcha Zissel, the Alter of Kelm, taught that we practice Mussar "in simple things, small things, to come through them to the greatest heights."[24]

6

Two Illustrations

TWO EXAMPLES of how all this theory plays out in the actual practice and work of Mussar will help make clear how Mussar plays its role in the lives of real people like you and me.

The first concerns Marianne, a Mussar student who has a teenage daughter with whom she was having much too much conflict for her liking. Their discord wasn't at a level so different from many mother-daughter relationships, but Marianne wanted to lift her relationship with her daughter to a higher level. Her ultimate objective was the wholeness of her soul, and she saw resolving this problematic relationship as key work she needed to do with that goal in mind.

Her predicament was that no matter what kindness and love she intended, as soon as her daughter did something that annoyed her, Marianne exploded and ripped into her daughter with all sorts of verbal abuse. She knew she was damaging their relationship, both now and for the future, yet the power of her emotions and the deep ruts of habit kept her from making any change.

I guided Marianne to work on the soul-traits that needed to be strengthened in order that she could take control of herself and the situation. In Mussar, the route to changing a relationship (or changing the world, for that matter) is to do the spiritual practice needed to change yourself. We focused on cultivating patience, equanimity, and humility, and most of all on the soul-trait of honor. Partly this was a matter of her learning new ideas—practically speaking, to inculcate the perspective that every human being, including an annoying teenage girl, is a radiant soul inherently deserving of honor. But the learning didn't stop there. To take that lesson and imprint it on her heart, so that she would really *see* the soul in the other, Marianne engaged in Mussar exercises like those I've described, which are designed to bring that about.

One day she called me, quite excited. Her daughter had been repainting her room in preparation for the new school year and had accidentally kicked over a can of green paint. On the beige carpet. Right in front of her mother.

"At that exact instant," Marianne told me, "as the green paint was seeping into the carpet, I saw before me in my mind two doors. One was really familiar and well used, and behind it I could see myself yelling, 'You idiot! You clumsy imbecile!' and a lot more. The other door was a new one for me. Behind it, I saw myself saying, 'What a mess! Let's clean this up.' And I saw that the choice was mine."

Marianne's spiritual practice had given her a measure of free will she'd never had before. With appropriate pride she reported, "And so I said to her, 'What a mess! Let's clean this up.'"

To this I responded, "Marianne, you just gave a gift not only to your daughter, but also to your grandchildren. Because you just changed the kind of mother your daughter will be."

It's important to reiterate that Mussar is not another kind of "self-help" system that showed Marianne how to improve herself on the functional interpersonal and psychological levels. What Marianne was consciously working on, and what Mussar is concerned with, is overcoming the sorts of obstacles that prevent you from realizing the potential of your soul—and sometimes that does mean dealing with issues as concrete as how you eat, speak, or even dress. Mussar differs from self-help because it encourages you to do all this not in order to gratify some as-yet unfulfilled personal and worldly desire, but because this is the path you must walk in order to bring the soul to wholeness and holiness.

Mussar would never suggest that you can expect to find fulfillment by getting what you want, especially because its teachings wisely point out that our desires are endless. Instead, we are told to aim higher, toward the highest virtues the biblical tradition identifies, because that is the route to fulfilling the soul's potential. That's a masterful strategy, because when we refocus our vision beyond worldly indulgence, we also gain exceptional clarity about what exists on this plane, too. By connecting to higher truths beyond material concerns, even the tiniest details of our lives come into new focus so that they can be addressed and transformed.

Here is another story. Rob is a Mussar student who found himself caught in one of the most primitive of situations, one that is so ancient the Torah actually warns us against it directly. "Do not bear a grudge," we are told.[1] But how could he not? Eighteen years ago, he and his wife were blessed with the birth of their first child, a son. They planned the circumcision ceremony for the eighth day, as Jewish law dictates, and they happily invited all their friends and family to the celebration. As it happened, Rob's father did not get along with Rob's wife's parents and so, when he called his father to invite him to the ceremony, Rob added, "And, Dad, please make an effort to be civil to Sarah's parents."

Well, Rob's father took such offense at this comment that he did not attend the circumcision of his own grandson. Not only that, he stopped speaking to his son, who was only too happy to reciprocate the favor. As a result, father and son did not speak for eighteen years. In that time, Rob's father never met his own grandson.

One of the soul-traits Rob worked on in his Mussar practice was forgiveness, which, one might have expected, would bring up the deep grudge he was bearing and provide an opening for healing. But that actually wasn't what happened. When he thought of forgiving, the grievance seemed, on a deep inner level, too unjust. Wasn't his father responsible, after all?

While forgiveness didn't actually create illumination for Rob, when the soul-trait of generosity came into focus, a light went on. Confronted by the Mussar understanding of generosity, which entails stretching yourself to give beyond the boundaries of the comfortable or usual, a new course opened up before him.

Rob wrote a letter to his father as an act of conscious generosity. And his father wrote back. Rob and his wife had been married for twenty-five years by this time and decided to celebrate with a party. Rob invited his father, who lived in a distant state. His father came and met his grandson for the first time.

Mussar had opened the way to healing, inwardly and in relationship. It had provided Rob with the tools he needed to free himself from the dictates of his primitive, grudge-bearing nature and to entrust the governance of his life to his higher self, the soul, which seeks both *sh'lemut* (wholeness) and *shalom* (peace). This was a fruit of his Mussar practice.

Seek for it like silver and search for it like hidden treasure.

—Proverbs/*Mishlei* 2:4

PART TWO

The Map

7

Humility

ANAVAH

Occupy a rightful space, neither too much nor too little.
Focus neither on your own virtues nor the faults of others.

> Generally, man finds his delight in examining his own
> virtues, in discovering even the smallest of his positive
> attributes and the most minute faults of his friends, for
> he can then find reason to be proud even when in the
> company of great ones whose little fingers are thicker
> than his loins.
>
> —Rabbi M. M. Leffin, *Cheshbon ha'Nefesh*

SOON AFTER I HAD FINISHED giving a talk, an elderly woman approached me. I greeted her, and she started to say something. "You have a wonderful, wonderful . . . ," she began, speaking slowly and stretching out the words, giving me lots of time to guess what it was she was leading up to. "Voice," I finished her sentence in my mind, since I had just addressed the group. No, I then thought, maybe she was about to say "way with words," since people do say I am articulate. And right after that, because I felt I had just made a really good presentation, I upped the ante to "presence." Before I could speculate any further, however, her sentence arrived at the station to which her words had slowly been winding. ". . . wife," she pronounced, her eyes smiling warmly. Oh, I thought. Then, "Thank you," I recovered. "How do you know her?"

I've never had a more graphic illustration of my own instinctive craving for praise and honor. Having blindly stepped in it up to my ankle, there was no way I could deny where I stood. Here was my spiritual curriculum.

Where Your Curriculum Begins

I've emphasized that your interior world is the realm of soul, and the soul-traits that are turned up too high or too low define your spiritual curriculum. But where to start the course? In *Duties of the Heart*, Rabbi Bachya ibn Pakuda helps direct our attention by posing a question: "On what do the virtues depend?"

His answer is clear: "All virtues and duties are dependent on humility."[1] This is a principle later Mussar teachers have endorsed—the first leg of the spiritual journey involves the cultivation of humility. The importance they place on humility is underlined in the Talmud,[2] where we read: "One who sacrifices a whole offering shall be rewarded for a whole offering. One who offers a burnt-offering shall have the reward of a burnt-offering. But one who offers humility to God and man shall be rewarded with a reward as if he had offered all the sacrifices in the world. As it is written, 'A contrite and humbled spirit is a sacrifice to God. God does not ignore a broken heart.'"[3]

The Mussar teachers stress that humility is a primary soul-trait to work on because it entails an unvarnished and honest assessment of who you are. Without this accurate self-awareness, nothing else in your inner life will come into focus in its true measure—and it is no accident that the word that means "soul-trait" in Hebrew is *middah* (pl. *middot*), which literally does mean "measure." Without humility, either you will be so puffed up with arrogance that you won't even see what really needs some work, or you will be so deflated and lacking in self-esteem that you will despair of being able to make the changes that are lit up so glaringly in your self-critical mind.

Humility and Self-Esteem

Unfortunately for us, humility sounds so much like humiliation that it's easy to get a very wrong impression of this soul-trait. In the traditional Jewish understanding, humility has nothing to do with being the lowest, most debased, shrinking creature on earth. Rav Abraham Isaac Kook, who was the first Ashkenazi Chief Rabbi of Israel, says it well: "Humility is associated with spiritual perfection. When humility effects depression it is defective; when it is genuine it inspires joy, courage and inner dignity."[4]

Mussar teaches that real humility is always associated with healthy self-esteem. Lack of self-esteem leads to unholy and false feelings of worthlessness. One student in a Mussar course developed this insight from her own experience. She had the habit of sitting in the front at public gatherings and of wearing colorful clothes. When she was learning about humility, she decided to try toning herself down for the next event she attended. "This time, I packed my suitcase with beige, black, white, and brown clothes and made the choice to sit in the back of the room." Despite this retraction of self, she reported, "I had a great time, so much so that some people noticed and asked me what I was up to." But what really struck home was the realization she had that the sitting in the front and the colorful clothing were reflections "that I lacked a solid foundation in self-esteem."

She responded by focusing her Mussar practice on "rebuilding my self-esteem and having it based on a foundation of loving-kindness and humility." She could see the effect: "Recently, I have begun to feel a difference. As I develop my own internal love and respect for myself and become less other-directed, I do not need to be acknowledged by others for what I do. I have always sought the approval of others. Now my motivation is more internal and true to my own self."

Let's be very clear, though, that being humble doesn't mean being a nobody, it just means being no more of a somebody than you ought to be. After all, Moses, who is considered the greatest of the prophets, is described in the Torah as "very humble, more than any other men who were upon the face of the earth."[5] If a leader as great as Moses was so humble, there is surely more to humility than the shrinking meekness we ordinarily associate with the term.

Not This, Not That

Every aspect of our lives is experienced by us through the lens of the ego, and when that glass is distorted or obscured, we will no longer perceive any of the details of our lives accurately, as they are. Too little humility—what we'd call arrogance or conceit—is easily seen as this sort of spiritual impediment. Even scripture is remarkably concrete on this point: "The arrogant cannot stand in Your presence; You hate all who do wrong."[6]

Rabbi Rafael of Barshad[7] told a story that captures just how unfitting it is to think overly highly of oneself: "When I get to heaven, they'll ask me, why didn't you learn more Torah? And I'll tell them that I wasn't bright enough. Then they'll ask me, why didn't you do more kind deeds for others? And I'll tell them that I was physically weak. Then they'll ask me, why didn't you give more to charity? And I'll tell them that I didn't have enough money for that. And then they'll ask me: If you were so stupid, weak and poor, why were you so arrogant? And for that I won't have an answer."

Because they abhorred arrogance, the followers of the Novarodok branch of Mussar were legendary for the exercises they undertook to reduce and deter excesses of ego. Their teachers would send them into a hardware store to ask for bread, and then into a bakery to ask for nails. They'd often get chased out of the store for those antics, but they learned that their self-worth did not depend on other people's appraisal and that they could get by in life with a whole lot less pride than they might otherwise have thought necessary.

But the opposite is equally true. Humility taken to the extreme also throws a veil across the inner light of the soul. The rabbis in the Talmud make this point very forcefully through a story that begins: "The humility of Rabbi Zechariah ben Avkulas caused the destruction of the Temple in Jerusalem."[8] This was a cataclysmic event in Jewish history that is still mourned today. How could a virtue like humility cause so terrible a catastrophe?

To understand, we have to enter the story a little earlier, when a man named Bar Kamtza sought revenge on the Jewish leaders of Jerusalem who had offended him. He went to the Roman governors to inform them that the Jews were rebelling. To prove his point, he told the Romans to send a sacrifice to the Temple. Normally such a sacrifice would be offered up, but Bar Kamtza caused a minor blemish on the animal that was unnoticeable to the Romans, but that he knew the Temple priests would see. Because a sacrifice must be blemishless, Bar Kamtza knew that the priests would be bound to refuse to accept the offering. This refusal would be the "proof" that the Jews were in rebellion against Rome.

When the sacrifice came before the priests in the Temple, they immediately spotted the hidden blemish, as Bar Kamtza knew they would. But what he may not have anticipated was that they immediately understood what was going on. Someone suggested that they go ahead and offer the sacrifice anyway. Rabbi Zechariah ben Avkulas, however, argued that if they did that, people would draw the incorrect conclusion that it was permitted to offer blemished sacrifices.

It was then suggested that Bar Kamtza be killed to prevent him from telling the Romans and endangering the Jewish people. Rabbi Zechariah ben Avkulas responded, saying, "If we do so, people will incorrectly think that those who inflict blemishes on sacrifices are put to death."

As a result of the priest's unwillingness to accept either course of action, Bar Kamtza succeeded in his plan. The sacrifice was denied, and as Bar Kamtza had planned, the Romans took this to mean that the Jews were in rebellion. The Romans attacked and ultimately destroyed the Temple. The Talmud concludes, "The humility of Rabbi Zechariah ben Avkulas caused the loss of our home, the burning of our sanctuary, and our exile from the land."

There is no understanding this statement in any way that we usually define the term *humility*. This story offers us a new insight into the traditional Jewish concept of humility.

Rabbi Zechariah ben Avkulas showed humility because he did not act with presumption—neither by offering a blemished animal in seeming contravention of the rules, nor by condoning murder—but he actually manifested *too much* humility, because he shrank from the task he had been handed. He held the fate of the Temple and his people in his hands, yet he seemed to say, "Who am I to make such unprecedented decisions that will potentially mislead the people as to the law?" This was his excessive humility. His sense of himself was flawed because he saw himself as less capable than he actually was of solving a real-life dilemma of great consequence.

To clarify the picture even more, let's add for consideration another enigmatic reflection on humility from the Talmud that says: "Anyone who sets a particular place for himself to pray in the synagogue, the God of Abraham stands in his aid, and when he dies, people say of him, 'This was a humble person.'"[9]

Now that's curious, don't you think? Where is the humility in sitting in the same place every time you pray in the synagogue? The answer is that by fixing yourself to one spot, you free up all the other space for others to use.

Adding this story to the one on the destruction of the Temple helps us to frame a Mussar definition of humility as "limiting oneself to an appropriate space while leaving room for others." Sitting in a predictable place, you make room for others to occupy their own spaces, too. Rabbi Zechariah ben Avkulas gave up too much of his "space," considering that the space a person occupies can be physical, emotional, verbal, or even metaphorical.

We hear an echo of the same notion in the description of the seating arrangement in the ancient Jewish court, the Sanhedrin. The Talmud[10] reports:

> There were three rows of disciples of the sages who sat before [the judges], and each knew his proper place. If they needed to appoint [another as a judge], they appointed him from the first row, and one from the second row came into the first row, and one from the third row came into the second row, and they chose another from the congregation and set him in the third row. He did not sit in the place of the former, but he sat in the place that was proper for him.

Humility Is Not an Extreme

Our definition of humility fits the Rambam's concept that humility is not the opposite of conceit, which would be self-effacement, but rather stands between conceit and self-effacement.[11] Humility is not an extreme quality, but rather a balanced, moderate, accurate understanding of yourself that you act on in your life. That's why humility and self-esteem go hand in hand.

We can graph this teaching as follows:

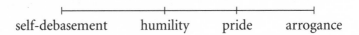

self-debasement   humility   pride   arrogance

Arrogance has an insatiable appetite for space. It claims. It occupies. It sprawls. It suffocates others. Every statement in its voice begins with "I." The opposite extreme is self-debasement. Shrinking from occupying any space whatsoever, it retracts meekly inside itself. Its statements would never dare to begin with "I," although, in fact, if we listen carefully, they all do, because, whether we see ourselves as nothing or as everything, we are still preoccupied with the self, and both of these traits are, therefore, forms of narcissism. In Jewish terms, they are two variations on the theme of idolatry. Both extremes—whether we see ourselves as a god or a worm—are severe distortions of truth. Neither expresses humility. Neither is true so neither reflects accurate self-knowledge. The truth is toward the middle range, where there is room for self and other.

Role Models of Humility

Our primary role model for the space-making nature of humility is none other than God. In an interesting turn of phrase, just as God is about to create Adam, the text reads, "And God said, 'Let us make Man in Our image, as Our likeness.'"[12] For centuries, sages have wondered about the use of the plural pronoun *Us*. Why is the description of the creation of man phrased in the plural? Who is this "us" that God is referring to?

The medieval commentator Rashi says that we learn from this passage that God is humble. How does he draw that lesson? He explains: "Since man is in the likeness of the angels and they would be jealous of him, for this reason, God consulted them." He goes on to say that this verse teaches "proper conduct and the trait of humility, that the greater one should consult and take permission from the lesser one."[13]

The lesson is that if God Himself is so humble as to take second opinions on the Creator's own actions, shouldn't we be at least that humble ourselves? We act with humility by making space in our lives to listen to others, even if they happen to hold a lesser station or rank or intellectual attainment than we do.

All the Mussar masters have been masters of humility and offer us earthly role models of this trait. A man once gave Rabbi Eliyahu Dessler what seemed to him to be excessive honor by referring to him directly in the third person, calling him "ha'Rav"—the Teacher—as in "Would ha'Rav like to do this or that?" Rabbi Dessler responded by asking that he not be called by that title. "You can injure a person speaking like that," he said.

Witness, too, Rabbi Yisrael Salanter's statement about himself. He said, "I know that I have the mental capacity of a thousand men." This was surely not arrogance on his part, just uncommon honesty and accurate self-knowledge. He followed it up by noting, "Because of that, my obligation to serve God is also that of a thousand men." He knew his space and his capacity to occupy it.

Occupying Your Rightful Space

Do you express humility by limiting yourself to taking up just the appropriate space while leaving room for others? Next time you sit on a bench, watch how much of it you occupy. There is no need to cringe on the edge, because you're entitled to sit. Yet there is also no justification for sprawling into a space that ought to accommodate someone else. Or when someone shares a piece of news with you, do you come right back with your own concerns, filling the space they've opened, or do you make room to follow up what the other person has introduced?

One Mussar student reports on how her insights in this area have changed her behavior. Now, she says, "when friends, family, and associates tell me their troubles, I no longer rush in with my brilliant advice or suggestions as to how to solve their problems. My capacity for self-restraint has developed, and I no longer feel as much need to look smart, wise, good, etc." Understanding that her behavior was meant to gratify her own needs at the expense of caring for others, she said, "I'm now willing to take up less space in this domain."

Another student also sees a role for humility in interaction with others. "Before I learned Mussar," he said, "when in a group setting, I always chose to add something to the discussion." He says he works hard to remember to take only the space he requires. "I ask myself, 'Is this comment *absolutely* vital to the discussion at hand?' and often wait longer before giving my view."

Big Spaces and Small Spaces

When you understand humility in terms of the space you occupy, it's important to clarify that we are not all meant to occupy the same amount of space. Some people appropriately occupy a lot of space, as would be the case for a leader—think of Moses again. But if a leader laid claim to even more space than was appropriate, they would be Pharaoh. And we have already learned from the case of Rabbi Zechariah ben Avkulas that a leader who shrinks from his responsibilities—that is, takes up less space than appropriate—can also create disastrous consequences.

At the other end of the spectrum, it may be entirely appropriate for a more solitary person to occupy a less than average volume of space. Were people of this nature to force themselves to speak up more, be more outgoing—in other words, to fill more space—the consequences could be negative at the level of soul. Nor would such people be serving the soul to withdraw themselves even further than is suitable for them.

The right amount of space is also situational. When police officers direct traffic, we accept that they are occupying a large public space. But when those same police officers go to their child's school for parent-teacher night, were they to try to occupy as "large" a space as they do on the street, they would appear arrogant and presumptuous.

The Well-Situated Ego

We read the following enigmatic saying in the Talmud: "Rava [a disciple of the sages] said: 'Who possesses [haughtiness of spirit] deserves excommunication, and if he does not possess it he deserves excommunication.'"[14] The lesson we are meant to take away is that there is great spiritual danger in having an ego that is overinflated—and just as much spiritual danger in being devoid of self-esteem.[15]

Proper humility means having the right relationship to self, giving self neither too big nor too small a role in your life. Rabbi Chatzkel Abramsky, a well-known leader of the Jewish community in England, was once called to testify in court. His lawyer asked him, "Rabbi Abramsky, is it true that you are the greatest living Jewish legal authority in Europe?" The rabbi replied, "Yes. That is true." At that point the judge interjected and said, "Rabbi Abramsky, is that not rather haughty on your part? I thought that your laws and ethics teach you to be humble." To which Rabbi Abramsky responded, "I know we are taught to be humble. But what can I do? I am under oath."

The more you accept extreme inner attitudes that either build up the ego or tear it down, the more you deviate from truth. The inner voice that says, "You're hot!" and the one that says, "You're not!" both originate from the same source, and both mislead. The core issue is that these different voices draw our focus toward self, and that distracts from soul, which is really where we should keep our focus.

If you're unsure whether humility is a soul-trait you need to work on, ask yourself this: Do you leave enough space in your life for others, or are you jamming up your world with your self? Or is there space you ought rightfully to occupy that you need to stretch into? Your answers are the measure of your humility and define how humility figures into your spiritual curriculum.

The goal would be to have it said of you (as it was of one of the Mussar masters of the nineteenth century), "He was so humble he didn't even know he was humble."[16]

> A small deed done in humility is a thousand times more acceptable to God than a great deed done in pride.
>
> —*Orchot Tzaddikim* (The Ways of the Righteous)

8

Patience

SAVLANUT

Whatever may obstruct me from reaching my goals, it is possible to bear the burden of the situation.

Woe to the pampered one who has never been trained to be patient. Either today or in the future he is destined to sip from the cup of affliction.

—Rabbi M. M. Leffin, *Cheshbon ha'Nefesh*

NOT A DAY GOES BY when we don't face some sort of frustrating delay or obstacle, and too often our response is to strain against how things are. That tends to happen to me when I'm rushing somewhere in my car, but those feelings may suddenly sneak up on you while the water fills the tub ever so slowly, or as your child struggles with clumsy fingers to master the complexity of a shoelace, or on those days when nothing—not your Internet server, not your spouse, not the postman, *nobody!!*—does things when or how you want.

Impatience seldom makes things happen faster or better and usually only causes us grief. It's like an inner blaze that burns us up without giving off any warmth. That would be bad enough, but it is also a short step from impatience to rage, and we all know what harm can come to ourselves and others because of uncontrollable anger.

I'd be remiss not to point out right at the outset that there are circumstances where we should not be patient and where patience is not a virtue. When confronted with injustice or the needs or suffering of another person or other situations where our actions could make a difference, we have no business patiently taking our time. Patience comes into play when it is our own burden we are bearing, or when there really is no course of action available to us at that moment to alleviate the situation.

Walking in God's Patient Way

Who wouldn't be delighted to deepen their ability to meet life's challenges with more patience? We get very clear support for doing so from the Bible, where it tells us that we should "walk in His ways".[1] This simple but forceful idea—sometimes called *imitatio dei*, emulating God—is the ultimate blueprint for the spiritual life and tells us that we should model our lives on godly virtues. That's how we move ourselves closer to the highest potential we have from birth, and when we act with heavenly virtue in our personal lives, we help to make this world a little more like heaven.

In practical terms, we emulate God by practicing virtue or, as I like to call it, living in "virtuous reality." The sages tell us: "As God is called merciful and gracious, so be you merciful and gracious; as God is called righteous, so be you righteous; as God is called holy, so be you holy."[2] As God is forgiving, so too should we strive to be forgiving. We are guided to emulate God in all the divine attributes of mercy and righteousness, though not the attributes of severity and justice that we can also find in the Torah. Because we want the world to be infused with qualities of goodness, we have a responsibility to become vessels for those same virtues. That prescription includes the trait of patience.

No matter how you may conceive of God or the creative force that stands behind the universe, there is no doubt that this ultimate source of life is endowed with patience, especially when compared to us. Think of the pace of earthly eras, creeping along as slowly as glaciers advancing and retreating in an ice age. Stars and galaxies are born, mature, and pass away. And as for us, what the Mussar tradition offers as evidence for God's patience is the fact that our lives are sustained, even when we do wrong.[3] It's not hard to imagine a universe where there is absolutely no margin for error, where punishment is instantaneous and total, but that isn't the world we live in. God is patient and preserves our lives even when our actions happen to hit way off the mark, to give us time to come to deeper realizations, make amends, and return to a straighter way.

"From this, man should learn to what extent he, too, should be patient and bear the yoke of his fellow."[4] Since God is patient, then we, who are encouraged to guide our lives by "walking in His ways," should also be patient.

Suffering Impatience

Where we get into trouble with impatience is in our reactivity. The problem confronting you may be entirely real: You're late. You need it now. There will be consequences. But whatever the problem, no matter how great or how small, it is one thing to face those life issues just as they are, and quite another to slop grief, worry, regret, impatience, and other such mental condiments all over the situation. Reactions like these only increase our burden by adding a whole extra dimension of inner suffering (and often hurtful behavior) to an already difficult experience.

Can you identify situations that tend to try your patience?

In the chapter on patience in the classic Mussar text *Cheshbon ha'Nefesh* by Rabbi Menachem Mendel Leffin,[5] the author sets up his discussion by pointing out that there are many cases of people extracting delight from what we'd agree are painful and unsavory experiences. By way of illustration he mentions the experience of tasting vinegar and pepper, which are sour and sharp but which can add zest and flavor to food (when used in the right way) and be a delight to the palate.

But "towering above all these are the spiritual delights in which the supernal soul [*neshama*] exalts—for example, the wondrous, sublime pleasure of acting righteously with everyone." He is pointing to something that we have all experienced because it is innate within us, which is the deep and satisfying pleasure we get from doing good, especially with other people.

Continuing to work toward his consideration of patience, he points out that in many situations we can do right by planning and careful action. But for "those serious incidents which come upon us unavoidably and which we were powerless to prepare for or which we could not deal with once they transpired, God has provided us with a remedial regimen—patience."[6]

Patience is here depicted as a tool we can call on to help us endure when we find ourselves in difficult circumstances we did not choose and could not avoid. In this he is revealing something essential about patience as this attribute is understood in the Jewish tradition. The Hebrew word for patience is *savlanut,* which can also mean "tolerance." The same root[7] gives rise to words that mean "suffer" and "endure" and also the noun for a porter who carries goods. We can learn something fundamental from this pool of words that derive from the common source: patience means enduring and tolerating, and the experience may even bring us elements of suffering.

We get a hint of the same message in the English word "suffer," which means both to experience pain and to tolerate, or put up with. So patience is not just about waiting, it's about bearing. A story told by a Mussar student reflects on this core aspect of patience. She had been in a car accident that caused her back problems and that, in turn, had an impact on her ability to work. "I think about all the patience I have had to have to get to this point. Patience with my back and physical limitations. Patience with the legal process. Patience with my attorney, who wasn't always available exactly when I had a question or a need."

She realized that the root of her problem with being patient was "accepting what I cannot control. It is not that difficult to surrender and say to myself, 'I have done all I can; it is in the hands of God.' What is so much more difficult is to be at peace about it and to really let go. I find that tolerating the uncertainty of the outcome, and accepting the burden of an outcome that is unwanted, are both hard." Here is the "bearing" that is essential to patience.

The converse is that if you are the kind of person who finds it easy to be joyful in traffic jams and to whistle happily in mile-long bank lines, then you have little need for patience. You're already well equipped with tranquillity or equanimity, and so you are not that reactive to the delays and obstacles that tend to send most people spinning into a rage. Patience comes into play when you are already ticked off, when the situation already has you starting to fume. It's then that you reach into your pocket to pull out your patience, which helps you bear the burden that is pressing on you.

Opening the Space between the Match and the Fuse

The problem with impatience is that it usually takes only a split second for its first glowing embers to ignite into flames that course through us even before we've become aware that they have started up. Impatience snuffs out consciousness, and before I even know it's happening, I'm leaning on my horn, or you're going hoarse yelling at your child or cursing the postman. At this point we don't even recognize ourselves, and there is little to be done but to try to rein in these feelings enough to minimize any damage we might do.

It's so much better to be able to catch our impatience as it is arising and to nip it in the bud. To do this we need to recognize the fact that we are getting impatient and then take responsibility for our impatience. This is much easier said than done.

For example, it is common that when a couple is getting ready to go out for a pleasant evening, one of them is always ready before the other. And it is always the same one who is ready first and waiting at the door while the other one has to make one more phone call, or change shoes or tie or dress one last time, or check on something or other. Time passes, impatience grows, and by the time they are both in the car heading out for the evening or to visit friends, they are not even speaking to each other.

The tendency is for the one who is always ready first to become righteous and blame the other one for bad behavior. While it surely isn't good to be unpunctual and to waste other people's time, what the impatient person tends to be blind to is that he or she has the personal freedom to choose to call upon the power of patience in that moment, in order to bear the situation without smoldering and then igniting and acting out.

When you find yourself in a situation that is triggering your impatience, instead of giving all your attention and energy to finding fault with the person who is so clearly at fault, you can choose to be patient and take responsibility for your emotional response to that situation. You make the choice of whether you buckle or call on patience to help you bear the burden of the situation. My teacher, Rabbi Perr, calls this awareness and exercise of choice "opening the space between the match and the fuse."

Witnessing and Naming

Being able to call on patience in the way I am describing depends on having cultivated your awareness of the telltale signs of impatience so you can spot them right in the instant that they begin to stir. The practice is to witness and name the feelings just as they come up, which requires that you say to yourself, "I'm feeling impatient" or "There's impatience." Just by forming those words, you are holding open at least a tiny crack through which the light of consciousness can still shine, and if you can do that, then at that point what is going to happen to that impatience is suddenly no longer so certain.

There are obstacles to the sort of awareness I am noting here. One is the common condition of simply being disconnected from one's own feelings. Too often people who are impatient and act it are unaware of their own behavior. When the inner lights are dimmed like that, spiritual progress is stopped in its tracks. Another equally common obstacle is denial. In this case, people actually do know their patterns but refuse to acknowledge and take responsibility for them. Rather, they deflect what is real and could be painful and difficult, and instead cling to false analyses and excuses.

Truth and consciousness are preconditions to exercising free will. Only when the light of awareness is glowing brightly can we see the truth and choose to follow a course that is guided by our values and goals, not by our "animal soul":[8] instincts, emotional reactions, and habits. And the brighter awareness glows, the more freedom of choice we have.

Many techniques work to increase the strength of conscious awareness to open that space between the match and the fuse. Meditation does this, and it is also one of the main outcomes of the "Accounting of the Soul" practice that is described in part 3 of this book. The challenging thing is, you have to commit yourself to doing these sorts of practices at those times when awareness is *not* being tested, so their effects will be there right at hand when it is. This tests your discipline. If you suddenly found yourself having to climb up many flights of stairs, you'd be very glad that you had kept up your physical conditioning before it was called on. If you were a gunfighter in the Wild West, you'd work on your draw before you needed it for a shoot-out. The same is true for the inner life. As my first meditation teacher repeatedly said, "Do spiritual practice now, so you'll have it when you need it!"

Patience and Humility

The situations in which we can feel impatience are numberless, but there is one common factor that unites them all. We only burn with that particular fire when the focus in the situation is on *me*. You are delaying *me*, misleading *me*, berating *me*. You are interfering with *my* plan or standing in the way of *my* needs. Sometimes the only inner voice I can hear is my ego, loudly promoting all its important needs and plans and drowning out any other voice that might whisper within.

We all tend to see ourselves as the prime actor in a drama that swirls around us. Some of us believe that all that heavy action is playing out according to a script we ourselves have written. Others see it the opposite way, playing the victim to the forces that press in on their own little stronghold. Despite the obvious differences, both these attitudes see the whole of life as pivoting around a separate identity that stands at the center of a very personal universe.

But the truth is different. We are neither so central nor independent as all that. We are actually wired into all kinds of larger circuits and systems, from the molecular to the social, and we don't control many of the factors that have a role in shaping our lives. Least of all can we expect to rule the timetable according to which life takes place.

The Mussar teachers encourage us to contemplate these truths, because when we realize a deeper understanding of our rightful place in the universe, this helps us avoid getting all worked up when things don't go just precisely as we'd like. Why should everything go our way, considering how small we are and how many other agendas and needs are always involved? When we do hold in sight how integrated we are within the grand schemes that make up and sustain the world, we see ourselves situated amid the large wheels turning and rivers flowing, moved by hands that are not our own. Whatever pleasure or pain we may experience, our lives are taking place within great cycles of time, space, and material, even though we often have our eyes focused so directly in front of our noses that we don't perceive the truth of that largest picture.

We truthfully have so little control over so many features of our lives that it doesn't make any sense at all to put ourselves through useless suffering as if we did have control. And that's just what we do when we slip into impatience.

It's important to sort out what is actually within our power and what is not. And the remarkable thing is that in both cases, we are better off to be patient—patient with the things that are within our control to change, and patient with those that aren't.

Fruits of Patience

Patience doesn't mean that we become passive. We still need to make a genuine effort to set the pace and trajectory of our lives, but we don't need to react to every delay or deflection as if it were a denial, whether that means a denial of our selves or a denial by God. In those moments when I am good at being patient, I live in the here and now, without straining against reality. I walk a middle path, not leaning to the one extreme of being inactive and fatalistic—because that way I negate the powers I do have, limited though they might be—nor veering to the other, where impatience reigns.

There is a story in the Talmud[9] about Rav Preida, who had a student who was so slow that he could not grasp a lesson unless his teacher taught it to him four hundred times. One day, while Rav Preida was teaching this student, someone came and told the rabbi that he needed his services when he had finished teaching. That day, after he had completed the four hundredth repetition, Rav Preida asked the student if he had grasped the lesson, to which the student replied that he had not. "Why is it different today than other days?" the teacher asked, and his student answered that from the moment the other person had come to speak to Rav Preida, the student had been distracted, thinking to himself, "Soon the master will have to get up ... Soon the master will have to get up ..." Rav Preida then replied, "If that is so, let me teach you the lesson again." He then repeated the teaching an additional four hundred times. When he had finished, a heavenly voice called out to Rav Preida, "Which reward do you want? Either four hundred years will be added to your life, or you and your generation will be received into the World-to-Come." He answered, "I request that my generation and I merit the World-to-Come." To this the heavenly voice replied, "Give him *both!*"

Such are the fruits of patience.

9

Gratitude

HAKARAT HA'TOV

Awaken to the good and give thanks.

Ben Zoma used to say: "A good guest says, 'How much my host toiled for me! He put so much meat in front of me, so much wine, so much bread—all his exertion was just for me!' A bad guest says, 'What did my host toil for me? I ate just one roll, just one piece of meat, I drank just one cup—all his exertion was for his own household!'"

—Babylonian Talmud: *B'rachot* 58a

A PSALM OF THANKSGIVING

Shout for joy to the Lord, all the earth.
Worship the Lord with gladness;
come into his presence with singing.
Know that the Lord is God.
It is he that made us, and we are his;
we are his people, and the sheep of his
    pasture.
Enter his gates with thanksgiving,
and his courts with praise.
Give thanks to him, bless his name.
For the Lord is good;
his steadfast love endures forever,
and his faithfulness to all generations.

—Psalms/ *Tehillim* 100

THE HEBREW TERM for gratitude is *hakarat ha'tov,* which means, literally, "recognizing the good." The good is already there. Practicing gratitude means being fully aware of the good that is already yours.

If you've lost your job but you still have your family and health, you have something to be grateful for.

If you can't move around except in a wheelchair but your mind is as sharp as ever, you have something to be grateful for.

If your house burns down but you still have your memories, you have something to be grateful for.

If you've broken a string on your violin, and you still have three more, you have something to be grateful for.

What's Good in Your Life?

When you open yourself to experience the trait of gratitude, you discover with clarity and accuracy how much good there is in your life. Whatever you are lacking will still be missing, of course, and in reaching for gratitude no one is saying you ought to put on rose-colored glasses to obscure those shortcomings. The obstacles to appreciating the good can also be very real, especially when life is riven by suffering. But it is worth the effort to practice gratitude, especially since the one who benefits most is the one who is suffering. Recognizing the good affirms life, and more, because when you see the good in the world it sets your heart free to soar, to shout, and to sing a song of life.

Most of us tend to focus so heavily on the deficiencies in our lives that we barely perceive the good that counterbalances them. This tendency is bolstered by advertisers who attempt to convince us of just how inadequate and lacking we really are, in the hope we will try to plug our wants and needs by buying some product or other.

There is no limit to what we don't have, and if that is where we focus, then our lives are inevitably filled with endless dissatisfaction. It is also true that even if we are aware of our gifts, we tend to grow callous to those fine things that pepper our lives, so that after a while we no longer even see that they are there. We come to take the good for granted. When gratitude is a living reality well established in our hearts, however, we constantly refresh our vision so that we make accurate note of the good that surrounds us. This is the ethos that lies behind the ancient proverb, which asks, "Who is rich?" and then answers, "He who rejoices in his own lot."[1]

Live like that and you will suddenly discover that you want to give thanks for anything or anyone who has benefited you, whether they meant to or not. Imagine a prayer of thanks springing to your lips when the driver in the next car lets you merge without protest, or when there is electricity to light your room, or the food is adequate. Giving thanks can become a flow that waters the fields of life.

When gratitude is well established and flowing, it is a sign of a heart that has been made right and whole. Gratitude can't coexist with arrogance, resentment, and selfishness. The Chassidic teacher Rebbe Nachman of Breslov writes, "Gratitude rejoices with her sister joy and is always ready to light a candle and have a party. Gratitude doesn't much like the old cronies of boredom, despair, and taking life for granted."

Grateful to Whom, or What?

To what and whom should we feel thankful? In the Torah, when Moses is bringing down the plagues on Egypt, it isn't he who initiated turning the Nile River into blood and bringing frogs from the river. His brother Aaron invokes those plagues. The medieval commentator Rashi explains that the river had protected Moses when he was an infant, and therefore he could not send a plague against it. God was teaching Moses a powerful lesson in gratitude: we can open in gratitude even to inanimate objects.

Whenever Rabbi Menachem Mendel Morgenstern, the Kotzker Rebbe, would replace a worn-out pair of shoes, he would neatly wrap up the old ones in newspaper before placing them in the trash, and he would declare, "How can I simply toss away such a fine pair of shoes that have served me so well these past years?" I felt the same way when I gave away my old Honda that had ferried me and my family so reliably for eighteen years.

There is a story about the Mussar teacher Rabbi Eliyahu Lopian,[2] who was talking to a student after prayers and at the same time was folding up his *tallis* (prayer shawl). The *tallis* was large, and he had to rest it on a bench to fold it. After he had finished the folding, Reb Elyah noticed that the bench was dusty, and so he headed out to fetch a towel in order to clean the bench. The student to whom he was speaking realized what Reb Elyah was doing and ran to get the towel for him. Reb Elyah held up his hand. "No! No! I must clean it myself, for I must show my gratitude to the bench upon which I folded my *tallis*."[3]

Now if we learn from these stories that we can be grateful to rivers, shoes, cars, and benches, which help us involuntarily, how much more so to human beings who have free will and who help us consciously out of the goodness of their hearts? Or to the mysterious source out of which our lives have come?

When Leah, wife of the patriarch Jacob, had her fourth child, she named him "Yehuda," which means "I am grateful."[4] The name Jew derives from "Yehudi," the people of "Yehuda," revealing that gratitude is intrinsic to being Jewish. This idea is confirmed in the prayer book, where so many of the prayers express gratitude to God for all we have. Astoundingly, the prayer to God, "Who is good and does good,"[5] which is part of the blessing after eating, was introduced directly after the defeat of the Bar Kochba revolt and the fall of the fortress of Betar, where thousands of people were slain by the legions of Rome.[7] When the remains of the martyrs of Betar finally received proper burial, the sages ordained the recitation of this blessing for the goodness of God, as they found the goodness even within—maybe especially within—a catastrophe. This is their lesson to us.

In our lives, the Torah asks us to recite blessings for everything, from the most mundane activities, like eating, to the most extraordinary, like seeing a rainbow or the ocean, all of which help us focus on and appreciate that which we might otherwise take for granted.

Leah was thankful to God for the gift of another son, and our daily blessings focus on God's bounty as well. The fact is, however, that many people find it easier to thank God than to acknowledge the gifts received from other people. People are complex, and they give in such confounding ways. This can make it so much harder to feel grateful for their gifts or to thank them. But we need to be ready to give thanks to a fellow human being, even if he or she has not done anything special for us. Why? Because the soul-trait of gratitude holds the key to opening the heart. It is an elevated soul-trait, and a fine orientation to the inanimate, human, and divine dimensions of the world. The refined soul is a grateful soul.

Gratitude Doesn't Come Easy

Yet gratitude often doesn't come easily to us, and it usually takes some effort to develop this quality through practice. When we practice gratitude, we make an effort to heighten our awareness of the gifts we already possess, and so relieve ourselves of the exhausting pursuit of the ever-receding targets of those things we think we lack. No wonder gratitude satisfies the soul. It frees us from compulsive grasping, and so gives us back our lives.

In the Mussar classic *Duties of the Heart,* Rabbi Bachya ibn Pakuda tells us that there isn't a person alive who hasn't been given gifts, if only the gifts of life and hope, but we tend to suffer a kind of blindness that keeps us from seeing and appreciating what we have. He identifies three reasons why we fail to see the abundance in our lives for which we ought to be grateful, and it's worth paying attention to what he says because his insights are as true for us today as they were nearly one thousand years ago when he wrote them. As you read these points, see if you can identify how these factors play out in your own life and keep you from the gratitude that is the soul's satisfaction.

First, he says we tend not to feel appreciative because we are too absorbed in worldly things and in the enjoyment of them. He points out that physical pleasures can never be fully gratified and so we pursue them endlessly, which keeps us from gratitude for what we have.

Second, we are so used to our gifts that we don't even really see them any more. We have grown so accustomed to them that they appear to us as typical, permanent, unremarkable features of our lives. Because we just take them for granted, we don't see all the good that is in our lives, for which we really could and should be grateful.

And third, we are so focused on the travails and afflictions we suffer in this world that we forget that both our very being and all we own are among the good things that have been gifted to us.

The result of this foolishness, Rabbi Ibn Pakuda concludes, is that "many good things are left unenjoyed, and the happiness to be had from them becomes tainted either because people do not recognize the good in it, or they do not realize its value."[7]

This voice from a millennium ago is saying things that seem to be equally applicable to our lives today. Isn't he pointing to the common feelings of entitlement that keep many of us from recognizing the good and being grateful? We are experts in wanting and complaining, and even if the problems are real and things aren't perfect, we don't give due appreciation to what we already have in hand. Yes, the glass is certainly half empty, but it is also half full. Someone once challenged me, "What could a prisoner in a concentration camp be grateful for?" "Being alive," I answered.

Even for the Challenges

The poem "Thanks," by W. S. Merwin, includes the lines:

> back from a series of hospitals back from a mugging
> after funerals we are saying thank you
> after the news of the dead
> whether or not we knew them we are saying thank you
> in a culture up to its chin in shame
> living in the stench it has chosen we are saying thank you[8]

And it goes on to describe all sorts of other contemporary issues, and still the chorus resounds, "We are saying thank you."

How can that be? Why on earth would anyone want to say thank you for the police at the back door, the beatings, the crooks, the animals dying around us, the forests falling faster than the minutes?

Merwin is challenging us to stretch to a very radical kind of gratitude. What he is proposing won't be easy or natural for us, because he is throwing open the simple certainties of "good" and "bad" through which we tend to see the world. But how useful and even true are these categories? We cheer for the good that happens to us and mourn for the bad, but are we really in a position to pass such clear judgment as to which is which? How certain can we be that something that happens to us is really for our good, and something else bad?

A story about the sage Rabbi Akiva says this perfectly. He used to say, "A person should always make it a habit of saying, 'Whatever the All-Merciful does, He does for the good.'" He backed this up with a story from his own experience.

Once, Rabbi Akiva was walking along the way accompanied by a rooster, a donkey, and a lamp. He came to a certain place and looked for room at the inn, but he was turned away. When that happened, he said, "Whatever the All-Merciful does, He does for the good." So he went with his rooster, donkey, and lamp and spent the night in an open field.

The wind came and put out the lamp, a weasel came and ate the rooster, a lion came and ate the donkey. He said, "Whatever the All-Merciful
does, He does for the good."

On that very night, a marauding troop came to that town and took
into captivity everyone in the town. Rabbi Akiva was spared.[9] Had his
rooster crowed, had the donkey brayed, had the light glowed, he would
have been discovered.

The message is clear. How can we evaluate what is happening right
now when we don't know what will happen next? It's only against the contours of that bigger picture that we can grasp the meaning and direction
of our present circumstances. Only then can we possibly know what is
good and what is bad—and even then we can't really be sure because
events continue to unfold. "Did I not tell you?" Rabbi Akiva concluded.
"Whatever the All-Merciful does, He does for the good."

Blessings in Disguise

It isn't hard to find real-life examples of terrible things that befell people
that turned out in the end to be "blessings in disguise."

What spared my teacher Mrs. Perr's family from destruction in the
Holocaust was the "disaster" that occurred when the invading Russians exiled her family from Poland to Siberia early in World War II. It was this
harsh fate that took them out of the path of the Nazis and spared their lives.

I met a Holocaust survivor who had emerged from the war penniless,
stateless, and traumatized. He left Europe behind and made his way to
Uruguay. He and his family lived in South America for many years, until
they left that unstable place to settle in the United States. They were able
to immigrate because they had become quite wealthy. The source of their
wealth was a veritable monopoly the family held on the manufacture of
soap in Uruguay. The patriarch of the family had learned how to make
soap as a forced laborer in a concentration camp.

In my own life, had it not been for the painful downturn in my own business fortunes that I wrote about in *Climbing Jacob's Ladder,* I never would
have discovered Mussar, and I would not be writing these words today.

As we continually try to make sense of our experiences, there is wisdom
in receiving whatever comes our way with an attitude of thankfulness. This

attitude reflects an "advanced" level of gratitude practice. The method here is to set ourselves to seeing that even in the troubles we face in this world, we can find good and something to be grateful for. Just because our limited human eyes don't permit us to perceive that the apparent disaster that has landed in our lap will turn out to be for the best, when we cultivate that very attitude, its truth begins to become visible to us. The Mishnah goes so far in this direction as to instruct that "one is obligated to say a blessing for evil." [10] The sage Rava explained that this teaching was given "to indicate that one must accept [evil] with gladness."

The rabbis challenged him, asking for examples of how this can be the case. The answer that comes back is that our limited vision doesn't permit us to know with any certainty what is good and what is bad, despite appearances:

> For instance, if a flood took one's land. Eventually that will be a good thing, because his land gets covered with sediment and becomes more fertile. Now, however, it is a bad thing. And in regard to a good thing, like, for instance, if one found something, it appears for the moment as a good thing even though it will become a disadvantage to him because if the government hears about it, it will confiscate the object from him. [11]

From where we stand at this moment, we just can't know which is which, and so we bless for the good and we bless for the apparently bad, too.

There is a famous individual in the Talmud, [12] named Nachum Ish Gamzu, who personifies this attitude. He is a righteous person who comes to the last days of his life destitute, blind, without the use of his limbs, and beset with illness. And yet as each of these devastating conditions descends on him, no matter what is happening to him, he always says of it: "*Gam zu l'tovah*"—"And that is also for the good." [13]

One story involving Nachum Ish Gamzu took place when the Jews wanted to send a gift to the court of Caesar and the pious Nachum was chosen to be the emissary. He set off with a chest filled with gems and pearls. Along the way, some people secretly made off with his jewels and refilled the chest with ordinary dirt. When he discovered the switch, Nachum's response was only to say *gam zu l'tovah*—this too is for the good—and to carry on with his mission. Other equally disastrous events take place and he responds in just the same way. How could that be? How could it be for the best to find yourself having just presented a gift of a bucket of dirt to an enraged Roman emperor? The answer is that at this point, the story isn't over.

Enter prophet Elijah (in disguise). He reveals that the dirt in the chest actually has magic properties. Caesar is overjoyed and rewards Nachum by refilling his chest with jewels and sending him on his way with great honor. *Gam zu l'tovah*—that too is for the best.[14]

Here is the practice. When something apparently "good" happens to you, you offer the blessing, "And *that* is also for the good." And if something "bad" happens to you, "And *that* is also for the good." On the last broadcast of his television show, when the comedian Jerry Lewis was being thrown off the air, he quoted the saying that Nachum Ish Gamzu referred to above, which Lewis had learned from his mother: "*Gam zu l'tovah,*" he said on camera. "And that is also for the good." No doubt this is a difficult spiritual practice, but when done sincerely, it has a powerful impact on your life.

Saying Thank You

Though there is great spiritual value in seeking the good in everything that happens, we have to be careful not to set ourselves up to being too much of a Pollyanna. All we want is to affirm that in everything that happens there is the possibility of good, if only we could perceive it, and while it may not be visible now, perhaps in time we'll see the bigger picture. And perhaps that bigger picture will include dimensions that are beyond this world and beyond our known experience, as the Jewish tradition affirms repeatedly in telling us that the real recompense for our lives is not in this world but in the World-to-Come.

We have a tendency to live our lives mired in our feelings of deprivation. No one has to look far to find someone who has more money, or is taller, healthier, or luckier in love. Comparing ourselves like this can create bitterness in the soul, as we poison ourselves with judgment, grasping, and self-recrimination. Cultivating gratitude counterbalances this tendency. When we take on the curriculum of reminding ourselves to be grateful, we change our perception of our lives, and with that, we actually change our lives, too.

In undertaking to practice gratitude, it is important to call thankfulness to mind and then to express and act on the feeling of gratefulness we have fostered.

This is just what I found myself doing one week when I was working on the soul-trait of gratitude. During that very week, I got an e-mail from a student who was very unhappy because of all the things she saw to be wrong with the Mussar course she was taking. As far as I could tell, all the problems were on her end, like the fact that she had an old computer that didn't like attachments, and that she seemed to be so overwrought that she was blaming instead of problem-solving. Taking the whole situation into account, I offered her a partial refund on her course fee. That seemed fair to me, but obviously not to her, because she sent me back an even more aggressive response, one that got under my skin. Even though what we were arguing over was less than $100, I sat down to write her a blistering reply that would be sure to put her in her place. Just then, the unbidden thought of "gratitude" flickered into my mind. Remember that you are cultivating gratitude, I reminded myself. What can you find to be grateful for in this situation? Nothing was evident to my eyes at that moment, so I determined that I would not reply to her until I could begin my response with the words "I am grateful to you for . . ."

The first few ideas that came to my mind had to be thrown out. "I am grateful to you for being an idiot." "I am grateful to you for showing me just how wrong a person can be." Meanwhile, I calmed down, and then it struck me that there was, in fact, one thing in this vein that I could validly say. I could say to her, "I am grateful to you for showing me what this situation looks like from your point of view." This was true. She was telling me what the unsatisfactory situation looked like to her (even though it was her radically different viewpoint that was so infuriating).

Once I had settled on articulating my gratitude to her for sharing her perspective, I was able to see that her position actually had validity, too. If I had bought a toaster at the department store, I told myself, and I took it back after a few weeks because it wasn't working for me, I'd expect a full refund. That's just how she saw this situation. Standing on my rights, we had a fight on our hands. Liberated by the practice of gratitude, I could see the situation from two perspectives, both of which had merit.

I gave her back her money, and we both came away from the situation satisfied.

An Attitude of Gratitude

You can see from this story that gratitude does not just mean uttering a polite thank you when someone confers a benefit. The goal is to do the work it takes to weave thankfulness deeply into the very fabric of your being, permeating everything you do. To achieve that level, said Rabbi Yerucham Levovitz,[15] you must "keep talking like a fishwife" (i.e., endlessly) about everything you receive.

Although gratitude practice requires that we put our feelings into action, the essence of the soul-trait is the inner attitude we maintain. We learn this from a story told about this same Rabbi Levovitz. The rabbi had a special fund from which his yeshiva students could borrow money. One year a young man borrowed some money to travel home for Passover.

On returning to the yeshiva, the student returned the money and expressed his thanks. Immediately his teacher reproached him because there is a Jewish value that when a beneficiary expresses gratitude, he or she diminishes the good deed and undercuts the selflessness of the doer. The boy got the message.

The next year, the same boy again borrowed money from the fund to travel home. This time, though, he had learned his lesson and returned the money without a word.

"Where's your gratitude?" Rabbi Levovitz chided him.

The baffled student burst out, "But Rebbe, last year I thanked you, and you rebuked me. This year, I didn't thank you, and again you rebuked me. What am I supposed to do?"

His teacher explained, "It is certainly forbidden for you to express any verbal thanks in this situation. But the *feeling* of gratitude inside you should have been so strong that it would have been hard for you to remain silent. I didn't see you experiencing any struggle to remain silent."

This story points out that the very essence of gratitude lies in the heart and not in behavior. An inner attitude or stance of thankfulness provides us with resources that help us face whatever we encounter in our lives. A grateful heart is a solid platform from which to reach out to take care of others as well as ourselves because this orients us toward the resources we have, not what we lack. An attitude of optimism and joy ensues, and it is to foster that outlook that we practice gratitude throughout our day. The intention is that the seeds we plant in practice will sprout, and then we will find ourselves experiencing flashes of gratitude as we go about the ordinary activities of our life.

> It is good to give thanks to the Lord
> And to sing praises to Your name, O Most High
> To proclaim Your goodness in the morning
> And Your faithfulness at night.
>
> —Psalms/*Tehillim* 92

10

Compassion
RACHAMIM

Kindness, empathy, and care arise from standing so close,
feeling what the other feels.

> Compassion is an extremely noble trait. It is one of
> the thirteen traits attributed to the Holy One, Blessed
> be He, as it is written: "Compassionate and gracious."[1]
> All that one can do in cultivating this trait, he should
> exert himself to do. Just as one would want compassion
> in his time of need, so should one have compassion on
> others who are in need.
>
> —*Orchot Tzaddikim*

THE MORAL PRECEPTS of Judaism demand that we be compassionate to every soul. Singled out repeatedly as especially needing our compassion are the poor, widows, orphans, and others in need. The Torah repeatedly hammers away at our obligation to help those who are vulnerable and needy. The tradition is so insistent that we be living vessels of compassion that the Talmud asserts that "anyone who is not compassionate with people is certainly not a descendant of our forefather Abraham."[2]

The Hebrew term for compassion—*rachamim*—shares its linguistic root with the word *rechem*, which means "womb." That compassion is somehow connected to motherhood has led many commentators to link this soul-trait to the emotional bond of mother to child. Compassion is seen to be the embodiment of the strong ties of love, kinship, and tenderness a mother feels for the baby she carries within her.

Rabbi Samson Raphael Hirsch,[3] for example, notes the connection between the words *rachamim* and *rechem*[4] and draws the conclusion that we

should have compassion in our hearts just as a mother has a loving, emotional bond to the child of her womb. He writes:

> Compassion is the feeling of empathy which the pain of one being
> of itself awakens in another; and the higher and more human the
> beings are, the more keenly attuned are they to re-echo the note of
> suffering which, like a voice from heaven, penetrates the heart.[5]

Is Compassion a Feeling?

Rabbi Hirsch's words are beautifully expressed, but we can still ask, is he
right? Is compassion a "feeling of empathy," as Rabbi Hirsch says? Before
we can fulfill the many commandments we are given to be compassionate,
and before we do what we can to cause that soul-trait to take firm root in
our hearts, we have to grasp what is really meant by compassion in the
uniquely Jewish view. That requires that we add into the mix a number of
other references where the term *rachamim*—compassion—figures prominently. It is, in fact, a very common term in the Torah,[6] and the way it is
used adds more dimensions to the simple focus that rests on the mother-
child relationship.

In a psalm we read: "As a father has compassion on his children, so
God has compassion for those who are in awe of Him."[7] This single line of
scripture gives us two additional points to note about compassion. Not
only is compassion a quality that is somehow related to a mother and the
child of her womb, here it is set out in the image of a father-child relationship. In addition, compassion is portrayed as a divine quality, exhibited
by God, "who crowns you with loving-kindness and tender compassion."[8]
One very frequently used name of God is *Ha'Rachaman*—the Compassionate One—and the two notions of a father's compassion and God's
compassion are brought together in the daily prayer that contains the line
Ha'El Ha'Av Ha'Rachaman—"God, the Compassionate Father."[9]

That God is seen to be compassionate is fundamental to a Jewish
view of the divine. The high point of the closing prayers on Yom Kippur,
the holiest day of the Jewish calendar, is the recitation of the thirteen
divine *middot ha'rachamim* (attributes of compassion)[10] of God. This is
also the central refrain of the forgiveness prayers that are repeated peri-
odically throughout the year. When do these thirteen attributes of com-

passion that we invoke on Yom Kippur and in these special prayers make their appearance in the Torah? They show up in the immediate aftermath to the sin of the Israelites building a Golden Calf to worship, when Moses successfully pleads with God not to wipe out his people who have sinned, but instead to be compassionate and forgiving. So it is appropriate that we, too, call on the compassion of God as we confess our own weaknesses and transgressions.

We can see that this notion of compassion is related to the mother's womb and to the father-child relationship as well, and is also a quality that God manifests for all of us. This gives us our first important conclusion about compassion, which is that it is *an attribute of relationship* and that it can exist in relationships of many kinds.

We'll need to look more closely at how compassion shows up in relationship, but before we do that, we need to investigate whether compassion is indeed an emotion, as Rabbi Hirsch and others describe it to us. Is compassion simply the kind of empathetic feeling a parent has for a beloved child, and which we hope and pray God has for us, who are like children of the divine? When we look at one further way in which the term *rachamim* is frequently put to use in the Jewish tradition, we will have to call into question the idea that compassion is an emotion.

Tradition teaches that God's original intention was to create the world solely with the attribute of judgment.[11] We can still see the results of this intention, because the fundamental laws of nature are themselves immutable. If you put your hand in fire, it will be burned, no matter what you might say or think. A world created according to the quality of judgment requires that everything be a specific way, with no deviation whatsoever.

But we are told that God realized that the world (and especially people) could not survive if the world were set up so that strict justice was exacted instantly for every error or wrongdoing. A world run only according to the principle of stern justice would leave no room for free will, learning, change, or growth, because every single time you did something wrong, mechanical rules would mete out results instantly and without variation. To forestall such insufferable rigidity, God included the attribute of compassion as an essential feature of creation, right alongside judgment.[12]

A midrash explains the necessary interplay of judgment and compassion in creation by telling of a king who had some fragile glass cups. He said to himself, "If I pour hot water into them, they will expand and break, and if I pour cold water into them, they will contract and shatter." So what did he do? He mixed hot water with cold water and poured the mixture into the cups, and they did not break.

So it was when it came time to create the world. A midrash tells us that God reflected, "If I create the world with only the attribute of compassion, no one will be concerned for the consequences of their actions, and people will feel impunity to act badly. But if I create the world with strict judgment alone, how could the world endure? It would shatter from the harshness of justice. So I will create it with both justice and compassion, and it will endure." [13]

A Building Block of Creation

Compassion is so fundamental to the world that the Talmud says it is one of the ten elements through which the world was created. [14] The mystical tradition in Judaism has picked up on this depiction, and so it comes down to us that *rachamim* is one of the ten primary emanations that underlie all of ongoing existence in the universe. Compassion is the meeting and balancing point for the channels that bring down loving-kindness, on the one hand, and strict judgment on the other. Compassion blends these energies and so achieves and promotes balance between the necessarily hard and rigid and the equally necessary soft and caring.

So we see that far from being just an emotion, compassion now appears as a fundamental feature of the way in which reality has been constructed or, if you prefer, of the way in which God runs the world.

A poignant example from the Talmud makes this case by asserting that even the exile to Babylonia, which was an enormously catastrophic event in Jewish history that is still mourned to this day, also had within its harshness a measure of divine compassion. "Rabbi Chiya taught that the Holy One, Blessed be He, knew that Israel could not withstand the cruel decrees of Rome, and therefore He exiled them to Babylonia." [15] This sort of compassion is not just an emotion, a feeling of empathy, but an action that takes care of the other.

That compassion is something other than an emotion is confirmed in the Mussar text *Orchot Tzaddikim*, where some examples are given of the firm guidance that is the responsibility of parents, whose compassion for their child might well involve rules, consequences, and even punishment, in order to bring the child to the right way of thinking and acting: "Though it may seem cruel to do so, such cruelty is compassion."[16]

All these teachings from tradition lead us to the conclusion that compassion is not what it may have seemed at first—the emotion a mother feels for the child she carries in her womb. If not that, then how are we to understand compassion?

Close Identity

One feature that we can identify that unites all the ways the term *compassion* is put to use in Jewish thought is the notion of closeness. The soul-trait of compassion emerges from an experience of being very, very close to another, or from a feeling of closeness, or equally from an effort to draw closer to the other.

Put another way, compassion is an inner quality that grows within us out of the perception that we are not really separate from the other. We have a commonsense appreciation that we are all separate beings, but the truth is that we are very much connected at several levels. Could there be a better image for this intimate connection than the physical proximity of fetus to mother, where two beings so totally overcome duality by situating one of them within the other? That is a beautiful and revealing image, but such closeness is not a feature of only the mother-child relationship. And so tradition also includes images of the father-child relationship, and of the relationship of God to each of us. The key and common point here is closeness in relationship, which can potentially exist in any relationship.

Compassion then appears to depend upon the internal connectedness that arises from a sense of shared identity, as the you and the me are mingled in a oneness that transcends our perceptions of separate identities. When that close connection registers with a resonating impact within me, I am able to feel your pain (and your happiness) as if they were my own. We express this in common language when we say that we are "touched" by someone else's story or experience. To be touched is to have a physical connection, to join.

If you get a thorn in your toe, you don't say, "I have nothing to do with that toe down there," because you recognize the connection. Or if you are chewing and accidentally bite your tongue, you don't run to get a hammer

and start smashing your teeth. When we experience being so close to one
another that the membranes that separate us are permeated, then I will
live in the recognition that you and I are as connected as I am to my own
foot or mouth. This condition of intimacy precipitates compassion.

We find examples of closeness setting off compassion in the Torah, such
as when God responds to the people who have returned from wayward-
ness and drawn close once again. In 2 Chronicles 30:9 we read: "The Lord
your God is gracious and compassionate. He will not turn his face from
you if you return to him." The same process appears in Nechemiah 9:27:
"When they were oppressed they cried out to you. From heaven You heard
them, and in Your great compassion You gave them deliverers." Drawing
close sets the stage for compassion.

Identity with the other as the basis for compassion is precisely what
the Torah invokes when it hands down the commandment to be loving
to the stranger in your midst. The rationale for doing so is our shared
identity as strangers: "You shall love the stranger, because you have been
strangers in the land of Egypt." [17]

Rabbi Moshe Cordovero, a great Mussar teacher and kabbalist of the
sixteenth century, demonstrates the link of compassion to closeness by
drawing the picture of the negative case. He asks how compassion can be
fostered and answers that compassion can be nurtured through Torah
study. But he immediately warns that "great caution must be exercised to
avoid becoming aloof through one's learning, which could cause great
harm." [18] Aloofness—with its sense of being remote and distant—is inim-
ical to compassion. So it is that a recent study of executioners in the
United States documents that in order to do their job of killing people on
behalf of the state, these people set an emotional gulf between themselves
and the prisoner: "And the closer they are to the killing," the article reports, "the higher their level of disengagement goes." [19]

We are led to the conclusion that compassion is not primarily a feeling.
It is something more fundamental than that. Compassion may indeed involve feeling. It also may breed action. But these qualities do not take the
definition far enough. The soul-trait of compassion may be more accurately defined as the inner experience of touching another being so closely
that you no longer perceive the other one as separate from you. The two
are made one, as the baby in the mother's womb. In that state of inner
identification, feelings will be shared as fully as if they were your own. You

will leap to care for the other as naturally as you care for yourself. Because the other is no longer other.

Compassionate Feeling and Action

Though it is not its defining characteristic, compassion does have an important emotional component. My oneness with you means that whatever you are feeling is also stirred within me as my own emotional experience. Your sadness is my sadness. Your pain is my pain. Your confusion is my confusion. Your joy is my joy. Compassion may not be an emotion, but it cannot exist without full emotional contact with the other.

When you make real contact with someone who is suffering, and you feel their needs and their pain or their trying situation, this sets up the conditions for compassion to arise in you.

What is it that turns empathetic connection into compassion? The answer resides in the Jewish insistence that inner qualities only reach a state of sh'lemut, "wholeness," when they are brought out into the world of action. Having a good heart is not the final goal that Mussar sets for us, as Rabbi Shlomo Wolbe clarifies: to really elevate our soul-traits we must put them into action.[20]

A number of crucial soul-traits require action or else they are incomplete, possibly even illusory. Chesed, loving-kindness, is not some sort of loving feeling you have toward another person in your heart, but for chesed to be real you must take action to sustain that other person. Similarly, rachamim—compassion—does not come into being just by feeling empathy. The depth and richness of the emotional connection must be translated into action that expresses concretely how truly moved you are to take care of the other. It is the action you take that turns a relationship or a shared emotion into compassion.

So it is that Rabbi Bachya ibn Pakuda challenges us in Duties of the Heart:

Express compassion when you encounter the impoverished, the poor, and the diseased; with people who are outside the mainstream of society, who do not know how to improve their lot, who do not know how to conduct themselves, who are imprisoned by enemies, who have lost great fortunes, who regret having transgressed, and who weep for the consequences of their sins.

All the situations Ibn Pakuda identifies where compassion is called for represent what tradition calls "stern judgment." Our compassion is what we can offer to offset these outpourings from the side of judgment. Notice, though, that Ibn Pakuda doesn't say "feel" compassion, but rather "express" compassion.[21] The emphasis is on the actions we take. The two steps prior to action that have had our attention—joining ourselves to the other person and sharing in their feelings—become worthy of the name compassion only when they are put into action. For our response to be truly compassionate, we must not just feel with another person but also try to act on their behalf.

Defining Compassion

Compassion is a deep emotional feeling arising out of identification with the other that seeks a concrete expression. Compassion flows between equals or from the more powerful to the less powerful, as we see in the Torah, where it never expresses human feeling for God. It does, however, apply to a human king caring for subjects[22] and to God caring for humanity.[23] These defining features help us understand what touches and moves people to act as they do when they manifest compassion.

It was 1942 and the Nazis were rounding up Jews in France. The pastors of the town of Le Chambon-sur-Lignon in southern France gathered together their parishioners and asked them to shelter Jews, even though they would be putting their own lives at risk. They hid Jews in homes, on farms, and in public buildings. Whenever Nazi patrols showed up, the Jews were sent into the countryside. One of the villagers recalled: "As soon as the soldiers left, we would go into the forest and sing a song. When they heard that song, the Jews knew it was safe to come home." The villagers provided Jews with forged ID and ration cards and helped them get over the border to Switzerland.

It is estimated that three thousand to five thousand Jews were saved. One reason given for this display of compassion is that these French villagers were Protestants descended from persecuted Huguenots. Their history of persecution as a religious minority connected them to the persecuted Jews. Out of this feeling of shared identity came action: "Things had to be done and we happened to be there to do them" is how one villager put it.[24]

Compassion comes into being only by being put to use. It is like a skill or a tool that gains its full value only when used. And like a skill or the use

of a tool, it can be cultivated. When the Rambam discusses the commandment we are given to emulate God by "walking in His ways,"[25] he says,
"Just as He is called gracious, so you should be gracious. Just as He is
called compassionate, so you should be compassionate." We are enjoined
to be compassionate, taking God as our model. Because we more easily
perceive our separation than our oneness with others, we slip into judgment more easily than we rise to compassion. We need to be told to walk
in God's footsteps by acting to cultivate compassion in our hearts.

Imitating the divine trait of compassion is not just a lovely ideal. We
are assured that it is within our grasp to do so, however, because "He will
bestow upon you [the attribute of] compassion and show mercy to you."[26]
The capacity for compassion is innate within us. But to bring that quality
from potential to actuality, we need to take steps to confront the obstacles
to compassion.

Self and the Other

The primary barrier to being compassionate is the sense that you and I are
separate from each other. We have our separate family, a personal name,
our own property, and, more fundamentally, the sensibility of being an au-
tonomous entity. Our personal life so easily becomes a preoccupation—
seeking only what the "I" wants and needs—that we come to live within a
walled fortress called self. When we live in this separateness—you in your
fortress, me in mine—how could we possibly identify with one another?

Compassion can come into existence only when you lower the barriers
that ordinarily wall off and isolate your own sense of self. Opening up to
connecting so closely with another that you actually feel that other person's pain will be possible only when the high walls of ego are reduced.[27]
Only then will it be possible for compassion to well up and flow into passionate action on behalf of the other.

A habitual ego-bound perspective gives rise to the well-ingrained tendency to look at others with eyes of judgment. What appears before us
when we look at another in this way are that person's accumulated deeds
and habits as they stand right now, which we judge from our own vantage
point. When we lower or transcend the boundaries of self, however, and
draw closer so that we can feel within us the truth of that other person's
experience, and so see with eyes of compassion, we still ought to see that

person as they are now, but something else will also be added to that picture. We will also see more deeply to perceive the untainted soul that is the kernel of that being—the image of the divine that is reflected in ourselves as well. This perception leads us to suspend our own sense of judgment of the other. Through close identification we become more generous, forgiving, excusing, overlooking, patient, and forbearing, just as you would expect someone to be to you, if only they would feel what you are feeling.

This was the practice of Rabbi Noson Tzvi Finkel, the Alter of Slabodka. His compassion emerged from his perception of the holy dimension of the person who stood before him:

> He loved people with an extraordinary and excessive love, a love without restraints; he had a limitless affection for humanity—for any human, regardless of who or what he was. He was also extremely sensitive to any humiliation of any person and he fully participated in other people's suffering. The source for these qualities is that he saw in people the image of God, a part of God from Above. Every human was, for him, like Adam—a creation of God's own hands—before his sin and fall . . . whose holiness is part of the nature of every human even after the Sin, even after the sins of all later generations and all the terrible descents and falls.[28]

The interplay of judgment and compassion is presented to us as a notion of how the cosmos is put together. This is not just an abstract concept but also a dynamic process that is alive and effective in our own lives as well. Compassion has us believe that a person is inherently holy and has the capacity to change, so the deeds we might find ourselves judging do not really reflect who a person is at the core, nor could be. As a result, compassion has us see a person more favorably than his or her deeds currently warrant. Said a different way, judgment assesses a person based on the reality of who he or she is now, while compassion recognizes as well a person's soul-nature. This is how compassion offsets the force of judgment.

Varieties of Compassion

Yet all of that identification and shared feeling will become compassionate only when put into practice. According to the Mussar masters, compassion can come in two forms.

There is "compassion in the form of compassion," when our feeling along with the other leads us to act kindly, softly, and gently. The second type of compassion comes as "compassion in the form of judgment." In this case, our shared feelings with the other call for action that is firm, hard, or possibly even harsh.

The classic example of compassion in the form of compassion is the redemption of the Jews from slavery in Egypt. It has been argued that the Jews in Egypt did not deserve to be redeemed from slavery. There are traditions that say that while in Egypt, the people of Israel assimilated, did not keep what they knew of tradition (which was incomplete, in any case, because the Torah had not yet been received), and, worst of all, became idolaters. The prophet Ezekiel reveals, "I also said to them, 'Cast away, every one of you, the detestable things that you are drawn to, and do not defile yourselves with the idols of Egypt—I the Lord am your God.' But they defied Me and refused to listen to Me."[29]

Why, then, did God redeem the Israelites and free them from the oppression of slavery? That was solely because of God's compassion. "And HaShem said: 'I have surely seen the oppression of My people, who are in Egypt, and have heard their cry because of their taskmasters, for I know their sorrows.'"[30] The way the prophet Isaiah puts it fits well with our view that compassion is based on the experience of nonseparateness: "In all their affliction He was afflicted."[31] It was based on this identification that HaShem acted compassionately and "brought forth Your people Israel out of the land of Egypt with signs, and with wonders, and with a strong hand, and with an outstretched arm, and with great terror."[32]

Compassion in the guise of judgment appears in the story of the eviction of Adam and Eve from the Garden of Eden. This seems such a harsh punishment for the very human error of not following instructions. They aren't even given a second chance. But this apparently stern judgment can also be seen to be an act of compassion on God's part. In the first instance, God could have eliminated the errant couple from the world in a stroke, but did not do so. Second, the world of Eden was perfect and it demanded perfection. Then as now, this is more than humans can handle. By exiling us from Eden, God put us in a world where human imperfection is tolerated and so made it possible for us to survive.

That biblical story brings to mind another example that can be understood in the same way. I mentioned briefly in the last chapter the story about my teacher, Rebbetzin Shoshana Perr, whose family was living in Poland at the start of World War II. They escaped to Lithuania, but in 1941 the Russians who controlled Lithuania began rounding up "clerics and clerical students" for deportation, among them Rabbi Nekritz (Mrs. Perr's father and so Rabbi Perr's future father-in-law). His wife wouldn't hear of being left behind, and so the entire family, with babies, was shipped out to endure the rigors of life in Siberia. This apparently stern judgment concealed divine compassion, however, because their exile removed the Nekritz family from the path of the Nazis only weeks before they invaded Lithuania, where they killed all the remaining Jews. Exile at the hands of the Russians ensured that the Nekritz family all survived. A later agreement between Stalin and the Polish government-in-exile freed all Polish refugees, and the Nekritzes eventually made their way to the United States.

Modeling our own pursuit of wholeness on the traits of God requires that we, too, need to be capable of acting in both ways—with compassion in the form of compassion and compassion in the form of judgment. We aspire to having the spiritual dexterity to shift from one type of compassionate action to the other, as the situation requires and according to how our sensitivity guides us.

We get a hint that our wise ancestors wanted us to grasp the multiple layers embedded in compassion because the Hebrew term they bequeathed us—*rachamim*—is unique among the soul-traits: its name has no singular form and is always stated in the plural. Or possibly they wanted us to understand that despite our apparent duality, compassion is one and so are we.

> One's compassion should extend to all creatures, and
> one should neither despise nor destroy them, for the
> wisdom above extends to all of creation—inanimate
> objects, plants, animals, and humans.
>
> —*Tomer Devorah*

11

Order

SEDER

Order creates inner alignment, peaceful and prepared.

Take time, be exact, unclutter the mind.
> —Rabbi Simcha Zissel Ziv, the Alter of Kelm

THE SOUL-TRAIT of order[1] is all about the middle way. Too little order gives birth to chaos, while at the other end of the range, too much order ties us up in obsessive rigidity. The best in life lies between these extremes, and we are well-advised to seek that moderate course.

Rabbi Eliyahu Dessler[2] provides three reasons why we should make an effort to bring order into our lives. First, knowing that things are well arranged creates a feeling of inner satisfaction and confidence that everything is under control. Another reason is even more practical—order helps you find things when you need them and saves you the time you would lose looking for them. And a third reason is that many things will function only if they are arranged correctly, like a machine that requires every one of its parts to be in good working order, often in a specific sequence, to run properly.

That such practical guidance emanates from a Mussar teacher of Rabbi Dessler's stature reveals something about our spiritual life as the Mussar masters see it. The path to spiritual growth they illuminate is hidden right in front of us, right there *within* the ways of this world. The order you create on your desk, in your car, and with your clothes, your financial papers, your tools, your kitchen utensils, and so on is not just good management, it is actually bona fide spiritual work. Nothing less.

Spiritual Order

Rabbi Dessler was the product of the famous Mussar yeshiva located in Kelm in Lithuania, which was founded in 1862 by Rabbi Simcha Zissel Ziv.[3] Rabbi Simcha Zissel was one of the primary disciples of Rabbi Yisrael Salanter, and he grew to be the person who did most to propagate his teacher's thought and methods.[4] In 1906, at the age of fourteen, the boy who became Rabbi Dessler entered the Kelm Yeshiva, becoming one of its youngest students. Except for several years during World War I, Rabbi Dessler would reside at the yeshiva until 1928.[5] In 1920 he married Bluma, the great-granddaughter of the Alter of Kelm, founder of the yeshiva, and in total he passed eighteen years living and learning in Kelm.

At Kelm, Rabbi Dessler was immersed in an environment that made a high priority of order. The Alter saw this quality as a major aid to self-perfection, so order became a pillar of the Kelm way of Mussar. His views on this soul-trait were based on the Torah, which he saw standing entirely on principles of order. After all, only one moment separates Shabbat from the weekday. One hairbreadth is the difference between a kosher and an unfit slaughtering. A small volume of water can render a kosher *mikveh*[6] unfit. Details are small, but they matter, often crucially.

Mussar in the Kelm Yeshiva focused primarily on the cultivation of inner attitudes and states. External disorder was taken to be a reflection of internal disarray. A person whose possessions are messy is likely to have thoughts that are also jumbled. If you are not careful about the cleanliness of your house, you are also likely to be lax about the purity of your spirit.

The Alter highly valued order in his own life. He allowed nothing to interfere with his fixed times for learning, even when people would bang on his door. At home and even while traveling, he followed a schedule of learning. He would say: "People set aside fixed times for their personal business, for resting, and for eating, and they receive people only at certain hours—and no one complains."

There is an oft-repeated story that Rav Simcha Zissel once went to visit his son Nachum Zev, then a student in a distant yeshiva. The first thing the father did was visit his son's room. On inspection, he found the boy's possessions in order. From this alone, he could tell that his son was doing well in the yeshiva. Only then did he go to see his son.

The Alter's successor and son-in-law, Rabbi Tzvi Hirsch Broide, was a classic product of this devotion to order that characterized Kelm. His daily timetable was arranged with almost military precision to such a degree that it was said that you could set your watch according to Rav Tzvi Hirsch's comings and goings.

Even Rabbi Dessler's appearance conveyed Kelm's emphasis on order. His clothing is reported to have been simple but always immaculate. While his wife was alive, she used to inspect him and brush off his hat and tie before he departed for the yeshiva. After she passed away, before leaving the house Rabbi Dessler would always carefully examine his beard in the mirror to make sure it was neatly combed.

Servant of God

Kelm Mussar recognizes the practical consequences of disorder, and even more, its spiritual costs. Spiritual living requires order just as much as does our material life.

In the Jewish view, the spiritual seeker is meant to be a servant of God. Our paragon here is Moses, who is called just that: *eved HaShem*, a servant of God.[7] The first line of the book of Joshua repeats this phrase, again calling Moses *eved HaShem*. Psalm 36 begins: "To the chief musician, A Psalm of David, the servant of the Lord." In Leviticus God says: "For to Me are the Israelites servants, My servants that I have redeemed from Egypt."[8]

That the proper attitude for spiritual living should be that of a servant is very counter-cultural to the modern mind. The French, Russian, and American revolutions that set the course for the modern era, as well as innumerable anticolonial wars of independence, were all attempts to overthrow regimes that propagated servitude. So too the American Civil War. Not many national constitutions laud the value of being a servant. But the Jew is meant to serve. Our answer to God's commandment is "We shall do and we shall hear." Doing comes first. We will serve.

We'll circle back to see the connection between being a servant of God and perfecting the inner trait of order. First, though, we need to understand what it is to be one who serves God.

Being a servant of God means striving to align my will to that of the Master. I desire to unify my will with God's will within my own life and to delight in that unification. Rabbi Gamliel used to say: "Do His will as if it

were your will that He may do your will as if it were His will."[9] The servant
of God seeks an alignment of what he or she wants with the divine will
and submerges personal will into the divine will.

Serving in this way requires that I strive to rise above my own personal
habits of thought, speech, feeling, and action. I also need to pull myself
back from following my eyes and heart in pursuit of unsanctioned and
unsanctified personal gratification. The divine will that I seek to know
and follow is good and true in a much larger way than whatever serves my
own narrow self-interest.

Being a servant who aligns his or her will with the divine will makes
you a very useful human being. In time, your efforts will be judged to have
been right and good. Right alongside, the doors to personal happiness will
be opened wide to you. There is no long-term satisfaction to be gained by
pursuing and even temporarily gratifying the desires of the little personal
will. Contrast Moses, *eved HaShem* par excellence, who is described in the
Shabbat Amidah prayers as "Moses will be happy with the gift of his portion because a faithful servant You have called him."[10]

Happy. A servant.

It is because being a servant of God can be described so well as an
alignment of your will with the divine will that practicing order becomes
a key step in spiritual life. Alignment without order is inconceivable. As
humans we are endowed with free will and so it is perfectly possible for us
to choose to be chaotic, but when we make it a conscious practice to be orderly, we are aligning ourselves outwardly—and inwardly—with the universal order.

The essential value of practicing order is that by voluntarily aligning
ourselves with an orderly way of living, we draw ourselves closer to the divine way of being. When we are orderly, we emulate one of God's intrinsic characteristics, and that draws us closer to God.

Rabbi Aaron Kotler[11] taught along these lines. He saw that practicing
order in time and space replicates the deep pattern of organization in the
universe. It's that order we see in every aspect of creation, which has many
parts, all interrelated and perfectly suited to one another. The sun rises at
its appointed time and traverses its annual cycle, the oceans stay within
their borders, the animals have the food that they need to eat, water evap-
orates, rain falls, and the physical world operates in an orderly way. Even
change happens according to orderly principles. If rivers run higher and

faster, the rate of erosion can be measured. Even tsunamis obey the laws of physics. Because all of creation runs on orderly[12] principles, the Torah, which embodies the blueprint of the world, is orderly as well. The opening chapter of the Torah describes creation itself in terms of the emergence of order from primordial chaos.

Order also helps us with other forms of divine service because it is impossible to track one's service to and emulation of God without order. The rabbis who have drawn the commandments from the Torah have enumerated the ways to serve God and have given us the *seder* (order) according to which each should be performed. For example, we are commanded to eat matzo and drink four cups of wine on Passover. At one point it is matzo, and a second later—beyond the eighteen minutes that it takes to leaven—the matzo would be forbidden on Passover. There are measurements for how much matzo is the minimum required to fulfill the commandment,[13] and how much wine constitutes a "cup."[14] And of course, all of these acts are organized in a specific sequence, which takes place at the Passover Seder (the same word: "order").

There are rules to guide how large a *tallis* (prayer shawl) must be and how much charity one must give. A *mezuzah* is always placed at an angle to the doorpost on which it is hung in order to reconcile those who said the mezuzah should hang upright and parallel to the doorpost and those who said it should be placed horizontal and perpendicular to the doorpost.[15] Prayers must be said in a specific order, by a specific time, as laid out in the prayer book, which is called the Siddur (from the same root, meaning "order"). To develop a deep feeling of connection with God in your prayers, you must focus all your attention on your prayers, and this requires orderliness. All in search of order. All in commitment to the divine service.

An Image of Disorder

Consider the consequences of disorder, and you will be strengthened in choosing order in your life. The Torah gives us a direct teaching in this regard in the famous story of the Tower of Babel.[16] The Hebrew word for sin, *averah*—like its English counterpart *transgression*—means "straying across a boundary." The tower builders' efforts to reach out to touch heaven were sinful because they transgressed the limits and constraints that are laid into the deep structure of the universe. Stretching for heaven, they failed to honor the distinction between the human and the divine. Since they flaunted order, their punishment was to suffer disorder, as represented by their inability to communicate with one another. Failure to honor the need for order brings on chaos.

This cautionary tale applies to our lives, too. How much time, energy, emotion, and life is diverted into the channels that spring from disorder? Where are the Haggadot for the Seder? Where is my *tallis?* Who forgot to set the clock? Why didn't you take the soup out of the freezer? Why would I buy milk if it wasn't on the list? It's in here somewhere. I almost got there.

How many relationships are challenged or even destroyed by lack of attention to order?

Without order, you are bound to be wasting something—whether time, resources, things themselves that get lost, relationships, and so on. Not wasting is a Jewish ethical principle.[17]

Any management consultant will tell you that you have to get organized if you want to be effective, but our concern goes far beyond that. Our concern is how living in chaos throws up impediments to being attentive to the divine will. And isn't a life at the other end of the spectrum, which would be obsessively rigid, every bit as much an obstacle to spiritual living?

Picture chaos, with stuff flying and piles of junk and cluttered thinking and a clanging ruckus: who could possibly hear the fragile voice of truth whispering in the midst of the tornado? And in contrast, but equally disabling, where order has been taken to the point of extreme inflexibility, even if you heard the divine will, would there be anything you could do to meld your own personal will to the will of God, so unbending would your ways have become?

Practical Order

Mussar is inevitably and insistently a practical discipline, and so if all we did was assert that the soul-trait of order is essential to practical living as well as divine service, that would be like saying "don't steal" and expecting to have put an end to theft once and for all. Knowing something and living that truth are not one and the same thing. The gap between the two is where Mussar plays its most important role.

Ask yourself whether disorder is one of your handicaps. Some of us know right away because the mess is visible, maybe right from where you are sitting at this moment. On the other hand, you may have to look a bit, since more of us have figured out ways to keep the clutter out of sight, whether that means in a certain closet or in the secret of our private lives.

Or are you one of those rarer hyperorganized people, who take extreme fastidiousness beyond the golden mean and have made the soft flesh and pliable sinews of life into cement and iron?

Slovenliness and obsessiveness are two extreme qualities that we seek to avoid. The healthy range lies in the middle.

Next you must wonder how you are going to learn to get a grip on that room, those drawers, that pile on the floor, the boxes in the basement, your bank account, your priorities. Or, in the less common contrary case, how can you loosen up that iron fist that has you organizing every paper clip on the desk with obsessive precision?

It is common (though insightful) Mussar guidance that to control or diminish one trait, our efforts are not to be focused on that trait itself but rather on one of its corresponding partner traits. This is an important and not-obvious principle that makes a great deal of sense when you think about it. It applies very well to the soul-trait of order. Telling a disorderly person (who could be yourself) to clean up his or her act and get organized is a lot like telling a fire to cool down. It may be what you want, and it may be what is right, but is it likely to be successful?

Instead of fruitlessly yelling at the fire to cool down (to pursue this metaphor), you need to ask yourself, "What's the 'water' in this case?" In other words, what's the corresponding trait that will, if strengthened, cause the obstacles to orderliness to evaporate as if by themselves?

Let me give a few suggestions, based in Mussar sources. Since disorder leaning into chaos is more common than the problem of obsessive order, I'll focus on disorder, though the same way of analyzing and applying can be useful to one who is rigidly obsessive as well. It's up to you to figure out how to employ the general teaching in your own situation.

It may not be obvious at first why cultivating certain traits serves to counteract issues of order. That's what I will endeavor to explain. Often the connection between traits is subterranean, and so we are fortunate to have had the Mussar masters who have come before us, excavators that they were.

Undermining Disorder

The first of the countervailing traits I'll suggest is that most central of qualities, humility. Recall the definition of humility we developed in the chapter on that soul-trait: humility means occupying your appropriate space, neither too much nor too little.

The Torah provides a story about order that links clearly to humility. It describes how the people of Israel were told to organize themselves in formation for camping and traveling in the desert: "The Israelites shall camp with each person near the banner, under the flag of their ancestral house. They shall camp at a specified distance around the Tent of Meeting."[18] Each tribe is then positioned in a certain direction with respect to the central tent.

We read in a midrash that when God told Moses that the Jews were to be arranged in this specific formation, Moses complained that if he specified such an organization, there would be protests. "If I tell Yehuda to camp in the east, they will say they want the south, and so it will be with each and every tribe."[19]

This story underlines the human tendency to rebel against imposed order. It doesn't matter if the order that is being foisted on us is good, right, useful, or sensible. As long as our "rightful space" is being imposed, we don't want it: "If I tell Yehuda to camp in the east, they will say they want the south." Not that the south is necessarily better than the east or the north, it's just not what you told me to do, and that's the point. Sound familiar?

Disorder is often the child of a rebellious ego that resists humbly occupying a rightful space. All that it whispers in your inner ear can be reduced to "I want" or "I don't want."

I want to have fun, and cleaning up after myself is no fun.

I want to keep accumulating stuff, and organizing it is not something I enjoy.

I want my leisure, and setting things in order is work.

Or . . . I don't want to take responsibility for my stuff. I don't want to do that. I don't have to.

No matter what follows the word "I," there's no mistaking that the subject is "me." Hence the antidote here would be humility. All the methods for cultivating humility that the Mussar masters have formulated over the centuries come into play here.

The subject is large and, I think, the point is made: one approach to undercutting and disarming that inner voice that gives all sorts of reasons and incentives to maintain clutter and chaos is to employ the techniques the Mussar teachers have developed for fostering genuine humility. Order is, after all, a kind of submission of will, and humility fosters submission in place of the ego's self-assertion.

Another soul-trait that bears on order is *kavod*, meaning "honor." The Mussar teachers have had almost as much to say about honor as humility, since the two are actually very closely linked. In this case, what I have in mind is that disorder inevitably involves some sort of dishonor. The only question is, what or who is the target of the dishonor?

When you live with other people and you are content to make a mess in shared spaces, you dishonor the people you live with.

When you are careless and sloppy in your business dealings, you dishonor the people you work with.

When you can't keep anything straight for your customers, clients, or students, you dishonor the people you work for.

And not just people. It's interesting that we use the phrase "unholy mess" to describe a situation that has really been trashed, because to be disorderly also dishonors the inanimate things that are also part of our lives and may also be our responsibility.

The real "unholy mess," of course, is the disorder we bring to divine service, in whatever forms we might serve God, which dishonors HaShem.

Honor is due to all human beings not because of the greatness of their achievements but more simply because they embody an inherently holy soul. When you activate this inner sensibility, you want to keep things in order not just for order's sake, but also for the higher purpose of honoring the people with whom you share relationships. All of us are, after all, made in the divine image, and so when we dishonor people we dishonor God, and when we honor people we honor God.

A story about Rabbi Shimon ben Elazar in the Talmud[20] has him riding along on his donkey, feeling proud of his learning, and then meeting an ugly man. The man greeted the rabbi respectfully, saying, "Peace be with you, Rabbi!" The rabbi did not return the greeting, and, moreover, said: "Simpleton, how ugly are the children of Abraham our father! Are all your townsmen as ugly as you?" To which the man replied: "That I do not know; perhaps you should go to the Creator who formed me and say to Him: 'How ugly is the creature You have made!'"

Rabbi Shimon recovers, but the story has already delivered its caution not to set ourselves up as judges over others. *Pirkei Avot* (Ethics of the Fathers) has Hillel saying, "Do not judge your fellow until you have stood in his place." Cultivating an attitude of honoring others helps supplant the tendency to judge people that is so well entrenched in many of us. This is important because, as the famous analogy puts it, when you insult the pot, you insult the potter.

I have worked to foster honor by holding a phrase in mind and then turning my mind to the phrase whenever I encounter someone. I've used a phrase I've created—"each one a holy soul"—as well as one drawn from Proverbs: "The soul of man is the candle of God."[21] Calling a phrase like this to mind is a very effective way to instill a sense of honoring others.

The wisdom of Mussar tells us to be humble and then the resistance to order will evaporate. Honor others and order will come about as a natural consequence. Learning this and putting it into practice is a true gift of Mussar. The inner way to a more productive life will be opened and, much more significantly, the channels to divine service will be cleared. Effort is focused on countervailing soul-traits, and the fruit of the effort is order.[22]

The Clasp on the Necklace

Mussar itself also depends on order. Ideally one's Mussar time should be the same every day—a fixed time that works with your schedule. Set this plan in advance and do your best to keep to it.

One of the core Mussar practices is keeping a daily journal, a practice that I will describe at greater length in chapter 28. The thrust of Mussar journaling is to record your own experiences. As simple as that may sound, many people report difficulty in sustaining the practice. Working with students to solve this problem, I have learned that it is easier to keep the journal if the practice is made to coincide with the preexisting order in your own life. One woman contacted me and told me she had to drop out of a course I was leading. "Why?" I asked her. "Because I can't keep the journal in the evening," she answered. "Have you tried doing it in the morning?" I inquired. "You can do that?" was her answer.

Now I recommend that people place their diaries somewhere along the paths they already walk in their life, where they will see it and encounter it and be reminded to write in it. Beside the coffee pot? Under your tooth-brush? On your pillow? The journal practice has great effect if done consistently; order can be put to work to support the practice.

Rabbi Shlomo Wolbe says in the name of the Alter of Kelm that order can be compared to the clasp on a pearl necklace.[23] The pearls are what make the necklace, and they are definitely more important than the clasp, but without the clasp the pearls will fall off and scatter, and all that will remain of the necklace is the string alone. Similarly, a person contains an abundance of strengths, intellect, character traits, and qualities. But without order, all these virtues will scatter, and he or she will be left with nothing.

Seeing the soul-trait of order as the clasp on a string of pearls provides a useful metaphor for bringing our focus on order to a practical conclusion. When we conceive of order as a midpoint, we are reminded that what ultimately matters in regard to order is to be personally and inwardly "centered." Order helps create an inner sense that the things that matter have been properly arranged and tended to and, as a result, that the details of life are under control. Calm and unworried, at that point the channels to the divine will are as open and unencumbered as they can get, and the possibility of serving—and happiness—will have become real for you.

Ken yehi ratzon. May it be God's will.

> Who orders the stars in their heavenly constellations as
> He wills.
>
> —From the Ma'ariv Aravim prayer
> recited during the evening service

12

Equanimity
MENUCHAT HA'NEFESH

Rise above the good and the bad.

As long as a man's mind is settled, his intellectual spirit
quietly stands guard, spreading its light upon his mind
as if it were a torch atop the edifice of his body.

—Rabbi M. M. Leffin, *Cheshbon ha'Nefesh*

MY FIRST EXPOSURE to Mussar included a lesson on inner peace
unlike any I had ever encountered before. It was words of Rabbi Yisrael
Salanter that surprised me so. He said: "As long as one lives a life of calmness and tranquility in the service of God, it is clear that he is remote from
true service."[1]

All notions I held about the spiritual life pointed in the opposite direction. Isn't spiritual practice supposed to make us more calm? What's the
point of cultivating an inner life if it doesn't result in greater tranquillity?
But Rabbi Salanter's meaning is clear. From his perspective, if you have
come to a place in your life where all the waters are becalmed and the
waves have been stilled, there is a very good chance that you are in a coma,
or at least deeply asleep. It is not a good place to be.

Equanimity and tranquillity are attractive in these turbulent and uncertain times. It's so seductive to think of a total escape from the storms
and turmoil of life. The place of infinite and permanent calm beckons so
invitingly that we can easily overlook the possibility that the serenity we
seek would be nothing but a velvet-lined jail cell.

Rabbi Salanter's view cuts right across that grain. Comfort, sweet and soft,
invites us to snuggle down and fall asleep, and that can't be our spiritual

goal. Many Jewish teachers liken life to a ladder or a narrow bridge. Would you want to be asleep?

Neither Rabbi Salanter nor any other Mussar teacher has been interested in the soft sell, but rather truth, and especially the truth about our lives. And I confess without reluctance that the truth of my experience is that struggle continues. Despite the years of practice and learning, I continue to be challenged inwardly and to experience daily effort to lift myself up against inner forces that are primed and ready to pull me down, in betrayal of what I hold as my own values, my potential, and the vision of a human being the Torah presents.

What we encounter here is a very Jewish view of life. Your spiritual practice will give you many gifts, but don't expect it to relieve you of your human nature.

Human Nature

There is a story told about Rabbi Elyah Lopian,[2] a great Mussar teacher of the last generation, who had responsibility for the spiritual lives of boys and young men in a yeshiva. One student came to ask permission to go home for the weekend to attend a family celebration. Rabbi Lopian knew that the boy came from a very secular family, and he was concerned about what the boy might be exposed to at home, like immodestly dressed women. "Aren't you concerned about that?" he asked the boy. "Oh no," the boy replied. "I have a plan. I won't look." To which the saintly Rabbi Lopian replied, "I am ninety-two years old and I am blind in one eye and I still look!"

Such is human nature, and Mussar doesn't point us toward a complete transcendence of who we are, as if the goal is to become something other than human, like an angel. Our efforts will be rewarded and we will make progress in our climb toward the light of holiness, but we should know that the effort will be continuous. Rabbi Adin Steinsaltz writes:[3]

The Jewish approach to life considers the man who has stopped going—he who has a feeling of completion, of peace, of a great light from above that has brought him to rest—to be someone who has lost his way. Only he whom the light continues to beckon, for

whom the light is as distant as ever, only he can be considered to
have received some sort of response.

Does this mean that the inner trait of equanimity is not only unattain-
able but maybe even undesirable? That would be an understandable conclusion to draw, but it would be totally incorrect. The Mussar teachers do
tell us that equanimity is a very important inner trait to cultivate.

Calmness of the Soul

Jewish sources use several terms to name the soul-trait of undisturbed
equanimity, the most descriptive of which is *menuchat ha'nefesh*, calmness
of the soul.[4] The Mussar teachers see the importance of a calm soul, but
they don't see that inner state as a final station called "Peace and Tranquillity" where the journey ends, even as life continues. Instead, they view equanimity as an inner balance that coexists with a world and an experience that
accepts turbulence and even turmoil, because that's just the way life is.

In the Jewish view, the goal of spiritual life is not to reach an enlight-
ened state in which all the questions and conundrums of life are unknot-
ted with finality, but rather to become much more skilled at the processes
of living. This view applies fully to the soul-trait of equanimity, which does
not spell the end of our struggles, but rather is an inner quality we can cultivate to equip ourselves to handle the inevitable ups and downs of life.

The Mussar teachers want us to be a calm soul who is like a surfer who
rides the waves on an even inner keel, regardless of what is happening
within and around him. Even as the waves are rising and falling, the calm
soul rides the crest, staying upright, balanced, and moving in the direction
the rider chooses. Equanimity is a quality of being centered in yourself,
though at the same time being exquisitely sensitive to the forces that are at
work all around, or else you will be vulnerable to being tossed around by
the sorts of unexpected waves that crash in on every life.

Equanimity in the Mussar usage does not suggest that feelings are idling
in neutral. It isn't a kind of numbness. You still register the ups and downs
of the feelings—those are the waves—but you stay awake to the experience from an undisturbed place. When you are submerged in your feelings without at least a flicker of self-awareness, the light of consciousness
is extinguished, and the doors to connection and choice are closed. But if

awareness is calmly present, even amid the storms of life, your soul maintains its connection to others and to the divine source and your free will is preserved.

Tests

The situations—large and small—that crop up in everybody's life and disturb our inner peace are not just painful inconveniences, the Mussar masters say, they are tests.[5] As such, it is open to you to pass or fail. Where you get tested is in those specific soul-traits where you yourself are vulnerable. A situation that presses on a well measured and strong trait really is no test at all, and what you will do in response is no stretch. But if you are a person prone to anger and someone steps on your toes (literally or figuratively), or if you are sorely tempted to steal and someone leaves an open purse right under your nose, or if lust gets you every time and the hotel desk clerk is just your type, then here we have a test.

The Alter of Novarodok made preparing for these life-tests a central feature of the Mussar he taught. His view was that we all tend to be very pious and God-fearing, so long as there is nothing particularly difficult challenging our willpower. He warned that when those sorts of troublesome challenges do come our way, as they inevitably will, we are likely to find ourselves unprepared and at risk of crumbling. We're wise to make the commitment to learn and practice at those times when we are not being tested so that we will have resolve and resources at the ready when challenge and trial do come to us, as they will. "The refining pot is for silver and the furnace for gold, but God tests hearts," the book of Proverbs teaches.[6]

The Alter of Novarodok once asked his students, "Do you know why the Master of the Universe created trains?" And before any of them could give a response, he answered himself, "In order to bring students to the Novarodok Yeshiva!"

A thoughtful student then questioned, "But Rebbe, if so, why does the train run in both directions?"

"That," said the Alter, "is the test."

Understanding and accepting the testing nature of life is essential to the cultivation of equanimity, because it is when you are being tested that you are most likely to be wrested from your inner balance.

The ideal response to a test is to rise to the occasion and to triumph with flying colors, which would mean stretching into the challenged soul-trait in a way that is both difficult for you to do and also good for the soul. The reality, however, has to be that you could go either way. That's why the test is real. If you pass a test, then that aspect of your inner being gets strengthened and you earn the right to move on—to face yet another set of challenges, as we have learned. Otherwise, you are likely to encounter the same test again at some future point.

I've seen this situation play out most clearly in relationships. Once the honeymoon is over, the relationship can look like nothing but tests. Too often people run from these trials, get divorced, and then proceed to find another relationship—that tests their weak soul-traits in exactly the same way.

Although we may regret it, curse it, and wish it were otherwise, it's inevitable that we keep coming into situations that challenge aspects of our nature where we are ripe to grow. Every life is peppered with these sorts of tests and trials. Why is life set up this way? Certainly not so we will inevitably fail and fall, but rather so we will keep being confronted by opportunities to grow. Life provides the real circumstances in which to mold character and cleanse the soul. From this perspective, our entire life is a curriculum, and as in any course, there are tests along the way. Our challenge is to meet these tests and to use them to purify and rectify and so clear our way to draw closer to each other and to God.

Tests Are on the Curriculum

When you think of the tests you have met and are meeting along your curriculum for growth, you'll likely think of negative challenges—lust, greed, rage, jealousy, arrogance, and the like. These are indeed common tests, but positive experiences can also become tests as we travel along our path. Success, for example, can sometimes be more of a challenge than failure. A run of success can lift a person on waves of elation, spurring a sense of invincibility. Intoxicating arrogance and dangerous greed will feed on success much more effectively than on failure. This is a phenomenon well-known in the business world, where it is a recognized and proven recipe for disaster.

So life keeps delivering tests to your doorstep, whether you happen to be living through dark days or when things are going very well. My observations of my own life as well as those of others convince me that you do yourself a favor by not pushing away from your struggles but instead embracing them, because they seem to be inevitable, woven right into the very fabric of life. In fact, if you are committed to your own growth, you won't even want your struggles to end because they are the very pathway to growth. The tests are the path. When we consider the ideal inner attitude you can adopt as you contend with your challenges, we are returned to the subject of equanimity.

The Independent Soul

In his chapter on equanimity in his nineteenth-century Mussar book *Cheshbon ha'Nefesh,* Rabbi Menachem Mendel Leffin sums up equanimity in a sentence: "Rise above events that are inconsequential—both good and bad," he writes, "for they are not worth disturbing your calmness of soul." His message is that the good that happens to you is as likely to cloud your settled inner state with mental agitation as is the bad, and in either case, the emotional overload is sure to have a negative impact on your life.

A classic Jewish story[7] attributed to the great kabbalist Rabbi Isaac Luria sets the standard for equanimity in facing the challenge inherent in both pleasant and nasty situations:

> A rabbi once came to one of the contemplative Kabbalists and asked to be accepted as an initiate. The Master said to him, "My son, may God bless you, for your intentions are good. Tell me, though, whether or not you have attained equanimity."
>
> The rabbi said to him, "Master, please explain your words."
>
> The Master replied, "If there were two people, and one of them honored you and the other insulted you, are they equal in your eyes?"
>
> The rabbi answered, "No, my Master. For I feel pleasure and satisfaction from the one who honors me, and pain from the insults of the other. But I do not take revenge or bear a grudge."
>
> The Master blessed the rabbi and sent him away. "Go in peace, my son. When you have attained equanimity, your soul does not feel the honor deriving from one who honors you nor the embarrassment arising from insults. Your consciousness is not yet ready to be attached to the supernal."

We learn something crucial about equanimity here. Calmness of the soul is described as a kind of *independence.* Even though you may be aware of honor as honor and insult as insult, your emotional state at any moment is not determined by the intentions and actions someone else (or life) sends in your direction. All sorts of feelings will come, as they do in all our lives, but when you are possessed of equanimity, your inner core is not left open to being whipped around by external experiences. You are freer than that.

This seems desirable, especially if we accept that life is bound to keep sending us struggles. We're going to be much better at guiding our way through life's challenges if we are not pulled off center by other peoples' emotions, wishes, and projections.

What makes our challenges so challenging, however, is the fact that they come at us charged with powerful feelings. This is the reality that makes the tests so hard. The bigger the challenge, the more we will experience feelings that will be difficult to sort out or even endure. The more you have mastered inner calmness, however, the better prepared you are to ride the waves of feelings as they arise in you.

Equanimity is the best mind state to be in when meeting a test. Think of being a general on the battlefield—would you want your soldiers to be all inwardly agitated and volatile, or calm, cool, and collected?

Still, we need to recognize that it isn't enough to say "yes to equanimity," as if that's all that's required to strengthen ourselves in that quality. If we really want to bring the balance and poise of a calm soul into the field of action of our lives, we have to take steps that will cause the roots of equanimity to work their way deep into our inner soil.

Distance Yourself

How are we to attain a settled mind that keeps its composure despite the vicissitudes of life? Rabbi Leffin uses the term "rise above" to help us find our inner stance, and this is helpful, though I would like to suggest an alternative that shows up more frequently in the Mussar literature and that I think is more practical: the guidance is to *distance yourself*.

In his famous letter to his son, Rabbi Moshe ben Nachman[8] advises: "Distance yourself from anger." And in the *Orchot Chaim* [Ways of Life] of the Rosh, we are advised, "Distance yourself from pride." This phrase, "distance yourself," shows up elsewhere as well.[9]

By "distance yourself" we are surely *not* being told never to be angry, proud, jealous, and the like, because Mussar teachers consistently assert that this would be an unrealistic goal—everyone experiences the full range of inner states, and in and of itself, every inner trait is neither good nor bad. More important is how we respond to what we feel. "Distance yourself," then, can mean only two things. Either we are to stay physically far from people who are angry, proud, and so forth, or we are being directed to develop some kind of *inner* distance from the experience of our own anger, pride, and other incendiary soul-traits.

Although there are definitely times when we ought to stand away from powerful outer forces (including "fools and sinners," [10] as we are warned), we need to be more concerned with the impulses and reactions that arise in us. We are solely responsible for the powerful inner forces that can lead us astray, and so these are our first priority. The guidance we are being given here is to cultivate an inner attitude that creates some distance between the stimulus that comes at us (whether from within or outside) and our reactions to it. We make this space by cultivating an inner capacity to bear witness.

When you have a strong inner witness, outer influences are seen for what they are. Your soul can clearly perceive "the honor of the one who honors you and the embarrassment of the one who insults you," and that lucid perception will help you keep yourself from being infected by sentiments that swirl around you. That same inner faculty will also keep you from being pushed around by the forces that arise within you—the distanced witness is not (or is at least less) susceptible to the tides of doubt, temptation, and jealousy, that wash through the interior world.

Beckoned by the Light

Do we still face struggles? Yes. Are the struggles real? Yes. Do the consequences matter? Yes. Do we still feel the full range of human emotions and drives? Yes. In other words, every aspect of your current life is real and important. You would be wise to embrace it because it's your soul curriculum. But cultivate the witness who will make you the master of the inner realm and not the victim.

Meditation prepares an inner witness. While sitting still and silent, many inner states will arise, and over time you can get quite good at simply living in their presence without feeling that you are a slave to any of them, whether repugnant or alluring.

Rabbi Steinsaltz describes the Jewish spiritual experience as a constant beckoning to the light. If we take that word *constant* seriously, then the light we seek must be present at all times and in all situations, no matter how murky or even dark they appear to us. Meditation strengthens the witness so we can remain inwardly aware and attentive to that light in every context in which we find ourselves.[11]

I know this experience personally, and therefore I understand why the metaphor of light is favored, but we are not speaking of real physical light here. There is a way of perceiving that includes a kind of shimmering meta-reality that isn't an aspect of any single thing in sight but encompasses all of it. I can shift into and out of that level of perception. Sometimes I only see the hard-edged stuff in the world. Other times I still see that stuff and also another reality breaching through, an intangible and luminous presence that radiates into all. The shell of materiality is infused with that illumination.

It is the job of the witness to keep an eye out for that light. When you realize that, and assign this task to your inner witness, and strengthen this practice, then over time the witness will make you more aware of the radiance that is a constant in the ever-shifting contexts in which you live.

An inner eye connected to the constant light won't give you a life of fewer challenges and struggles, but it will give you equanimity that will serve you well as you engage with these challenges. It's hard to imagine another inner state that you would want to bring to the trials that come your way, to better help you triumph. Maybe that's why the Alter of Kelm tells us: "A person who has mastered peace of mind has gained everything."

The essence of a person of faith is equanimity.

—Rabbi Bachya ibn Pakuda,
Duties of the Heart

13

Honor
KAVOD

Each and every one, holy soul.

Rabbi Akiva had twelve thousand pairs of students. All
of them died over thirty-two days between Passover and
Shavuot because they did not show respect toward
each other.

—*Yevamot* 62b

MANY OF US act as if we were born with a clipboard and have been assigned the task of evaluating everyone we meet. I see this tendency in myself, and maybe you can recognize it in yourself as well. You walk into a
room and immediately scan the crowd, taking in everyone who is there,
and putting them all through an instant evaluation. It can get pretty ugly,
and few of us would likely ever verbalize the sorts of things we routinely
run through in our minds as we mentally dress down other people.

"She wore that?"

"Just look at that dumb face!"

"Loud!"

"Such a slouch. Stand up straight, why don't you?"

"She smokes?"

I'll stop and let you continue. What sorts of things do you say (only to
yourself, of course) when that judgmental frame of mind has a grip on
you, and you are moving through life as if someone appointed you to be a
judge whose job it is to assess whether or not people measure up?

Let me ask, can you detect even a hint of honor in that attitude? Honor
not for what people have done, or how they do it, but in recognition of the

simple fact that we are all human, which means invested with a soul and possessing enormous gifts not of our own making?[1]

And further, what is the outcome of that judgmental attitude? Does it ever lead to anything positive, or is it the root of feelings of disappointment and dissatisfaction in everyone around us?

The Honor of a Person

The rabbis in the Talmud[2] open up this subject for us by sketching a hypothetical scenario. It's the evening of the festival of Purim and you are walking to synagogue to hear the traditional reading of the Megillah ("scroll"), the Book of Esther. Along the way, you have the misfortune to come across a corpse lying in the road. Jewish law obligates us to give a dead body a proper burial, no matter whether it is a Jew or a non-Jew or a stranger or a criminal. But burying a body takes time, and if you stop to fulfill this commandment, you will surely be unable to fulfill that other commandment, to hear the Megillah reading. What to do? Do you stop to bury the body or continue on to synagogue?

The answer in the Talmud is that you should bury the body. The reason given is that the honor due to a human being[3] is so great that it suspends even a negative precept of the Torah. What the rabbis are trying to teach us here is that every human being—even a dead one—is due honor. Now if the obligation to honor the humanity that resides even in a corpse is so compelling, imagine how much more we should honor a living person. Tradition puts such emphasis on honoring others that the sages tell us that the calamitous destruction of the Second Temple was brought on by the baseless hatred that existed among people of the time.[4]

When we consider the laws and injunctions that the rabbis have decreed, often they encourage us to do things that are very good but to which we are not naturally and easily inclined. We don't need much inducement to eat, wash, beautify ourselves, or gratify our needs, and what the rabbis have to say about these sorts of activities is only that we should be moderate in our participation in them and sacralize them. We don't generally need to be told to do them—in fact, not fulfilling these activities is considered to be "affliction." But in some areas of life, the rabbis see that we clearly have our work cut out for us. Good though they may be for us, doing certain activities doesn't come easily. To accustom ourselves to performing these sorts of actions, we need to learn, to be guided, to practice, and to hold ourselves accountable.

For many of us, honoring other people falls into this latter category. It just isn't easy for us to take responsibility for honoring others. It is much easier for us to be critical and harshly judgmental, seeing only others' flaws and failings. When our eyes focus only on the soiled garment, ignoring the divinely inspired being within, there really isn't anything much to honor.

Honor, respect, and dignity are due to each and every human being not because of the greatness of their achievements or how they have behaved, but because they are home to a soul that is inherently holy. Nobody created their own soul; everybody has been gifted with a rarefied essence. This is a teaching of Rabbi Chaim of Volozhin,[5] a forerunner of the Mussar movement, who explains that one should honor all people simply because they are the handiwork of God.

The Challenge to Honor

We need tradition to draw our attention to this deep reality because it isn't readily evident to us. Our eye easily falls on the flaws in the trappings. That's like focusing on the gift wrap and ignoring the present within. Imagine someone sent you a painting by Picasso or Chagall, and all you could see was the dirty, tattered packaging in your hands?

So why do we do it? Why do we set up standards against which to gauge others and then spend so much of our mental energy appraising how people are measuring up? I'd be surprised if anyone ever did that other than as an externalization of the standards against which we judge ourselves. And because we are anxious about how we ourselves are stacking up, we judge others. When we find them wanting, we appear better and greater to ourselves.

Whether we admit it or not, most of us want honor and feel we are not getting it, certainly not in the measure we feel to be our due. So the factor that drives us to be so critical of others is nothing other than our own search for honor, especially in our own eyes.

There is a profound and sad reality in this. Many people just don't love themselves enough and in the right way. In the Mussar work, we are always looking for soul-traits that we can elevate and improve, and that means we are awake to our imperfections, but even that self-awareness and effort ought to happen in an atmosphere of self-honor.

It is a truth that we are worthy of honor. The Jewish tradition, by and large, encourages us to find a balance that represents healthy self-esteem, a proper measure of honor. The discernment can be delicate. The respect that is due to others is due to you and me as well, not because we are perfect, or even great, or even good. Your greatness is not attached to your identity but rather to the fact that you are human and your essence is a gift of incomparable beauty and majesty. The healthiest and strongest way to tackle the practice of elevating soul-traits is by setting that inner work in a context of self-honor.

A Trait and Its Opposite

The Mussar teachers are insistent that you make a very clear distinction between the honor you ought to give to all souls—including your own deep inner being—and the desire of your hungry ego to slurp up every bit of honor it can possibly get its greedy hands on. They warn us stridently about this tendency of the ego, and Rabbi Salanter relates it to a general Mussar principle: a person "must endeavor to acquire within his soul each character trait and its opposite. Even more, he must train himself so that at the time he needs to exercise a character trait relevant to himself, it will be awakened within him and its opposite forgotten. On the other hand, at a time when its opposite is required to be employed on behalf of his fellow, this opposing one should be awakened, and the foundation of the trait should be momentarily forgotten."[6]

Honor is the perfect example of this need for "a trait and its opposite," about which he says, "For example, to flee from honor is a precious quality. As the Sages state: 'The desire for honor removes a man from the world.' However, the reverse is true concerning others, as the Sages said: 'Who is honored? He who honors others.'"[7]

Do not seek honor for yourself, but go out of your way to honor others. The real concern here is the place of ego in your life. Not seeking honor for yourself reflects humility; so too does honoring others. Committing your life to ego-based honor is not even wise because, when given free rein, the ego's desire for honor is never satisfied, and a life devoted to seeking honor will pass as a life unfulfilled.

Rabbi Salanter cites the sages' warning to "flee from honor."[8] Yet in their wildest dreams they never could have imagined the extent to which our modern culture would elevate personal honor and send us off on an endless and misguided search for pedestals onto which to hoist ourselves. Their warning stands for us now more than ever, since people didn't have magazines called *Self* and *Us* to lead them astray in nineteenth-century Lithuania. So severe are the effects of pursuing our own ego gratification that the sages warn us (as Rabbi Salanter quotes) that honor is one of the factors that "drive a person out of this world."[9] Does that mean actual death, or living a life that is not suited to this world? Either way, pursuing honor surely is not the way of the soul.

As for the other side of the equation, far from honoring others, who hasn't participated, or even delighted, in the public shaming of another person? While the tradition calls on us to honor others, it also warns with emphatic hyperbole to ensure we get the message: "Better had a man thrown himself into a fiery furnace than publicly put his neighbor to shame."[10] Yet too often we do just that.

Equally off the mark is our tendency to rue another person's good fortune instead of celebrating with them. "The other person's elevation must rouse us to joy," says Rabbi Meir Chodosh. "We must remember that his elevation and honor do not take anything away from us." He is alerting us to the root issue, which is the cravings of our egos. "In this way," he goes on, "we will become freed from thinking about ourselves and will see only [someone else who is doing well], and we will be glad."[11] In the Mussar tradition, this is called developing an *ayin tovah*, a good eye.

Who Is Worthy of Honor?

There is a direct connection between the ego's insistent but unquenchable craving for honor and that critical mind state in which we stand ourselves in fierce judgment over others, even to the extent of shaming them. We judge and criticize other people in a mistaken expression of the desire we have for love and honor for ourselves. The wisdom of tradition tells us that when we act like this, we've got the whole thing backward. Ben Zoma asks: "Who is worthy of honor?" And he answers: "The one who treats others with honor."[12] And elsewhere the rabbis caution: "Those who endeavor to gain honor at the price of another person being degraded have no portion in the World-to-Come."[13]

This is a cornerstone teaching around this soul-trait. We merit honor by giving honor. Yet our tendency is to withhold honor—or even shame—because we are hungry for honor. Could we get it any more wrong than that?

To turn things around, we have to develop the habit of offering honor to others. Rabbi Bachya ibn Pakuda tells a wonderfully illuminating story on this theme in *Duties of the Heart*:

> Once a pious person was talking with his disciples. As they passed a rotted dog's carcass, his students said, "How awful is the stench of this carcass."
>
> "How white are its teeth!" he responded.[14]

He looked, and within the rotting mess found something to honor.

The famous Chassidic sage Rebbe Levi Yitzchak of Berditchev spotted a man greasing the wheels of his wagon while wearing a *tallis* (prayer shawl) and *tefillin* (phylacteries). Instead of becoming furious at this apparent sacrilege, the rabbi turned his eyes toward heaven and proclaimed, "See, Master of the World, how holy are Your children! Even when he is engaged in greasing his wheels, he nevertheless remembers to pray to You!" Rebbe Levi Yitzchak trained himself to judge everyone positively.[15]

So too did Rabbi Yisrael Salanter, who said that when he first started learning Mussar, he became angry at the world but remained at peace within himself. As he studied further, he also became angry with himself. Finally, he evolved to judging others favorably.[16]

Honoring

Like every other soul-trait, honor is both a state of awareness and a deed. Soul-traits are virtues in action. It is not enough to *feel* reverence; one must *act* reverently. We act with honor when we honor the other (as well as ourselves) by treating all beings with the utmost respect and dignity. We act with honor when we listen carefully to the needs of another and respond; when we look beneath surface differences to see the shared ground upon which all beings stand. Honoring others requires that we make an effort to elevate people in our eyes, as Rabbi Elazar ben Shamua taught: "Let the honor of your student be as dear to you as your own, and the honor of your colleague as the reverence for your rabbi, and the reverence for your rabbi as the reverence for Heaven."[17]

I have heard it said in the name of Rabbi Aaron Kotler[18] that if you are driving along the highway and come to a toll plaza, and you have a choice between taking the automatic booth or the one that is staffed by a human being, you should choose the person. This gives respect to the human being, by making him or her feel useful, as opposed to unneeded, replaced by a toll machine.

I'm not often on a toll road, so I look for more accessible ways to give honor to others. One form of honoring about which the tradition has a lot to say is the act of greeting people. *Pirkei Avot*[19] urges us to "take the initiative in greeting any person you meet,"[20] and the Talmud[21] relates that no one ever greeted Rabbi Yochanan ben Zakai[22] before he greeted them, not even a stranger in the marketplace.

Rabbi Yochanan (not the same individual) put his guidance in colorful imagery worthy of today's ad writers: "It is better to whiten one's teeth for his friend [i.e., to greet him with a tooth-revealing smile], than to serve him milk."[23]

This is a practice any of us can do. All it takes is an encounter with another person and a willingness to say, "Hello, nice to see you." Imagine, *this* we call spiritual practice? How sensible. I urge you to try it.

Through practices like these, we actively honor others in concrete ways. When we are the first to honor another, we come forward from humility, and for this, others will honor us, too.

Honoring others in this way does not mean giving up the power and practice of exercising judgment, but puts the focus on moving away from unwise, useless, habitual, and even destructive acts of judgment. We start to move in that direction when we recognize that the roots of the problem lie in our own fears about our own inadequacies, of which we are only too aware, that make us fear that others will not give us the honor we feel we want and need. Our test is to recognize, internalize, and act upon the teaching of the sages: "The person who judges his neighbor in the scale of merit is himself judged favorably."[24]

The same Rabbi Akiva whose twenty-four thousand students died in just over the period of a month because they did not give each other mutual respect was a great proponent of the teaching, "Love your neighbor as yourself,"[25] calling it "the first principle of the Torah."[26] He taught: "Beloved is man, for he was created in the image of God."[27] This is a lesson you should fix before your eyes, like lenses through which you will see that every human being you meet is a holy soul.

> Rabbi Eliezer said: "Let the honor of your friend be as dear to you as your own."
>
> —*Pirkei Avot* 2:10

14

Simplicity

HISTAPKUT

Content with my portion.

An American visitor was passing through the Polish town of Radin and stopped in to visit the Chafetz Chaim.[1] Entering the great sage's simple apartment, he was struck by how sparsely it was furnished. "Where is your furniture?" the man asked. "Where is yours?" replied the Chafetz Chaim. "Oh, I am only passing through," answered the man. "I too am only passing through," was the Chafetz Chaim's reply.

WE LIVE IN A PHYSICAL WORLD, and though our aim is spiritual, the way of the soul runs right through the material realm. We should not mistake the material as the bane of the spiritual, because the whole journey toward wholeness can take place only by means of action in the physical world. The words of Rabbi Moshe Chaim Luzzatto[2] are very clear on this point:

> Even though man must be immersed in the physical, he is able to rise to wholeness through his worldly activities and the physical world itself. It is precisely through these that he attains a pure and lofty state. It is therefore his very lowliness that elevates him, for when he transforms darkness into light and deathly shadow into sparkling brilliance, he personally earns for himself unparalleled excellence and glory.

The Mussar masters tell us that this world is as real as it gets, and they urge us to make the most of our lives, here and now.

A story is told about Rabbi Yisrael Salanter walking down the street one late evening and seeing a shoemaker working by the light of a dying candle. "Why are you still working?" he asked. "It is very late and soon that candle will go out." The shoemaker replied, "As long as the candle is still burning, it is still possible to accomplish and to mend." Rabbi Salanter spent that entire night excitedly pacing his room and repeating to himself: "As long as the candle is still burning, it is still possible to accomplish and to mend!"

The time is now, the place is here. That's precisely what Rabbi Menachem Mendel Leffin writes in his revered Mussar text, *Cheshbon ha'Nefesh*,[3] under the heading, "Don't allow a moment of your life to be wasted." For a person even to warrant being called a human being, he says:

> The bulk of his time must be directed towards regaling in the delights of the supernal soul, progressively perfecting himself in this area daily. This is not true of the wicked, who waste their share in this precious life and die with nothing to show for themselves!

Though the soul needs this material plane in order to evolve in the direction of wholeness, the world we inhabit can also be a spiritual trap. The option of detouring away from the path of elevation is real, too. As the Talmud warns us, "For one who chooses to defile himself, the way is open."[4] Various sorts of cheese can bait this spiritual trap, since we are not all subject to the same temptations to veer from the straight way, but one of the most common impediments, especially in the contemporary world, is material possessions. Impoverished people can fall prey to seeing salvation in material goods, while the wealthy can become intoxicated and enslaved by what they own.

The Challenge of the Material

Our ancestors were well acquainted with poverty. Only if the rain fell in its proper season would there be food to harvest. Plant diseases and pests could wipe out a crop and bring the dependent population to ruin. Disease was prevalent and life expectancy short. Rulers and their tax collectors were rapacious. Material comforts were basic at best. And even though our world has made affluence much more accessible to so many, poverty is still a challenge in many lives.

These days, however, the challenges brought on by material goods are more likely to arise out of abundance rather than lack. The problem of bounty is no doubt different, but as far back as Mishnaic times, it was understood that wealth could be just as much a spiritual problem as poverty. Hillel taught, "The more possessions, the more worries."[5] What if thieves come to steal my wealth? What if they threaten me or my family? What if my investments fail? What if...?

The issue is not things themselves. Judaism values the things of this world, holding that everything ultimately stems from God and therefore everything must have goodness. The issue is how that good is put to work, because even the best of good can be put to evil uses—like bright minds composing precise train schedules to deliver innocent people to their deaths—and too much of a good thing can be harmful, as every doctor will attest.

The core issue, of course, is human nature. Things are not the problem—it's our inclination to become overinvolved with material possessions and pleasures that we have to be aware of and attend to. Rabbi Yisrael Salanter acknowledges compassionately that this is just a feature of our earthly natures:

> Insofar as man is a physical being—"dust from the ground"[6]—his heart inclines to the material. Therefore, he desires to "eat, drink, and be merry." He loves wealth and fortune, and longs for honor and dominion. He is full of self-importance and seeks to delight in bodily comforts.

The problem is that the allure of the material is endless, and ultimately the craving is insatiable. "Man is immersed in this pursuit with all his heart and soul," wrote Rabbi Salanter, "—to gather and collect, to further his acquisitions and increase his property. There is no end to all his labor, for there is no limit to his longing."[7] As the sages of the midrash have written, "No one leaves this world with even half his desires fulfilled."[8]

What the Mussar teachers decry is not the material world per se but our enslavement to it. Rabbi Dessler describes[9] people whose "hearts remain attached to their material, animalistic desires." "What a pity!" he writes. "They are like fish trapped in a net, or an animal inside a snare. They run back and forth to no avail."

This is our predicament, and to guide us in dealing with it, the Mussar masters taught the virtue of living a more simple life, and being content with what you have.[10]

Wanting versus Needing

Most of us could get by very well with less than we have and certainly less than we seek. Not only would we get by, we would actually be freed to give our time and energy to things that really do matter in this life. I know that it seems to me that I spend far too much of my time being of service to the things that I acquired with the intention that they would take care of me— servicing the car, repairing the computer, buying supplies for the household, replacing the old models, and on and on.

It was in eleventh-century Spain that the Jewish poet-philosopher and rabbi Shlomo ibn Gabirol wrote: "Seek what you need and give up what you do not need. For in giving up what you do not need, you will learn what you really do need."[11]

Do you know what you really need in this life? I invite you to pause and think about this for a moment.

Of course our lives depend on having food, shelter, air, water, clothes, and the like. Beyond that, I wonder if your answer has been influenced by the allure of the glinting baubles the world hangs before us. If everyone has a hot tub, I must need a hot tub, too. If everyone has a food processor, a PDA, a car, a television, a diamond ring, and a Borsalino hat, how can I be expected to live without these necessities?

A need is different from a desire. A need really is essential. A desire, on the other hand, is backed by an emotional force that turns it into a virtual demand: I have to have it. And it is our desires[12] that create trouble for us. Desires can commandeer our lives on behalf of their fulfillment. And when they go unrealized, they deliver up anxiety, anger, frustration, and unethical behavior that we want to avoid.

No one disputes that we need to satisfy our basic needs for reasonable comfort and safety. But the sages felt it so important to warn us against a life enslaved to gratification that they embedded their warning right in the daily recitation of the *Sh'ma*, the central affirmation of Jewish faith. The blessing cautions: "Don't stray after your heart or your eyes."[13] The rabbis who set the prayers to melody made sure we understood that they were warning us about the allure of the world by accompanying this phrase with notes that rise and fall in a beckoning way.

Making Life Count

How will you make your life count if you don't know what really counts in your life? Rabbi Ibn Gabirol counsels that you'll find out only if you make your life simpler. The new space you open up will invite the answer of what it is you really do need. Only then can you hope to live well, under the wing of truth.

Previous generations often practiced frugality just because money was truly scarce. The verb "to darn," which describes what my mother would do to socks that had holes in them, hardly knows that usage any more. We have to be careful, though, not to make a virtue of stingy self-denial. *Orchot Tzaddikim,* for example, provides an unflattering description of the extremely frugal individual, who "is of constricted spirit, for whom even a trifle suffices and he does not rush to obtain all of his needs." This is the sort of individual who "consumes not even a penny's worth of his own without dire distress."

Because frugality can be as negative and pinched as this description suggests, for voluntary simplicity to be good for the soul (as opposed to being merely miserly renunciation), it requires not only outer action but also a strong and positive inner attitude. Simplicity undertaken to bring the life you lead into alignment with your deepest values is a spiritual practice. Living frugally[14] then becomes a virtue in itself.

The Three Levels of Simplicity

Acquiring Less

Pulling yourself back from the relentless pursuit of things represents the first of what the Vilna Ga'on[15] clarifies as the three levels to practicing this trait. When you undertake to be satisfied with little and not run after unnecessary things, whether food, clothing, possessions, experiences, or mental states, you will have simplified your life. At this level of practicing simplicity, although you will be making do with less, you can still expect to feel the desires that you are training yourself not to fulfill.

Can you identify any things in your life that you might be willing to give up?

Resisting overengagement with the material world is no easy task in a culture that constantly creates new "needs" for us. Before you have a moment to appreciate what you have, you are bombarded with reminders of what you still lack. (No time for complacent enjoyment!) You might not even have realized that you were missing something until it was pointed out to you, complete with all the details of the social costs that will ensue if you don't comply. The mindset of acquisition can leave us constantly feeling great pangs of need. Of desire, the Talmud says, "Satisfy it, and it becomes ravenous; starve it, and it becomes satiated."[16]

Becoming Happy with What You Already Have

The Vilna Ga'on points to an even higher level of simplification that comes when you are actually happy with whatever you have. You're content with what you have and not bothered by whatever you do not currently possess.

"Who is rich?" asks Ben Zoma,[17] and he answers, "One who is content with his lot." That is not how we ordinarily define wealth; it is much wiser. No matter how many or how few your possessions, you will actually feel the reality of your riches only if you have an inner contentment with what you have. Otherwise, you will be forever measuring yourself against someone who has more, and in comparison you will not even see yourself as having anything: "One who has one hundred wants two hundred,"[18] our sages warn. Those who endlessly crave will not even enjoy what they already have: "One who loves money will not be satisfied with money."[19] And again from Rabbi Sh'lomo ibn Gabirol, "Whoever seeks more than he needs hinders himself from enjoying what he has."

The rabbis of the Talmud had a saying that applies here. "*Tafasta meruba lo tafasta*,"[20] which means, "He who grabs too much grabs nothing." To devote ourselves excessively to the stuff of the world is to be left with nothing.

Being content is entirely a matter of attitude, not a reflection on the extent of one's possessions. Rabbi Salanter's disciple, Rabbi Yitzchak Blazer,[21] points that out by citing a story from the Talmud:[22]

> Every day a heavenly voice is heard declaring, "The whole world draws its sustenance because [of the merit] of Chanina, my son, and Chanina, my son, is satisfied with a measure of carobs from one Shabbos eve to another." The text does not say, "and Chanina, my son, has a measure of carobs," rather, it says, "and Chanina, my son, is satisfied with a measure of carobs from one Shabbos eve to another." The crucial element is that he is satisfied with what he has.[23]

If being content with what you have is an attitude, it is not meant to be a fatalistic one. It's more positive than that. At its core, this inner attitude is about elevating the spiritual above the physical. It calls for transcending materialism[24] in favor of a way of living that acknowledges the primacy of the spiritual in your life. Rabbi Eliyahu Dessler speaks to this shift in how we live when we opt for material simplicity:

> When the focus of his life is on spiritual goals, a person automatically diminishes his material endeavors and the time he spends on them. To the extent of his yearning for spirituality, he is not dismayed by the lack of material success, for dismay is only felt where there is unfulfilled ambition.[25]

At this level of simplification, the practice shifts from being one of frugality, which implies denying yourself, to abstinence, which is a much more positive quality.

Abstinence is positive? Most of us hear the word *abstinence* and immediately think that we are being asked to give up something good and most likely enjoyable, leaving in its place loss and deprivation. Mussar teachings on abstinence can be just like that, but there are others that are much more sensitive and generous. What I have come to understand and appreciate—quite contrary to simple assumptions—is that spiritually focused abstinence is not a matter of denial but contains within it seeds of liberation.

Nowhere in my experience has this been clearer than in the observance of Shabbat. It's not something I grew up with, but in recent years as I have taken on more Jewish practice, on the Sabbath I have denied myself television, radio, video, computer, car travel, and many other aspects of everyday life. If you think that giving up these activities has impoverished my life, you'd be wrong. Six days in the week is ample time to accomplish everything I need to do for my daily life. And on the seventh, the absence of these more mundane activities opens a space into which other, more meaningful activities flow. I read, review the texts I studied that week, pray, meditate, walk, visit friends, rest, and study. I engage in more delicate and tender activities that have a hard time competing with the computer and the car on the other days of the week. But on Shabbat, the competition is rendered silent, and the spirit has its way.

We already encountered the Ramban's teaching that foreswearing indulgence in excessive or unsanctioned material pleasures is the very definition of holiness itself. To elevate yourself requires that you limit yourself even in regard to permissible and good things. Why? Because the primary target in sight here is to liberate yourself from the bondage of insatiable desire. And you are satisfied.

Nothing More to Need

The highest level of simplification that the Vilna Ga'on identifies is the feeling that you have everything. You could not possibly want anything more on the material plane.

The soul-trait of simplicity does not have its own chapter in *Orchot Tzaddikim,* but where that trait is discussed is within "The Gate of Joy." This elevated level of simplified living sets joy free in the heart. "The person who bears these things is free of the worries of the world. He also finds sufficient the little that he has." Released from craving and the relentless pursuit of more material satisfactions, perfectly content with what is, the heart bubbles forth with the joy that is its potential and natural inclination.

Have you ever encountered anyone who lived like this? Is it a way of life that calls to you?

Divine service is to be done joyfully, as the psalm says: "Serve God with joy."[26] The practice of simplicity and contentment makes that possible.

Simplicity in the Moment

There is another aspect to living with simplicity that might not be so evident but is just as important as the subjects we have been looking at. When you move yourself away from a life driven by desire for acquisition, and cultivate contentment with what you have, you will inevitably find yourself living in the present. The past is gone and the future unknowable. The Rambam said, "Only the ignorant sorrowfully mourn what's past. So worrying over the money you've lost is about as useful as worrying that you were created a human being and not an angel." The same happens to be true of someone who nostalgically lives in their victories of the past. Either way, win or lose, simplicity means letting go of the past and accepting what is now.

If you tend to glorify or mourn the past, you are just as likely to worry about the future. Against this tendency the Talmud counsels: "Do not worry about tomorrow's troubles, for you do not know what the day may bring. Tomorrow may come and you will be no more, and so you will have worried about a world that is not yours!"[27] The Vilna Ga'on agrees, also encouraging us not to tie ourselves in knots over the unknowable future: "Contentment, which is the foundation for keeping the whole Torah, means faithfully to believe that there is no need to worry about what tomorrow will bring."[28]

The alternative is to accept and live in the present.

This attitude affects Mussar practice, too. There are so many steps on the way of the soul. Here I am trying to focus on simplicity, but what about all the work I need to do on generosity and gratitude and honor and all the traits in my curriculum? It calls for mindful simplicity to be content to be fully engaged with only one thing at a time. When practicing Mussar, while you work to internalize and integrate one soul-trait, you don't fret about everything else. We work at one soul-trait at a time. Then we move to the next.

Simplicity Is about Trusting God

Ultimately, simplicity is about trusting God. All the worry, striving, desire, regret, and clinging that you pour into your possessions—those you have, those you lost, or those you aspire to—reflect your disbelief that you will be provided with just the right materials you need to fulfill your soul-mission in life. It's not likely to be all you want, but there is no end to desires or the craving for gratification, and no satisfaction to be won by chasing the illusion that begins, "If only I had . . ." Being content means accepting that you have been allotted everything you need for the present, according to a wisdom that is higher than anything your human mind can assess.

Though living a simpler life might seem at first glance to be a sacrifice, from a soul-perspective, it is nothing less than true liberation. It is the most practical thing you can do to extricate your life from the concerns of the material to devote to the spiritual. Simplicity brings you freedom: freedom from the bondage to possessions, freedom from insatiable desires, freedom from dwelling on the past and from making demands on the future.

> Ben Zoma said: "Who is rich? One who is happy with what he has."
>
> —*Pirkei Avot* 4:1

15

Enthusiasm

ZERIZUT

Just do it—enthusiastically!

The angels were praised for this good trait [enthusi-
asm]. As it is said regarding them (Psalms 103:20),
"(They are) mighty in energy, doing as He says, listening to the voice of His word." And, as it is written
(Ezekiel 1:14), "The heavenly beings dashed back and
forth like lightning." In truth human beings are just
that—humans, and not angels. It is therefore impossible for us to have the might of the angels. Nonetheless we should strive to get as close to this level as we
possibly can. King David used to praise his own share
of this trait by saying (Psalm 119:60), "I hurried—did
not delay—to keep Your commandments."

—Rabbi Moshe Chaim Luzzatto, *The Path of the Just*

IN TRADITIONAL MUSSAR YESHIVAS, the talks given by the spiritual
supervisor[1] are sometimes called *hisorerus,*[2] meaning "awakening." Rabbi
Yisrael Yaakov Lubchansky,[3] who delivered these talks at the Baranovich
Yeshiva in the years leading up to its destruction in the Holocaust, was a
master of the *hisorerus* talk, usually delivered to about five hundred
people on Saturday night in total darkness.

But there is another sense or interpretation for the word *hisorerus,* and
that is "inspiration." The soul-trait of "enthusiasm"[4] or "zeal" carries the
same sense of awakened energy.

Motivation is as much a key to spiritual endeavor as any other activity.
Meditation will have no impact if not done regularly. How can your

prayer life have any effect if you seldom rouse yourself to pray with concentration and passion? It is just a fact that your soul-traits will gradually
fade from your field of vision when you don't recite a morning affirmation or keep an evening journal. "If a person will not rouse himself—of
what benefit are all the Mussar talks?" asks Rabbenu Yonah.[5]

Of course, motivation is only part of the picture. There are ways to be
very energetic that still run you off the rails. A good head of steam, for example, is also potent for driving in the direction of evil. There is also the
modern curse of frantic rushing, which is a kind of headless enthusiasm.
And while we will see the importance of being energetic and enthusiastic,
even to the point of zealousness, this is no counsel to be rash and foolish,
as *Cheshbon ha'Nefesh* underlines:

> There are people whose process of deliberation is so short that it
> seems as if they conduct all their affairs solely according to the ad-
> vice of their animal spirits. About them, the verse (*Mishlei* [Proverbs]
> 21:5) states: "The thoughts of the zealous are superfluous and those
> who are hasty reap only loss."[6]

The warning the Mussar teachers give us is that rashness and frantic
busyness are just as much impediments to the trait of enthusiasm as is
slothful laziness.

Might you recognize tendencies of your own in any of these obstacles
to enthusiasm?

So bear in mind that when we are considering the soul-trait of enthusiasm, we're taking it as a given that there is a good moral compass in hand
and that effective deliberation has taken place. Proper, positive, balanced
enthusiasm is action done with a full throttle, once review, consideration,
and decision have set you on the right course.

Showing Up Is Not Enough

Judaism is a religion of commandments and actions, and its leaders and
teachers have stressed the importance of enthusiasm, because the proper
way to execute the divine will is with energy and alacrity (*zerizut*).[7] However, recognition dawned long ago that it is almost impossible to do the
same thing every day (more so several times a day) and not have those

activities become dull and mechanical acts of mere obligation, just going through the motions. Anyone who has attended a prayer service that seems to have as its main purpose racing through the requisite words in the shortest possible time in order to get out of there knows what I mean. That is so far from the intention, in which every observance is a precious opportunity crafted with care to help us connect to the spiritual in such a way as to make a lasting impression on the soul.

Because we get drugged into unconsciousness by repetition, and lest they become dead acts, prayer and observance need to be regularly boosted with an infusion of enthusiasm. And what is true in your service to God is also true in your life in other ways. To live with spiritual integrity and authenticity requires that you break through the smothering curtain of routine. You'll do that by consciously ticking up your enthusiasm a notch.

"You must know," says the sixteenth-century Mussar classic *Orchot Tzaddikim,* "that the trait of zeal is the foundation of all the traits." And later it adds, "The trait of zeal is an ornament to all the other traits and it perfects all of them."[8] If you are going to be generous, how much better to give with enthusiasm. Acts of loving-kindness should not be delayed but rather done with alacrity. Be zealous in defense of the honor of your friend. These are examples of some traits among the many that gain an important dimension when they are enlivened with enthusiasm.

The rabbis have found the basis for their teachings on enthusiastic action in the Torah's instruction on eating the Passover sacrificial lamb. The sacrifice is to be eaten quickly, and from this the general principle is drawn that we should not delay in doing what is spiritually beneficial. "When a mitzvah presents itself, don't let it go stale."[9] King David said of himself: "I was quick. I did not delay in keeping Your commandments."[10]

The standard reason for not delaying is that you might let the opportunity slip away from you. Rabbi Shlomo Wolbe explains, however, that a mitzvah delayed or done unenthusiastically is not a mitzvah that might go wrong, but one that already has gone wrong. It is a second-rate performance that has already been contaminated.

The lesson for us here is that merely showing up in life just isn't enough. Drifting along with no passion for living, or repeating the same good acts in a routine way, is a kind of sin. Your acts are contaminated.

Would you have thought of delay or a lack of enthusiasm as factors that contaminate your actions? One student got this lesson in the most ordinary of contexts, when she had to attend a meeting for one of her children. She approached the meeting with a negative attitude: "I doubted it would be useful to me. I resented the time I would have to take to schlep back and forth, the interruption in my day, which is already packed."

What snapped her out of her drift was her recognition that this meeting was for the benefit of her beloved child. How could she be so unenthusiastic when it might do him some good? "I took a deep breath and thought of *zerizut* [enthusiasm]. To do this task was not enough. To show up was not enough. I needed to get into a different frame of mind, to think about my kid and the possibility that I might learn even one thing that would be a benefit."

With those thoughts, something shifted in her. "I no longer saw this task as an imposition, an interruption in my too-busy day. This was a worthwhile thing to be doing."

Quick and Enduring

There are two different aspects of the trait of enthusiasm. The first is to be quick to take action. Our role model here is Abraham, who the Torah tells us "rose early in the morning." He did that three times: once to stand before God's place;[11] another time to expel Hagar and her son Ishmael from his household;[12] and finally to fulfill the difficult commandment he had received to take his son Isaac to Mount Moriah to be sacrificed.[13] His sense of service was so complete that he did not hesitate in the least to spring into action.

When windows of opportunity open in your life, these may also be invitations from God. Are you quick to recognize and act on the ones that are for the good?

The second aspect of enthusiasm involves finding and expressing the energy needed to complete a task. As important as it is to be quick off the mark, it is equally important to sustain energy throughout the whole enterprise. It's so common for people to begin something with a tank full of enthusiasm, only to grind to a halt when they hit a delay or when some unforeseen obstruction arises, they get bored, or something else gets in the way. It takes enthusiasm not to bog down, wander off, or pull up midcourse but to press on to finish the good deed with vigor. With regard to this, the sages said, "A mitzvah is judged only upon its completion."[14] As much as we like to comfort ourselves otherwise, good intentions are not enough.

Laziness Subverts Enthusiasm

Enthusiasm is one of those soul-traits that is best cultivated by understanding and addressing what obstructs it. The natural tendency of the heart is to be passionate and energetic, so setting free that innate power is more a matter of removing impediments than stoking the fire.

What is it that subverts and deflates your enthusiasm? Rabbi Moshe Chaim Luzzatto offers his guidance in *The Path of the Just.*

The first major stumbling block to enthusiasm he identifies is its direct opposite, which is laziness.[15] When laziness rules the roost, not much of anything happens, except that we remain stuck in our present circumstances, arrested like a bud frozen on the limb.

Laziness may seem benign, but Rabbi Luzzatto warns us about how insidious and dangerous that trait can be:

> The bad that comes from laziness does not come about in one fell swoop, but slowly and without notice. It comes in a sequence of one bad deed after another, until you find yourself sunk in evil.

Without even recognizing that it is happening, laziness carries us lower and lower until we ultimately become agents of evil: "The lazy man, though not actively evil, produces evil through his very inactivity."

What Rabbi Luzzatto has to tell us about laziness that we may not realize is that laziness is characterized by *heaviness:* "And see that the nature of a human being is very heavy."[16]

Like many Mussar teachers, he associates laziness with our physicality. If we were beings of pure spirit, we'd be light and active, but because we live in bodies, we are tied to the physical world. Controlled by the force of gravity, we are pulled down.

These are realities over which we have no control, but Rabbi Luzzatto does point out what is under our influence. It is up to us whether we succumb to these forces or, alternatively, make an effort to lift ourselves up into enthusiasm: "If you abandon yourself to this 'heaviness' you will not succeed in your quest," he concludes.

The Hebrew word for *heavy* also shows up prominently in the story of Moses's attempts to get Pharaoh to release the children of Israel from Egypt. There we read[17] that Pharaoh refused to pay attention to Moses's entreaties because his heart was literally "heavy,"[18] though the translation usually says "obstinate" or "stubborn." Here, too, we get an image that helps us understand what it is to be "heavy"—like laziness, it means to run counter to the way of spirit.

The Power of Rationalization

In a great stroke of irony, the Pharaoh accuses the Jews of being lazy (Exodus Sh'mot 5:8). We uncover here a feature of laziness that most of us will recognize all too readily. Laziness thrives on rationalization, for surely that is what the Pharoah was doing: rationalizing his own weakness by attributing it to others. The Alter of Novarodok has a poignant section in his book, *Madregat ha'Adam,* in which he runs through a list of ambitions a person might set for himself, and he responds to each one with the words, "if only."

I'd give so much to charity, *if only* I were wealthy.

I'd study and learn so much, *if only* I were smarter.

I'd be so helpful to my friends, *if only* I were stronger.

All of it is rationalization, of course, and nowhere do we find rationalization more perfected than in the case of the lazybones. A lazy person shines with brilliance in creating excuses for why he or she just cannot accomplish some task. King Solomon pithily captures this idea in the book of Proverbs: "A lazy person considers himself wiser than seven sages."[19]

Though *Orchot Tzaddikim* was written in the sixteenth century, the picture of the rationalizing sluggard it presents still resonates five hundred years later. In "The Gate of Laziness"[20] we read the following, based on sayings in the book of Proverbs:

If one says to him: "Your teacher is in the city; go and learn Torah from him," he answers: "I am afraid of the lion on the road," as it is written (*Mishlei* [Proverbs] 26:13): "The lazy man says: 'There is a lion in the way.'" If they say to him: "Your teacher is already in the province: get up and go to him," he answers: "I am afraid that a lion might be in the streets," as it is written (ibid.): "A lion is in the streets." If they say to him: "He is lodging right near your house," he answers, "The lion is right outside," as it is written (ibid., 22:13):

"The lazy man says: 'There is a lion outside; I shall be slaughtered in the middle of the streets.'" If they say to him: "He is in the building," he answers: "And if I go and find the door locked, I will have to return." They say to him: "It is open," but he still will not get up, as it is written (ibid., 26:14): "The door is swinging on its hinges—and the lazy man is on his bed." In the end, not knowing what to answer, he says to them: "Whether the door is open or locked, I want to sleep a little more," as it is written (ibid., 6:9): "How long will you sleep, you lazy man? When will you rise from your sleep?"

Here is rationalization exemplified. By clever argument we justify giving in to the heavy inertia that Rabbi Luzzatto has highlighted to us. That's why rationalization is called "advice of the evil inclination"—and is ultimately not only misleading but destructive.

Are you aware of the little voice that keeps you from being active and energetic in the cause of lifting yourself up?

In Jewish thought, that whispering is the voice of the *yetzer ha'ra*—the inborn adversary to your spiritual ascent. What convincing reasons does it offer you to ensure that you stay stuck on the couch, not learning, not practicing, not exercising, not visiting the sick, not doing the myriad things that you yourself would certainly rank as worthwhile activities, if you would only do them?

The *yetzer ha'ra* counsels, "Why bother?" "You're so tired." "There will be lots of others." "This isn't the last chance." This is how that inner voice tries to keep you from doing that which is positive—and leads you to do negatively. The Talmudic rabbis were well aware of how the *yetzer ha'ra* operates: "Today he [the *yetzer ha'ra*] says 'do this [sin],' and the next day he says 'do this [more serious sin],' until he says to him 'serve idols' and he goes and does it."[21]

The *yetzer ha'ra* is masterful at deploying rationalizations as it leads you deeper and deeper into wrong action. Sometimes rationalization justifies laziness. Other times it comes in the guise of careful and thoughtful deliberation, which paralyzes just as effectively. Rabbi Menachem Mendel Leffin exposes this tendency:

There are people who are intelligent and quick in a certain field of learning or in a certain craft but who lack ideas or experience in other fields. When faced with a situation with which they are unfamiliar, they think and reflect and ponder, and then they consult and think again interminably. This one's virtue is, in truth, one's problem. Because humans are intelligent, they can always find endless rationales that support different courses of action. Because of one's inability to reach a final decision, opportunity passes by or one delays an enterprise with one's hesitations for days or years thus sacrificing their benefits for long periods of time.[22]

If you view small transgressions—and even laziness itself—as seriously as the Jewish tradition views idol worship, then you will find a source of inspiration to lift yourself up in enthusiasm.

Dulled by the World

Rabbi Luzzatto points to another common factor that can punch a hole in your inner life through which your energy can drain out: the propensity to dull ourselves with the pleasures of the world. If that was true in his time, how much more so in ours! The allures of today's world include so much that was inconceivable in previous centuries—from the useful, like cameras and computers, to the things we could still get by without, like junk food and luxury vehicles. Not only objects but also comforts and pleasures are available in forms and to degrees that even the most prescient people of earlier generations could not have imagined.

Oscar Wilde summed it up incisively: "Comfort is the only thing our civilization can give us," he said.[23] This thought captures a truth about our world (though any parent, like me, who has had a child's pneumonia cured by antibiotics will attest that the modern world offers other goods as well).

The relentless, almost addictive, pursuit of nifty things, comfort, and relaxation that is a mainstay of our civilization has never been an ingredient in anybody's recipe for a satisfying spiritual life. As consistent and self-evident as that may be, I have found that it is usually fruitless to suggest even to someone who is committed to their spiritual life that they step back from the soporific pleasures of society. Most of us are so used to our comforts and enjoy them so much that it's a little like trying to talk a kid away from candy or a toy.

The pursuit of comforts and pleasure depletes spiritual energy simply because we have only so much energy in our lives. We waste precious energy by running after the shiny apple, and then we have nothing left for higher pursuits.

Can you remember when new technology was called "labor-saving devices"? We've learned since then that having more technology does not save labor, it just speeds up processes and raises expectations.

Can you see this at work in your own life? Do you get caught up in worldly activities that sap what energy you have, leaving less for spiritual endeavor?

Don't Worry, Be Enthusiastic

Laziness, excessive deliberation, rationalization, and pursuit of material pleasures all deplete enthusiasm. Before closing the list, Rabbi Luzzatto brings us one more factor to watch out for: *anxiety*.

Worrying and fretting can also deplete spiritual energy. In fact, anxiety is often what underlies other things we do that sap our enthusiasm. After all, isn't it our fears and worries that send us searching after shelter from the (real or imagined) storm, and right into the arms of Madison Avenue and its commercial masters?

Rabbi Luzzatto provides an accurate thumbnail description of our usual state of anxiety: "At one point you might be nervous about cold or heat, another time you might worry about accidents, then another time about illness, and yet another time about the wind, and so forth."

Most of us can identify with this picture, and yet who realizes that among all the costs of anxiety we have to include a spiritual toll as well?

We are not talking about worries that validly ought to concern us, like the world situation, or things over which we have some control. Rabbi Luzzatto cites the Talmudic dictum, "Things are different where there is a possibility of danger."[24] No, what he is talking about is that generalized state of anxiety that defines a person's stance in relation to the world. The "object" of the anxiety (earning the quotation marks because so often the things we worry about are anything but objective) is not at all important because the apprehension that has us sweating and twisting our hands is really groundless. One moment it's the weather and the next your health and the next traffic, and that's followed by scheduling and then "what if" and "what if" . . .

When we receive life through a screen of anxiety, we find that even when some worry proves to be unfounded and we can finally breathe a sigh of relief, we don't, because that anxious orientation quickly generates a perfectly functional substitute in a matter of seconds. In no time, we're tied up again over something else that might happen today, and if not today, maybe tomorrow, or surely by next week. Once the pattern has taken hold—a worried mind as opposed to a mind with worries—there is no end to subjects to fret over, real or imaginary.

Rabbi Luzzatto points out the "senseless concern when you compound one form of self-protection onto another, one fear or worry onto another." What he means is that you buy the house to protect yourself from the elements and then worry about the roof. So you put on a new roof at great expense. Then you worry about the new roof, so you hire a company to apply a sealant. Then you worry that they didn't give you the best chemicals, or that it will wear off in one rainstorm. So you buy insurance on the sealant that protects the new roof on the new house.

You might recognize that kind of worried mind in someone you know. Or maybe in yourself as well?

A person prone to anxiety will worry about any product that it might not work, or it will break, or it's the wrong one, or no sooner have you gotten it home than the manufacturer will come out with a better one, or maybe a cheaper one, or one that has more functions, and so on, and so on.

This state of free-floating anxiety can dominate a life, fill it up, and see a person off to the grave never having really lived, because he or she was forever tied up in knots, every minute of every day, over what might be. At that extreme, of course, anxiety can be a psychiatric disorder best treated by professionals. But many of us relate to the world through a filter of anxiety that falls well short of a psychiatric diagnosis but still disables spiritual growth. You can be quite functional and still never realize anything near the measure of your soul-potential in life just because of anxiety.

Worry of the kind concerning us here is a posture. It isn't based on facts but on attitude. The sooner we divest ourselves of our worrying stance, the better, because this way of seeing and receiving the world keeps us from truth.

Corrosive anxiety reveals an overattachment to this world and its objects and conditions. What will those worries matter five years from now, or ten? Or when you are in your final days? Or laid to rest? It is valid and useful to recognize that you are just passing through. Against that backdrop, how important are those worries?

Rabbi Luzzatto also counsels that recognizing God's role in your life will help to counter anxiety. When you have firm trust that whatever will be is just as it should be (however you might evaluate it, good, bad, or otherwise), there will simply be no place in your heart for baseless anxiety. Knowing that you are sheltered under the wings of the divine quiets all tremors of the heart.[25]

How to Cultivate Enthusiasm

So how should we stoke the fire of our enthusiasm? Simply saying to yourself, "I want to burn like a Roman candle" is about as likely to have the desired effect as saying, "I want to be happy" is going to make you happy. This is a teaching of Rabbi Yisrael Salanter. He says, "It is insufficient for man to improve his general will, to long for the good and to despise evil." That won't do it, but what will? Rabbi Salanter continues: "But he must seek the means of correcting each individual trait of his soul."[26]

That's a tall order, but it is the one we are handed. Rabbi Luzzatto helps us focus in by pointing to one soul-trait that, if cultivated, delivers up more energy and fewer hindrances to moving yourself in the direction of holiness. He tells us that we will do this by "awakening [to] the very many good things that the Holy One (blessed be He) does for you moment by moment"[27]—in other words, practicing gratitude.[28]

Hard as it may be to see, good is undeniably flowing to you in every moment. Sometimes that outpouring is very apparent, like in those moments when you receive a wonderful and unexpected gift. In the early days of the Seva Foundation, we had a board meeting at which a number of very good projects were proposed. We had about a hundred thousand dollars in the bank, and if we funded all the proposals, our account would be totally emptied. That didn't seem to be the prudent thing to do, but the group came to a consensus that prudence wasn't the trait we wanted to strengthen at that moment, and so we gave away all the money we had. That very same day, a supporter phoned to offer a gift of, yes, a hundred thousand dollars, completely replenishing our well. It seemed perfectly clear to us that God's goodness was flowing toward us in that moment.

Most often, however, we are in a state of indifference toward the goodness in our lives. It's not that it isn't there, it's just that you may not be paying attention to it because you're working at this, or trying to fix that, or holding together some other thing, and as you struggle with one challenge or another, you've got your eyes fixed on the goal, or maybe just the next step you need to execute. You don't pay attention to the good in most situations because you are focused on what needs improvement.

It is also so easy to take for granted the "ordinary" goodness in our lives. For example, when you wake up in the morning, the chances are very good that you will find yourself in a warm, dry bed. For me, after fifty-seven years of waking up almost every day in a warm, dry bed, somehow I just don't spring out of bed in the morning and exclaim, "Warm and dry again!" It just doesn't happen, not because it isn't a gift to live in a secure, heated home—something the majority of the world's people do not experience today, let alone the even greater majority of the past—but because the recognition of that truth is dulled by its consistency. We become inured and don't feel gratitude for great beneficence that we simply cease to see as gifts.

And sometimes, alas, it is very hard to see the good because it is overshadowed by pain and suffering. There is still good there in some form and quantity, but misery can screen our perception. A person with terminal cancer, for example, may have physical symptoms and existential pain that occupy the full screen of consciousness. That person may be attended by a loving spouse, children, friends, nurses, doctors, social workers, clergy, psychologists, nutritionists, orderlies, and so on, who daily or even hourly are delivering tremendous gifts of treatment and care. Though there may be little or even no inner space to recognize these gifts for what they are and to feel gratitude, as anyone who has experienced physical pain can well understand and empathize with, they are gifts nonetheless. There are people who in the midst of terrible illness or other suffering do find their way to be able to say thank you and to express the trait of recognizing the good.

Good is always present. God is flowing gifts our way in every moment, if only the benefaction of being kept alive, and usually so much more. Even death can come as a gift, when the pain is beyond bearing. We need to awaken to feel gratitude for all we receive, in this moment, and then in this moment, and then in this moment . . .

Another perspective on this teaching focuses not on the gifts we receive at every moment but rather on our moment-to-moment experience of gratitude for those gifts. This interpretation looks not at our awakening to the unending flow of gifts we can identify and appreciate, but rather invites us to be richly present in this moment with gratitude. You may already be well aware that you are grateful for specific gifts. You may be thoroughly convinced by argument and reason and experience that there is an outpouring of beneficence flowing into your life. But does your heart fill with the experience of gratitude in this moment? And can you sustain that experience into the next moment? This perspective addresses the problem that many of us have of seeing ourselves intellectually as being the recipients of gifts and wonders *in theory,* while in practice, our every moment is *not* infused (or maybe even tinged with) the feeling of gratitude.

What's the connection to the soul-trait of enthusiasm? When you truly realize that you receive gifts every day, and when that recognition really penetrates, then you will be spurred into action to be of service and do good and make good of yourself simply because it has become palpably clear to you that you are holding gifts in your hands. Living with awakened gratitude delivers fuel to make our actions more energetic.

When you spark the flame that ignites the fire, and so lift yourself out of the heavy lethargy or frantic worry that can paralyze your life, you will have begun a process that will build on itself. Rabbi Luzzatto put it this way:

> Just as enthusiasm can *result* from an inner burning, so it can *create* one. That is, one who perceives a quickening of his outer movements in the performance of a mitzvah [commandment] conditions himself to experience a flaming inner movement, through which longing and desire will continually grow. If, however, he is sluggish in the movement of his limbs, the movement of his spirit will die down and become extinguished. Experience testifies to this.[29]

> Lazybones, go to the ant;
> Study its ways and learn.
> Without leaders, officers or rulers,

It lays up its stores during the summer,
Gathers in its food at the harvest.
How long will you lie there, lazybones;
When will you wake from your sleep?
A bit more sleep, a bit more slumber,
A bit more hugging yourself in bed,
And poverty will come calling upon you,
And want, like an armed soldier.

—Proverbs/*Mishlei* 6:6–11

16

Silence

SH'TIKAH

Nothing is better than silence.[1]

The craft of a person in this world is to behave as if mute! The craft is not to be a babbler. This is something one has to learn: since the baby knows to talk, he babbles as it pleases him. Silence needs to be learned, because silence is a great skill, and by it you recognize the person of intelligence. The nature of a person is his solitude. Only in that does the soul and spirit develop their strength.

—Rabbi Shlomo Wolbe, *Alei Shur*

RABBI YOSEF YOZEL HURWITZ, or the Alter of Novarodok, as he is always called, was born in Lithuania in 1847. Just before the rabbi's marriage, his father-in-law died, and right after the marriage, the Alter took over his father-in-law's textile store and worked as a merchant.

One day, as he rushed through the streets doing business in Saint Petersburg, capital of czarist Russia, he ran into Rabbi Itzele Peterburger.[2]

"Where are you running?" Reb Itzele asked the Alter.

"I'm going to my place of business," he replied. "A person must have a source of livelihood. A person must have from where to live."

"I realize that," answered Reb Itzele. "But a person must also have from where to die."

That piercing comment catalyzed the Alter to redirect his life. By this time he was already a widower, and he decided to give up his business and devote his life to his spiritual search.[3] He arranged for his children's care and then entered a period of seclusion that lasted two years. He had himself bricked into a small room attached to the house of a benefactor. There was no door or exit. No one could enter or leave the room except by breaking through the wall. He communicated with the outside world by means of a bell or left messages by one of the two windows in his room.[4] He prayed, studied Jewish law and Mussar, and looked deeply within himself, in silence.

He sought the quiet that is the soul's balm. Have you experienced the thick silence of a forest that penetrates to the marrow? Or the morning after a snowfall when stillness spreads an incomparable blanket on the muffled world? The night sky, no wind? The voluptuous silence of a becalmed sea? A mind released from chatter to stillness?

The central statement of faith in Judaism is the *Sh'ma*, which reads: "Hear Israel, the Lord your God, the Lord is One." Only in silence is it possible to hear.

Guarding the Tongue

Rabbi Yisrael Salanter, teacher of the Alter of Novarodok, made silence[5] the final of the thirteen soul-traits that he listed on his basic curriculum for Mussar practice. What he said about silence, however, like most of what we come upon in the Mussar literature on this subject, is actually more about restraint in speech than about silence itself or about how contemplative quiet figures in the curriculum of the soul. In this chapter, we'll first explore teachings about careful speech and then look at what the Mussar masters have to say about contemplative silence.

Orchot Tzaddikim advises, "If you cannot find someone to teach you Mussar, remain silent, lest you speak foolishness."[6] Predictably (and most important), the interpersonal dimension of silence gets most of the attention of the Mussar masters.

They drew on older sources. "There is a time to be silent and a time to speak," wrote King Solomon in Ecclesiastes/*Kohelet*.[7] In the book of Job, after listening to his so-called friends trying to comfort him, Job finally erupts with: "Be silent and I will teach you wisdom."[8] In silence is wisdom, too. A wise person, therefore, is one who knows what to say and when to say it but also knows when to keep silent. And even a fool is judged wise just because he keeps silent.[9]

Jewish thought and practice is very concerned with the right use of speech because it recognizes that, like any powerful resource, speech can be both creative and healing and dangerous and destructive. An even greater source for the honor due to language is the Torah's message that God brought creation into being with speech. "God said, 'Let there be light. And there was light.'" Later on, so much of the biblical narrative is directed by the words, "And God spoke to Moses, saying . . . "

The rabbis of the Talmud gave their blessing to speech by considering, "Whoever gives charity to a poor person receives six blessings; one who consoles him with words is blessed with eleven blessings."[10] There is a positive power inherent in speech.

But the word also contains a menacing power—speech is judged more powerful than the sword because a physical weapon can injure only those in proximity, while speech can kill at a distance. "Death and life are in the power of the tongue."[11]

So much of the trouble in our lives and the trouble we cause others is rooted in our idle, accidental, or even destructive use of words. It is very important to become aware and take command of our tongues.

The primary Mussar guideline for speech is not whether something is true or not but rather what impact our words will have. If our speech may cause people financial, physical, psychological, or other harm (or even anxiety or fear), then we are enjoined to hold our tongues. The practice of careful speech is called *sh'mirat ha'lashon,* which literally means "guarding the tongue."

Four main types of negative speech are identified for us.[12] The first is degrading or negative statements spoken about a person that are actually true. Just because something is true doesn't mean we are free to say it, as in the example, "You don't want to go to that party. The Hoffmans are so boring." The fact that the Hoffmans really are boring is no excuse for damaging their reputation in the eyes of others.

When the negative statements are false, they are weighed more severely. It is a much more serious and damaging misuse of speech to say, "You don't want to go to that party. The Hoffmans are so boring" when, in fact, the Hoffmans are the life of the party.

Gossip is passing on to a person the negative things someone else had said. That would be like telling the Hoffmans that you had heard they were boring. Think of the hurt and the damage to relationships that would come from that wagging of the tongue.

Finally, we need to guard against making statements that don't come right out with negativity but only imply it. Here we might say, "Considering that they never went to university, you'd think the Hoffmans would be more boring than they are." This is still negative and harmful speech, in the guise of saying something faintly positive.[13]

All these sorts of speech are forbidden by Jewish law and tradition. We are forbidden to say these negative things, and we are also forbidden to listen to them.

I regularly conduct students in an exercise in which I pair people up and direct them to relate to their partner one instance in the last week when they said something *to* someone, or heard something *from* someone, that reflected negatively on another person who was absent. The point is not to assess whether or not the facts in the conversation were true, but simply whether derogatory, potentially damaging speaking took place in your presence.

I have done this exercise dozens of times, and to date not a single person has failed to come up with at least one instance of wrong speech in which they participated. This remarkable 100 percent record proves true what the sages said: only a minority of people may commit sexual offenses, while most people sin in matters of theft, yet everybody transgresses with the tongue.[14]

And so our sages "screeched like cranes about the promiscuous use of lips and ears."[15] Maimonides warns us that wrong speech is a transgression that is equivalent to murder, but more heinous because it kills three people: the one who said it, the one who heard it, and the one about whom it was said.[16] He established the law:[17] "Silence is a protective fence for wisdom." "Therefore, one should not be hasty in answering, and one should not speak excessively. One should teach one's students calmly and with satisfaction, without shouting and without being verbose. Solomon said, 'The words of wise men heard in quiet are better.'"[18] On this passage of the Rambam, Rabbi Shlomo Wolbe commented, "It is wonderful how true speech actually grows from the midst of silence!"[19]

Damaging speech, in contrast, is a sin that sullies our souls. The Vilna Ga'on, in his *Mussar Letter*,[20] is emphatic on the need to guard ourselves from this sort of transgression:

Our Sages said that all man's observance of the commandments and teachings are not enough to counterbalance what comes out of his mouth. "What should be a man's pursuit in this world? He should be silent" (*Chullin* 89a). One must seal his lips as tight as two millstones.

Giving even greater weight to our need for caution is the sages' warning that the consequences of wrong speech last for eternity. Everyone is called to give a reckoning after death, at which time even the incidental conversations between a man and his wife are reported. They said: "At the time of judgment in the World of Truth it is reported to a person how far the power of his frivolous speech reached that he spoke when he was in this world."[21] Murder, adultery, and idol worship are sins that cause a person to forfeit his or her portion in the eternal world—and evil speech is equivalent to all three.[22]

There is a story told about Rabbi Itzele Peterburger and his friend, the great Talmud scholar Rabbi Chaim Berlin. When both men were elderly, they made an agreement that whichever one of them died first would come back and visit the other to report on what death and the hereafter were like. Reb Itzele passed away first, and after a few days he came to his friend in a dream. "Well," asked Rabbi Berlin, "what has it been like?" Reb Itzele replied, "The profundity of the Divine judgment is immeasurable. The sins of the tongue are the worst of all."[23]

If transgressions of speech are weighed so heavily, so must the proper use of the tongue be rewarded. There is a story that tells us this is so. Rabbi Eliyahu de Vidas, a leading kabbalist of the sixteenth century,[24] tells of "the righteous Rabbi Lapidot, of blessed memory," who dreamed of the Torah sage Rabbi Yehuda ben Shoshan. Rabbi Yehuda appeared to him in his dream with a "face gleaming like sunlight, and each hair of his beard shining like a torch." Rabbi Lapidot asked Rabbi Yehuda how he merited this transformation. "The latter answered that it was due to the extent to which he kept silent, for he had never engaged in an empty conversation in his life."[25]

Silence Is Pregnant

Minding what we say highlights one important facet of the soul-trait of silence, but there are others as well. Silence has much more to offer us.

Beyond mastery of our speech is the act of quieting down itself, stepping back from a life saturated with sounds, many of them of our own making. Silence is a pregnant state out of which can emerge worlds of possibility we have no hope of knowing so long as our lives are overfilled with words and noise.

Certain sorts of insights and understandings about life, and about my life, don't ever come to me by talking, or even by thinking, but are the gifts of silence. It's only by entering silence that I can find my way to prayer. So it was with the men of the Great Assembly,[26] who would sit for an hour in silence before they began their prayer.[27] It is only in silence that the million concerns of my day become quieted enough that I can reach out to God. Otherwise, I'm just too busy and distracted.

People today can live their entire lives without a moment's peace. We are so used to living with all the spaces filled by noise that quiet can seem threatening. A lull in the conversation feels intolerable. To have nothing to say is a kind of failure.

Yet the soul needs silence as the body needs sleep. Sleep to refresh; silence to cleanse. Sleep to dream; silence to awaken to the deeply real. The Talmud points to this in saying, "There is no better medicine than silence."[28]

In Jewish tradition, wisdom consists in penetrating the superficial layers of reality to perceive the essence of things, and I have found that silence is essential to making that happen. Rabbi Sh'lomo ibn Gabirol says, "In seeking wisdom the first step is silence."[29] As Rabbi Akiva has told us, silence erects a protective fence around the wisdom you already possess.

It may be because our inner quiet is a route to God and wisdom that the Talmud places such a high value on silence. "A word [is valuated] for one *sela* [a coin], but silence for two *selas*."[30] Remember that the Talmud is a collection of many words, reflecting on the words that came before, and appreciating how highly the rabbis of the Talmud valued words makes their assessment of silence that much more remarkable.

Like speech, silence also has its shadow side. There are those whose voices have been taken away, or who turn their heads aside and remain silent, or who are so battered that no words are possible. Those are different situations, all reflective of an unhealthy silence.

The Mussar masters are referring to a silence that is life giving, not death dealing, entered voluntarily in pursuit of spiritual insight and wisdom. This is contemplative silence, taken on voluntarily as spiritual practice.

A soul deprived of silence loses track of itself. It is afflicted. Sooner or later, it will in desperation seek its need, or capitulate to negative forces.

Practicing Silence

Contemplative silence is practiced. The Mussar guidance for working on any soul-trait is that the first stage of practice involves developing sensitivity. And so as we focus our attention on the place of silence in our lives, we can expect to become suddenly very sensitive to the reality that our lives are filled to the brim with noise.

Paying attention to this aspect of our lives awakens us from our habitual numbness to the racket that pervades our days. Joggers have their portable music, people ride the subway with boom boxes, cars rumble with thundering bass lines. There is a soundtrack playing to accompany your visit to the doctor or dentist, your elevator ride, or even your wait on the telephone because "all operators are currently busy helping other customers." Jets roar overhead, television commercials screech.

The second stage in Mussar practice involves restraint. Our new awareness calls out for active steps to change the circumstances of our lives. Once we realize how rarely the moments of real silence occur in our days, we can restrain the input and the output of noise that swirls around us. We do have a choice.

Limitation on speaking is built into Jewish liturgical practice in the Amidah, the silent prayer that is the central feature of the thrice-daily prayer service. Of course, you would have to be making a regular practice of participating in the prayer service for this locus of silence to become a feature of your life. But even then, although this prayer may have been inspired at least in part by a recognition of the soul's need for silence, as it is now practiced, the Amidah is still filled with words, though these are recited silently to oneself.

The medieval kabbalists introduced what they called a *tzom sh'tikah*— a fast of silence. We ordinarily think of a fast as a time of abstaining from food, like we do on Yom Kippur. In a *tzom sh'tikah*, people refrain not from eating but from speaking.

Consider making your own fast of silence. At first you may find it too radical to cut out speech entirely, but it is enough to start by designating a day

on which you simply will have no radio, no television, no CDs, no videos
… no input of sound of any kind over which you have control. Try it, and
observe for yourself what effect limiting noise has on you. Rabbi Shlomo
Wolbe, a recent Mussar master, defines Mussar as "building an interior
life." Take on this exercise and see what silence does for that enterprise.

Spending ten or fifteen minutes just sitting quietly once or twice a day
will change your life. This focused concentration will spill over into all
areas of your life and generate peace, creativity, and inner healing.

Whether it is in the "silent" prayer in the liturgy or in a fast of silence
or meditation, even though our lips may be closed so that no sound emerges,
we still might not yet know quiet. That's because, in its essence, silence is
not merely an absence of external noise; it is also an inner state that goes
beyond quiet to stillness. Often the noisiest thing in my life is not a jet engine or a loud conversation but my mind itself.[31]

Hitbodedut

This chapter began with the story of the two years the Alter of Novarodok
spent in seclusion when he embarked on his spiritual path. Later in his
life, he sought solitude in an isolated hut in the heart of a thick forest. He
lived in that hut for nine years and would receive his students and visitors
there. Years later it was discovered that he had built a little hut even deeper
in the forest, where he sequestered himself for periods of time.

The sort of withdrawal the Alter practiced is called *hitbodedut*,[32] a term
that denotes the process of isolating the soul from all external stimuli.[33]
The practice of *hitbodedut* draws us into the experience of silence in the
service of wisdom. Our world (and maybe, even more important, Jewish
life today) is choked with words, filled with noise, and committed to drawing people into connection, so much so that it is almost a revelation to discover that tradition gives such an important place to the practice of solitude.
The soul needs contemplative solitude in order to digest learning and experience and convert it into wisdom.

The Alter did not invent *hitbodedut*. One of the great kabbalists, Rabbi
Chaim Vital[34] wrote about *hitbodedut*, saying, "One must seclude himself
[*hitboded*] in his thoughts to the ultimate degree. The more one separates
himself from the physical, the greater will be his enlightenment."

Even earlier, in the twelfth century, Rabbi Abraham, son of the famous sage Maimonides,[35] wrote a chapter called, "On Contemplative Seclusion," in which he said:

> *Hitbodedut* is one of the most honorable of the exalted qualities, and it is the path of the greatest of the righteous and the means by which the prophets attained revelation. It may be subdivided into external and internal *hitbodedut*. The purpose of external *hitbodedut* is the attainment of internal *hitbodedut*, which is the highest rung on the ladder of revelation; in fact, it is nothing less than revelation itself. . . . This level may be attained by the annihilation of the activity of that part of the soul that senses, (entirely) or mostly, and distancing oneself from that part that drives [one] in other worldly matters, inclining toward [God].

In the eighteenth century, *hitbodedut* was a central practice of the Chassidic master Rebbe Nachman of Breslov[36] and continues among his present-day followers, the Breslover Chassidim. Their practice of seclusion adds an active element, in that their method involves seeking out a private corner (at home or out in a park or a field or woods) where you pour out all of your needs and feelings to God, crying, weeping, laughing, singing.

Rebbe Nachman emphasized the value and importance of *hitbodedut* as a simple practice applicable to all people—men, women, and children— each on his or her own level. He wrote:[37]

> You must pour out your thoughts and troubles to God like a child complaining and pestering his father. You must pray for everything. If your garment is torn and must be replaced, pray to God for a new one. Make it a habit to pray for all your needs, large or small, and especially for fundamentals: that God should help you attach yourself to Him. You can meditate in thought, but the most important thing is to express your thoughts in speech.

In essence, though, *hitbodedut* means simply withdrawing and uncoupling from the ordinary connections and stimulations that fill our days. Once we have opened that fresh space in our lives, some people will find their hearts bubbling over with things they want to say to God, while others will just savor the silence and the time to reflect. Everyone will draw their own deep value from a period of retreat that *hitbodedut* inserts into our lives.

In *Tomer Devorah*, Rabbi Moshe Cordovero says that a person should seek out "communion in solitude [*hitbodedut*] with his Creator in order to increase and perfect his *chochmah* [wisdom]."[38] He echoes the words spoken four hundred years earlier by Rabbi Sh'lomo ibn Gabirol, who points to silence as the first step toward wisdom.

When Rabbi Perr built his new yeshiva building in Far Rockaway, New York, he built a hardly noticeable and seemingly inaccessible little room right atop the flat roof for practicing *hitbodedut*. I heard him once say in a class, "When are you living, tell me? You live when you have those rare moments of quiet. It's important to be able to be silent. It's important to let thoughts go in. Because when you are quiet a lot of things that will come into your mind will come not from your mind but *min ha'shamayim* [from heaven]. You grow from that. You become a different person from that."

Ask yourself: Do I allow myself enough (or any) time when I consciously release the connections that bind me into my life and that sustain me in all my existing perspectives and perceptions of life? Isn't it true that sometimes even our "holiday" time is planned to be just as full of noise and activity as ordinary life, and maybe even more so? Is it possible for me to make space to pull back, just for a limited period of time, to take a fresh look, to give my soul the time and space it needs to digest and integrate my experience and learning, even to get quiet enough maybe to hear the gentle, rustling voice of the divine?

If you are like me, it is a challenge to find time to practice *hitbodedut* in this modern lifestyle that intrudes on our inner lives so forcefully. But perhaps it increases your motivation to make time for *hitbodedut* to know that voices from tradition—like the ones I have cited from the eleventh through the twenty-first centuries—all tell us the very same thing, which is that if we do practice withdrawal, the fruit of our silence and seclusion will be wisdom.

The Still, Small Voice

Elijah the Prophet[39] had a vision. He was told: "Go out and stand at the mountain before God, and behold, God will pass, and a great wind breaking mountains and shattering rocks before God; God will not be in the wind. After the wind, an earthquake will follow; but God will not be in the earthquake. And after the earthquake, a fire will pass, but God is not in the fire; and after the fire, a still small voice.'" The Hebrew reads literally, "a soft, gentle rustling," the kind of voice that it would only be possible to hear in silence, both outer and inner.

Can you hear the same voice in this poem, "September on the Avenue," written in 1903 in Hebrew by Avraham Ben-Yitzhak?[40]

SEPTEMBER ON THE AVENUE

> Lights dreaming
> fading lights,
> at my feet are falling.
> Soft shadows,
> failing shadows
> stroke my path . . .
> Among the bare branches
> a light wind
> sounds
> and ceases . . .
> and a last leaf
> flutters down, trembling
> a moment more . . .
> and stillness.

In seeking wisdom, the first step is silence, the second listening, the third remembering, the fourth practicing, the fifth teaching others.

—Rabbi Shlomo ibn Gabirol

17

Generosity

NEDIVUT

The generous heart gives freely.

And God spoke to Moses, saying: "Speak to the Children of Israel, that they should take a gift for Me, from every person whose heart moves him you should take My gift. . . . And let them build Me a Sanctuary, and I will dwell in their midst."

—Exodus/*Sh'mot* 25:1-2, 8

THE JEWISH TRADITION DISTINGUISHES between two types of generosity.[1]

The first is the giving that comes because your heart is so moved that without even the flicker of a thought your hand rushes to dig into your pocket to give. In the Torah, this generosity is called *t'rumah*, which means "gift."[2] Generosity of this sort comes neither from obligation nor rational thought nor guilt but out of an irresistible feeling that stirs deep within. It's a movement of the soul and it generates an open-handed response.

The other kind of generosity, called *tzedakah*, is obligated giving, such as tithing and other acts that come from commitment, whether or not the heart is moved to act in that way.

The overall goal of Mussar practice is to help us fulfill our potential to really live as the holy souls we are, and it is impossible to imagine that we will shine forth in holiness if we act only from a sense of obligation. The passion and the flowering of the heart must be so much more. To move toward holiness, you must yearn for it. You must be propelled by a spiritual willingness—*nedivut ha'lev*—a generosity of the heart. We'll see, though, that these two forms of generosity are not so distinct as we might suppose.

Giving from the Heart

The concept of generous and spontaneous giving from the heart appears in the Torah in the section where the Israelites undertake to build a sanctuary so that God might dwell among them. Rabbi Meir Leibush[3] commented that the verse[4] actually means that God would dwell not literally in the sanctuary building but among the people. He concludes that each person is to build a tabernacle in his or her own heart for God to dwell in. The Torah wants us to see that the way we do this inner construction work is by perfecting spontaneous generosity.

Because we live in a money-centric culture, we tend to think of generosity only as a question of reaching into our wallets. But as with all soul-traits, generosity is a quality of the soul and so it can find expression in many ways. You can be generous with money and also with your time, your energy, and your possessions. The one who gives *terumah* gives because his or her heart is so enflamed with magnanimity that it would be painful not to give, and the heart finds a way to respond spontaneously, whether with money, time, materials, or in any other way.

This sort of generosity is not defined by the kind of action you take or the amount you give, but by the energy of the response itself. I am pointing to a spontaneous, open, trusting, voluntary, inspired, internal overflow that erupts from the inner depths in response to the needs of, or love for, another.

God is the model for this sort of giving. God needs nothing and yet gives abundantly. In this way, God is intrinsically a giver. A person can also be a giver by intrinsic nature. Most of us would need to train ourselves to reach this level of giving, but it is possible. Then being generous becomes who and what you are.

You have money in your pocket, so you give money. You have no money but there's food in your home, so you give food. There's no food in your home but there are ideas in your mind, so you give helping words. There are no words in your mouth but there is love in your heart, so you offer your heart itself.

In my years in India, I visited many Hindu holy places, including the town of Varanasi, which is located on the sacred Ganges River. Varanasi is a magnet for pilgrims, holy men and women, and beggars. In fact, the lanes leading down to the river are lined with beggars, who insistently entreat pilgrims for a coin. They are truly needy, helpless people. Many are lepers and polio victims, amputees, and people with unnamed afflictions. One of my teachers, Richard Alpert (aka Ram Dass), tells of walking down one of those narrow lanes in Varanasi and being overwhelmed by the sight of the endless line of crying beggars. He knew right away that he couldn't possibly give a coin to every one of the thousands of people who wanted and needed his help, so he decided he would give only to those he felt were the highest priority cases. That decision led him into an impossible calculation: Are people with no arms more or less deserving than people with no legs? What about one arm and one leg? One arm and no legs? No fingers? No toes? No nose?

It was hopeless to try to be rational in the face of suffering and need on such a scale. The mind is overwhelmed in that sort of situation. So he just handed his wallet over to his heart, and gave as his heart moved him, without calculation and without guilt.

The same impulse moved the hand of Rabbi Aryeh Levin. In his neighborhood of old Jerusalem, an old Sephardic Jew used to sit mending worn-out shoes. Every Friday, as Reb Aryeh passed by, he made it a practice to drop off a sum of money to the old shoemaker. "Had anyone stopped the good rabbi and asked him why he chose this particular shoemaker to support with a weekly stipend, he would have found it hard to give a rational answer. Some inner urge prompted him."[5]

The Stopped-Up Heart

The human heart is naturally inclined to give. Caring comes easily to that organ, but it is able to act on that inclination only when it is open. That isn't always the heart's condition. When our hearts are closed or walled off, we are suffering from a spiritual ailment that the Mussar teachers call *timtum ha'lev*, meaning a blocked or barricaded heart—literally, a stopped-up heart. Instead of being open, flowing, and generous, we are sluggish, constipated, and unwilling at our core.

Why does that happen to us? If the heart is primed to be generous and is ready by its nature, how does its flow get to be so obstructed that we live without being generous? And what can we do about it?

Sometimes we suffer from a stopped-up heart because it is we ourselves who willingly blockade our hearts. There are things we do to build barriers to separate ourselves from others. In India, you hear lots of disparaging stories about the beggars—that they are professionals who earn a fortune, or that mothers mutilate their children so they will be more successful at begging, and so on. These stories are very likely untrue. In a population of a billion people, a high proportion of whom are poor and without access to good medical care, it just isn't necessary to create the physical ailments that make people into beggars. So why do stories like these circulate? Because they are useful for building a wall around the hearts of people who are confounded by the requests being made of them. The heart is so sensitive that we fear it couldn't bear being opened to the full onslaught of the monumental suffering of all of India's beggars. Drawn by the heart to respond, yet threatened by fear of overload, how comforting it is to have a rationale for shutting down the center of feeling, giving yourself a reason to turn away from that overwhelming pain.

There may be walls around your own heart. The key is to be on the lookout for rationalizations that exempt you from being generous. With the goal of protecting your heart, you will tell yourself all the sound reasons you must turn away. You then become less generous, and the victim is as much yourself as the other.

It isn't all done *by* us, however; sometimes it is also done *to* us. Life experience can play its part in shutting down the heart. The heart wants to be available, but sometimes it is just not capable of keeping its shutters open in the face of the brutal battering it has been handed. A person who has suffered major abuse or deprivation (of whatever kind) might emerge so scarred that putting expectations of generosity on him or her could be just another form of cruelty. In this case, we can empathize with their need to close off their hearts.

And yet if it is you who has been a victim in this way, and if you accept that your life will be forever dictated by those experiences, then you do a different kind of damage to the heart. When our hearts are closed, we are the first among those who suffer from that closure. There may be good reasons why someone feels it is too risky to open up, but by tolerating that condition in ourselves, we accept an imposed blockage to our spiritual hearts. With a walled-off heart, our lives will be so much less than they could be, and the damage done is extended even further.

In this case, the barriers to generosity are likely to be built not of rationalization but of fear. When you let your imagination run toward being spontaneously generous, can you identify any fears that arise in you that cause you to hold back? Can you see how these fears are walls and gates that keep your own heart locked up and closed down? Can you find within these fears some traces of your own past experiences? Can you see how accepting these scars as unchangeable realities perpetuates and compounds the damage done by the original offense?

More common than being abused in harsh and scarring ways is the tendency to sacrifice the ways of the heart for the needs of the ego. The ego tends to look on life in terms of scarcity and ownership and at the world as a zero-sum game: if I am to win, someone else must lose. The ego sees the riches of the world as a fixed pie and works to get the largest slice, believing that someone will be left with crumbs. All of this works against the heart's inclination to spontaneous generosity.

Any of these scenarios may or may not apply to you. I present them as material for you to think about, as you take a look at your own heart and its possible areas of congestion. These may well show up in your life as unwillingness to be generous. Find out what is true for you. Being more aware of your own interior reality is the first stage of Mussar work, the stage of sensitivity.

The simple question to ask yourself is: Do I give spontaneously from the heart?

Liberating Generosity

If you become aware that blockages obstruct your heart, then one Mussar approach is to try to identify soul-traits that are the sources of the fear and clutching and to work on these specific qualities, rather than directly on generosity itself.

Another approach applies more for people whose hearts are being enslaved to ego, where the inner voice says, how can I give when I don't even have enough for *me*? Here you might cultivate a sense that what you do for others is actually a great gift to yourself. No one loses.

Rabbi Simcha Zissel Ziv, the founder of the Kelm school of Mussar, wrote his book *Chochmah u'Mussar* [Wisdom and Mussar] just for the purpose of explaining how bearing the burden of the other is a profound spiritual practice. "We have spoken about this bearing the burden of the other many times," he writes.[6] "This is the most inclusive of the attributes."

He brings as his example the story of Moses, who began his spiritual journey toward becoming the greatest of prophets by responding to the suffering he saw around him, from which he had been insulated by living in Pharaoh's palace. "He saw their suffering,"[7] the Torah tells us, and what he felt had a formative impact on his soul.

Generously bearing the burden of the other is also central to a story said to have been told by the Ba'al Shem Tov, the founder of Chassidism. He said that in hell, people sit around a great banquet table piled high with food. Each person is given a fork six feet in length, far too long for them to maneuver into their mouths. They are starving. In heaven, on the other hand, people sit around exactly the same banquet. But in heaven each feeds the person across the table. And in so doing, all are filled.

In stressing the practice of "bearing the burden of the other," Rabbi Simcha Zissel was working out details of a spiritual method pointed to by his own teacher, Rabbi Yisrael Salanter. In one of his most memorable sayings, Rabbi Salanter comments that "the spiritual is higher than the physical, but the physical needs of another are an obligation of my spiritual life." In order to follow a spiritual path, I have to pay attention to the needs of others. Generosity would be one of the most accessible ways to do that.

In yet another approach, generosity is not only the diagnostic question; it can also be the cure. The Chassidic teacher Rebbe Nachman of Breslov teaches[8] that anyone who does not practice generosity has "a heart of stone." And to alleviate that condition, he prescribes nothing other than doing acts of charity themselves.

Obligatory Giving: Tzedakah

Rebbe Nachman is prescribing generosity as a practice, and so we have now worked our way around to the other sort of giving that the Jewish tradition advocates, which is obligatory giving. This is *tzedakah*, a Hebrew word often translated inaccurately as "charity." The root of the word actually comes from a source meaning "righteousness," "justice," or "fairness." That gives a very different slant on obligatory generosity as the Jewish tradition sees it.

Giving *tzedakah* is one of the traditional obligations of a Jewish life. It has the weight of a commandment directly from the Torah, where the instruction is unambiguously stated in four verses, including:

When any of your brothers is poor in any of your cities, in the land which HaShem your God is giving you, do not harden your heart or shut your hand from your poor brother. You shall open your hand, and you shall provide him whatever he needs, whatever he is lacking.[9]

That primary handbook to Jewish observance, the *Shulchan Aruch*, states that everyone is required to give *tzedakah* appropriate to his or her capacity. A person cannot be considered pious—a *tzaddik*, from the same etymological root as *tzedakah*—unless he or she gives to others, especially the needy. To give less than 10 percent is considered miserly. The law cautions against giving beyond one's means, however, and so it also sets an upper limit of one-fifth of one's income, because it will be of no benefit for a person to become impoverished because of excessive giving.

I'll interject a reminder here that in the Mussar view, not everyone needs to cultivate generosity. There are people whose soul work is to become *less* rather than more generous. There was a story in the news recently about a man who felt unsatisfied after giving away his $45 million real-estate fortune to charity, and so he determined to give up one of his healthy kidneys to someone who was enslaved to a dialysis machine. "No one should have two houses when people were homeless, and no one should have two kidneys while others struggled to live without one," Zell Kravinsky said.[10] He did donate one of his kidneys and felt so good about it that he decided to go to the next step and give up his remaining kidney as well. He reasoned that it would be even more generous of him to free another person from dialysis, even though that meant taking his or her place on the machine. This is unbalanced generosity. To be "totally self-sacrificing," as he claimed, is not spiritual virtue, because a total denial of self is a transmutation of a total concern for self and a backhanded and contorted way of serving self. It is egotism dressed in the guise of humility and generosity.

The majority of us could do with a building up of our generosity. Even then, Mussar teachings would not set us the task of loosening all restraint on generosity. Generosity ought to be kept in check by a healthy dose of intelligent restraint. The ideal is to achieve a balance of these forces within ourselves. I have seen that sometimes couples (and even organizations) achieve this balance. One of them leans toward giving away everything, and that puts the other partner in the position of having to put on the brakes before they are made destitute.

The law says that even the poor person who receives charity is obligated to give *tzedakah*. The logic here is that the poor should not be denied the joy and reward that derive from performing the mitzvah of *tzedakah*. A midrash teaches: "When a person gives even a small coin, he or she is privileged to sense God's presence. Even the wicked who have no other virtue but the giving of *tzedakah* are deemed worthy to greet the Presence of God."[11] No one should be deprived of this reward.

The essence of *tzedakah* is that it is an obligation. Both the donor and the recipient are meant to play their part in a legalistic process of giving and receiving. In fact, the community can impose a "charity levy" and has the right to enforce it as well. Maybe *tzedakah* is really more akin to taxation, because the intention is to demand of all individuals a contribution to help meet the needs of the social group, no matter what their hearts might be feeling.

Where *tzedakah* varies from taxation is that the charity laws say that it is best to fulfill our compulsory giving with good grace, gladly, and cheerfully, with an attitude of care and concern. Yet if we don't feel any of those things and can't paste a smile on our faces, we are still not relieved of our obligation to give. The Talmud ranks the ways of giving *tzedakah* by telling us that one who gives even a small coin to a poor person is blessed with six blessings, whether or not the giving was done with a positive air. But one who kindly offers words of comfort to a needy person as well as a coin is blessed with eleven blessings.[12]

Giving and Love

I've explored obligatory giving in such depth mainly to set up the discussion of the role this practice can play in cultivating a heart of love and holiness. Rabbi Eliyahu Dessler addressed this very issue.[13] Most of us can easily see how the love in our hearts will lead us to open our hands to giving. When a parent loves a child, or spouses love each other, the gifts that are given spring from the soil of love. What concerned Rabbi Dessler, however, was the question of whether the flow of influence could go in the other direction. He questioned what impact the very act of giving has on our hearts. The question he prompts us to consider is this: do you give to the ones you love, or do you love the ones to whom you give?

Rabbi Dessler places giving and taking at the center of our moral and spiritual life. "When the Almighty created human beings, He made them capable of both giving and taking," he wrote. Rabbi Dessler concluded that it is better to be a giver and so considered how we can develop that quality in ourselves. For guidance, Rabbi Dessler drew on a paragraph from Rabbi Moshe Chaim Luzzatto's classic Mussar text of the eighteenth century, *The Path of the Just*, which reads: "External motions stimulate internal ones."[14]

Applied to generosity, the principle is that giving arouses the heart to love. By obligating ourselves to give according to rules and formula, we expose our hearts to repetitive acts of giving that leave their trace on our inner lives. The very act of giving itself ultimately makes us more charitable, merciful, and loving. "Love flows in the direction of giving," was Rabbi Dessler's teaching. This may also be what the Talmud means to convey when it teaches, "If you want to bond yourself to loving your friend, give to him for his benefit."[15]

Rabbi Dessler saw the impact that our deeds have on our soul-traits. We don't have to wait until our hearts are fully open and infused with natural generosity before we begin to give. To the contrary, acts of generosity awaken love and foster the soul-trait of generosity. The Mussar tradition's guidance is this: by accustoming yourself to giving, and developing the habit of giving, eventually your heart will catch up and you will become more generous and loving by nature. "Our hearts follow our deeds," is how it is put in the thirteenth-century text *Sefer ha'Chinuch* (The Book of Instruction).[16]

The Forces of Resistance

If you permit yourself to give *only* when you are moved by genuine feelings of generosity, you will suffer a loss. To be generous only when you are inspired serves effectively (if inadvertently) to maintain intact all the interior factors that inhibit your generosity. The fears and attachments that bind your heart and that keep your hand from opening go unchallenged. The result is that you do nothing to cultivate the loving-kindness that is the engine of generosity. Your heart, your life, and our world are poorer for that.

But when giving is mandated as a compulsory act, and what you happen to feel in your heart does not figure whatsoever into your decisions about giving, you disarm all possibility of rationalization and are inevitably brought face-to-face with your inner resistances. That setup offers up the possibility and the hope that you will engage with those ingrained resistances, so you can loosen their grip on your heart and thus move closer to becoming the more loving, generous person you have the potential to be.

Our hearts can experience many sorts of resistance to generosity. In fact, each of us is susceptible to particular types of inhibition that reflect the circumstances of our lives. A childhood that was not nurturing, for example, could strap a binding around your generous heart. Or if your adulthood has been lived in poverty, that might be the source of constraint. Only you can discover and know the patterns that are at work in your own life. But the tradition alerts us to be on the lookout for these factors and how they work within us.

The forces of resistance can have many roots, but they have one name in the Mussar tradition—the *yetzer ha'ra*, literally, the inclination to evil. You undoubtedly know the experience. Just as your heart is opening to give, you hear an insistent inner voice piping up that tells you to withdraw your open hand. That voice is the *yetzer ha'ra*.

The Mussar text *The Duties of the Heart*[17] offers a vivid description of how the narcissistic and selfish *yetzer ha'ra* makes every effort to discourage a person from giving generously. This donation will put you in grave financial danger, it might say. Or suddenly you will see a vision of yourself living in abject poverty. Or that voice will tell you that *any* donation is simply beyond your means. Or that the people you might give to don't deserve it. Or you gave yesterday. Or you need it more than they do. Or . . .

The *yetzer ha'ra* is very clever. It will only spout words and images that have the potential to inhibit your own heart. Why? Ultimately, not to prevent you from giving, but to challenge you to grow beyond the level of generosity where you are today. In this way, the *yetzer ha'ra* can be a force for the good. Take a moment to consider what carefully scripted lines your own *yetzer ha'ra* uses on you that keep you from stretching to a level of generosity of which you are capable.

Making a routine of giving regularly will surely bring you into direct encounter with your *yetzer ha'ra*. This will not be a comfortable experience, but it is a valuable one because it gives you a real opportunity to confront whatever inner patterns cause your personal constriction of the heart. This is surely what lies behind the comment in *Orchot Tzaddikim*, the sixteenth-century Mussar classic, that "a person who gives a thousand gold pieces to a worthy person is not as generous as one who gives a thousand gold pieces on a thousand different occasions, each in its proper place. For if one gives a thousand pieces at one time, it is because he was suddenly seized with a great impulse to give that afterward departed him." It's the very act of opening the hand one thousand times that is spiritually transformative. "About this our Sages have said (*Pirkei Avot* 3:15): 'All is according to abundance of deed.' They did not say 'according to greatness of deed.'"[18]

This image of one thousand gold coins that we encounter in *Orchot Tzaddikim* comes from Maimonides' commentary on this same verse from *Pirkei Avot* that "all is according to the abundance of deed." He writes that "the virtues of character do not come to a person through the greatness of their deeds but according to the number of deeds. Virtues of character come with repetition of right action many times over." Mussar teacher Rabbi Shlomo Wolbe comments, "It is a wonder. If a person thinks great thoughts about generosity, and has many profound new concepts about it, this thinking will not enable him to acquire the attribute of generosity. But if he gives one coin to a thousand poor people, through this he will surely acquire generosity."[19]

Our external actions bring about inner change, which we can understand scientifically: our behavior gives us experiences that carve new neural pathways in the brain. I have at times assigned students to find three situations every day in which to act with generosity—giving a donation to a charity, dropping a coin in a homeless person's cup, offering someone your seat on the bus, giving up your place in line at the bank, sending someone a gift, offering to teach someone something you know, visiting a sick person. The list of possibilities is endless.

One student had an experience around giving something other than money. She and her colleagues at work had been having difficulties, and she wasn't getting along with one in particular. "Our styles, worldviews, and priorities were quite different," she noted. With a focus on generosity practice, she said to herself, "Well, perhaps I can come to the relationship with generosity of spirit—which to me means not having always to be right, and to see that I don't have to change her. I will ask myself to be generous enough to give her way of being in the world space to operate."

She had the opportunity to put that resolution into action the next morning. "I approached her to try to recalibrate our relationship," she said, "and I did so with the soul-trait of generosity in mind. That intention changed my attitude, and in response, my colleague responded differently to me as well. I believe that entering the conversation with this spirit of generosity made the outcome positive and useful."

Gifts given with the express purpose of thawing a frozen heart will, in time, cause fear to melt away and trust to grow. Each act of generosity works to pry open the heart a little, like clearing a blocked stream one pebble at a time. The flow of spontaneity is then freed to follow.

It may seem strange to practice generosity in order to do work on your own heart. That might even seem somehow to undermine the very quality of generosity itself, since the intention also involves a reward to the giver. Therein lies some of the magic of generosity. It rewards all. In Hebrew, the phrase "and they shall give"—*v'natnu*—is spelled *vav-nun-tav-nun-vav*. That's a palindrome, a word that is spelled the same way whether you read it left to right or right to left. Such is the flow of generosity.

Giving Your Heart

All of this might lead you to conclude that the ultimate form of generosity is giving from a loving heart. Rabbi Simcha Zissel tells us this, and more. He looks closely at the phrasing of the section of the Torah dealing with *terumah* (generous offerings). A literal reading of the statement goes: "Whoever is of a willing heart, let him bring it, an offering of the Almighty." The question Rabbi Simcha Zissel asks is, "To what does 'it' refer?" He answers that this verse means that those who bring gifts should bring their hearts along with their offerings. It isn't enough just to give money or an object, even from the heart; God wants us to give our hearts themselves.

God wants your heart. Real generosity means not only giving something practical that will be of help to someone, it also means changing something in yourself. Wrapped up in our hearts are the inner qualities that can adorn our generosity. Will your gift be just a thing, or will it be accompanied by joy, or empathy, or commitment, or love, or any of the other soul-traits you cultivate in yourself? When you undertake to give your heart as well, you change an element of yourself. Each such act of generosity makes you into a more giving (or joyful, or empathic, or committed, or loving, or . . .) person. And when you change yourself, you change the world.

The tradition teaches that practicing generosity opens the heart, and that ultimately the reward for generosity is that the giver receives the gift of the presence of God dwelling among us. I can't imagine any difference between an open heart and the presence of HaShem.

> If you want to bond yourself to loving your friend, give
> to him for his benefit.
>
> —*Derech Eretz Zuta* 2

18

Truth

EMET

Be distant from falsehood.

> Even after the desires of one's heart have persuaded
> him to accept the false way as true, he still knows in
> his heart of hearts that the true path is "truer" than
> the other one. . . . Every human being thus has the fac-
> ulty of determining in his own heart where the real
> truth lies.[1]
>
> —Rabbi Eliyahu Dessler, *Strive for Truth!*

AT LEAST AS FAR BACK as the Talmud[2] we find references in Jewish
folklore to artificially created people, called golems. A golem looks and
acts like a human and has many of the features of humans, including the
ability to understand and think. What separates a golem from you and me
is that it comes into being only through purely artificial means. A body is
shaped out of earth or clay and water, until it looks like a human being.
Then the creature is brought to life, usually by the incantation of words.

The most famous golem was created Rabbi Judah Loew[3] in sixteenth-
century Prague. The rabbi assembled clay into a body and then chanted
powerful prayers over the prone form. Finally, he inscribed one word on
the creature's forehead, and the creature stirred.

The word was *emet*, which means "truth."[4] Such is the life-giving power
of truth.

The Test of Truth

Rabbi Shlomo Zalman Auerbach[5] was being considered to head a yeshiva in Jerusalem, and so he was invited to deliver a lecture before the community. Not long after he had begun, he was interrupted with a question. After a few seconds of silence, Rabbi Auerbach declared, "*Ta'isi*" (I'm mistaken). He then began a new topic, which was the focus of the remainder of his lecture.

When he returned home, his wife asked how it had gone. "Not so well," Reb Shlomo Zalman replied. "I had hardly begun when I admitted to a mistake. Actually, I had three different answers to offer. But I felt that the question was closer to the truth than any of my answers."

Rabbi Shlomo Zalman was hired for the position. Years later, the man who had asked the difficult question revealed, "When I asked him that question and he responded, 'I'm mistaken,' it was clear to me that with such a level of *emes* [truth], he should be our Rosh Yeshiva!" Rabbi Auerbach had passed the test.

And as for us?

Someone asks if you are free Saturday evening. You aren't busy, but you don't really like that person. So you fabricate a commitment and beg off.

You badly want the contract (or job, or invitation, or favor), and soon your lips start flapping in exaggerated self-praise.

You aren't confident that you will pass the exam, so you make sure to sit next to the best student in the class, just in case you need to glance over during the test for a hint to the answer.

You can probably come up with many more of your own examples of trivial (and maybe not so trivial) manipulations of truth that you commit. When you act carefully and no one catches on, they don't really even have any negative consequences, do they? And everyone does it, right? A study determined that an astounding one in five interactions in the general community is "utterly deceitful."[6]

We know it is wrong, and still we persist.

It's not like we haven't been warned. There is a saying in Hebrew that translates as "falsehood has no legs."[7] That could mean that falsehood has "no legs to stand on," that is, no basis or foundation, not set upon anything real. It could also mean that falsehood "has no legs to run with," that it can't endure over time. Eventually, falsehood runs out of steam and is overturned. A similar notion is expressed in the proverb, "True speech is forever, but a false tongue for a moment."[8]

So why do we lie? A student acknowledges that she "tells a story" "out of fear of being taken to task, to be seen in a negative light." Once she had to miss a board meeting because it conflicted with her husband's seventieth birthday party. "I found myself preparing all kinds of stories that would 'protect' me from these fears," she said.

Just as this story reveals, peel back the behavior and you are almost sure to discover that the source of the lie is a fear of one thing or other. We lie because we fear facing someone else's disappointment, or having disappointment ourselves, or fear of shame, or loss, or any number of other possibilities.

Are you aware of the ways in which you shade the truth? Can you identify the fear that motivates you to make that choice?

Beneath the fear you are sure to find is a soul-trait that is out of the middle range. This student's fear of "being taken to task" relates to the trait of responsibility, and "to be seen in a negative light" reflects the pursuit of honor. These are the root issues, and they tend to operate beneath the threshold of conscious awareness.

Can you relate your own fears to soul-traits that are operating in your own interior world?

It was not because of her inner awareness, but rather her commitment to tell the truth, that the student hosting her husband's seventieth birthday party eventually decided not to lie about the situation. What happened next was a revelation: "Instead of lightning coming down from heaven, I got congratulations for my husband's big birthday and a few 'your family comes first' remarks. It felt like a bit of my soul was being saved."

This is how truth telling is a test. When you make truth a practice, you will inevitably come up against the soul-trait (or traits) that underlie the fear that prompts the falsehood. Your commitment to truth thus serves you very well because the soul-traits that get revealed are clearly ones that figure into your spiritual curriculum. When you lie out of fear, you are failing yourself. But when you face the fear and look beyond it, you pass the test. Open before you are your next steps on the way of the soul: you can focus on the soul-traits that are generating the emotions that are motivating your negative behavior. This awareness will reveal how insubstantial the fear really is, and yet what a strong grip it has on your behavior. That awareness is essential to equipping yourself to meet the test of truth and falsehood. In time, truth itself will become an inner strength you can rely on.

The Simple Truth

The Jewish tradition condemns lying and celebrates truth telling, much as we would expect. As we explore this soul-trait, however, we will find that neither life nor the Mussar teachings invite us to take a simplistic approach. Truth is delicate. Its fabric is so easily stretched and torn. Truth is versatile—look at how many causes will readily sacrifice truth to some other goal. Truth can be simple, but more often it is deceptively complex, and not always singular. And as the Alter of Novarodok teaches, we are easily confused about truth, because truth can appear before us in the guise of falsehood, just as falsehood can show up in the trappings of truth.[9]

Truth often takes the form of falsehood when revolutionary scientific discoveries are announced. For example, in the eighteenth century Edward Jenner announced that a form of vaccination prevented smallpox and was promptly denounced as a quack. Only later was it proven that this apparently specious discovery was, in fact, correct. And on the score of falsehood masquerading as truth, we need only cite all the medical cures that really are bogus—such as leeching and cupping and many others that are popular today—even though they may be believed in assiduously.

Because we want to understand and develop the quality of truth as an optimally calibrated feature of our inner life, we don't focus on truth as if it were something hard, objective, and external.[10] Rather, the truth we'll investigate is subjective. The test we apply in our search for truth is therefore not strictly empirical. You'll see that the Jewish tradition understands that truth is situational, and we ourselves are part of the situation.

The Beautiful Bride

Let's jump right in with a tricky example. I can imagine that you've been in a situation much like this one, where obligation and truth are on a collision course with each other.

Among the many commandments that are religious obligations for Jews is the duty to praise a bride.[11] The commandment is "to praise." And there before us stands the bride: awkward, ungainly, unkempt. What can you possibly say that would qualify as praise? You can't find a single quality that allows you to fulfill the commandment. Not with truth, anyway. So do you lie, or do you tell the bald truth about what you see before you?

This situation is the focus of an argument between Shammai and Hillel, two major characters who show up repeatedly in the Talmud.[12] Shammai takes the position that a bride should be praised according to the positive qualities that she personally possesses. In other words, you are supposed to keep looking her over until you succeed in finding at least one praiseworthy quality, hard as that may be to do, and then to sing her praises for what you have found.

Hillel presents a different opinion. He states that *all* brides should be praised as being "beautiful and gracious."

To that Shammai retorts: "What if a bride limps or is blind, should one praise her as being 'beautiful and gracious'? Has not the Torah told us, 'Keep your distance from falsehood'?"[13]

Shammai has made a good point, invoking the very clear principle stated in the Torah: do not lie. When Hillel responds, he doesn't meet Shammai head-on over the verse from the Torah. Instead, he presents an analogy: "When a person buys an inferior article in the market, should one praise it in his presence, or should one find fault with it in his presence? It appears to us that one should praise it for him."

This analogy isn't one I'd personally try to defend—equating a bride to purchased merchandise—but let's try to get around that to the essence of what Hillel is saying about truth.

Hillel tells us that we should not be primarily concerned with how our words correspond to verifiable reality, but rather for the impact our statement will have on another person. The article (or bride) may be very blemished—anyone with eyes can see that—but does that obligate us to speak that truth? His answer is no, not if a person will be hurt by our speech.

So where does this leave us? Are we supposed to view truth in speech as an absolute, as Shammai seems to recommend? Or are there circumstances where it is justified—or maybe even better—not to tell the truth, such as when the goal is to serve a higher purpose?

We face this problem all the time as we choose what to say, and what not to say, in our every interaction. What guidelines do we follow? Are we supposed to speak the bald and honest truth at all times, regardless; or is it better to adopt a more relativistic position, changing what we say according to the circumstances and perspective?

Lying

On only a moment's reflection, it becomes clear that most lies are told to protect oneself or hurt someone else. These sorts of manipulative or malicious motives for deceit can never be excused. Twisting truth in a self-serving or harmful way has negative consequences for the whole world, since lying erodes truth, which is one of the pillars of the world, as Rabbi Shimon ben Gamliel teaches.[14] Lying like this undermines the only standard that enables us to trust one another.

And that's not all. There are also spiritual consequences to lying. Deceit undermines the soul of the person who is not dedicated to truth. When we habitually lie, flatter, boast, cheat, and otherwise deny truth, the impact registers at our deepest internal level. Soul-traits that are out of balance are kept that way, or driven even further toward pathological extremes. In *The Path of the Just,* Rabbi Moshe Chaim Luzzatto tells us that lying is a spiritual illness.[15] Ultimately, contact with the soul is lost completely. It is taught in the Talmud that a habitual liar is unable to perceive the Shechinah (the Divine Presence).[16]

The simple (though devastating) conclusion is that lying can damage worlds, both outer and inner.

But life is complex, and surely there are circumstances where our truth is not the right thing to speak. Some people equate "truth" with speaking their minds, but speaking your mind may simply be articulating your unexamined prejudice or bias. And even when there are facts to call on, and you have the facts straight, sometimes the honest truth can be a brutal stick. I know from stories I hear my wife tell about her work as a palliative care physician that as some people approach the end of their lives, they really don't want to be told that they have a terminal diagnosis. Is it right to impose that information on them, in the name of being truthful? And are we justified in speaking out even truthfully to ease a pain of our own, when doing so shifts that pain onto someone else, who is hurt by our words?

What standard is the right one for us to adopt? Truth is unreliable and can even be harmful. On the other hand, falsehood is dangerous and so often damaging. And surely we cannot give ourselves permission to abandon truth whenever we happen to get stumped for an answer. Such relativism is a slippery slope.

Truth as Task

Because Mussar encourages us to extract a curriculum for our own growth from our life experience, our job here is not to resolve the philosophical arguments but to be on the lookout for an assignment that we can find embedded in this issue that applies in the real circumstances of our lives. Here's what I see.

Shammai would have us make our personal perceptions our guide to truth. On the other hand, Hillel says that we need to challenge ourselves to see truth not only through our own eyes but also through the eyes of another person who is tied into the situation. Surely every groom considers his bride "beautiful and gracious." Hillel advises us to review the matter patiently until we can enter into the perspective of the groom, through which we will also come to see the bride as "beautiful and gracious."

Hillel's position guides us away from our typical tendency to see things only from our own singular perspective. He encourages us to stretch ourselves to see things through the eyes of other people. Truth involves not only speaking accurately, but even more important and earlier in the process, seeing accurately. And since truths are often multiple, so must be our perspectives.

Seeing a situation from the vantage point of others who are involved is one principle we need to apply to truth. Another is to be sensitive to the results that spring from our "truth." The Chafetz Chaim, a twentieth-century Jewish sage who codified the laws concerning right speech,[17] didn't set "truth" as the highest standard for speech. Just because something is true does not give us license to say it, because saying things that are true can still do enormous harm, and it is *the potential for harm* that is the ultimate guideline that the Chafetz Chaim puts to us to help us direct our speech.

This latter principle lies behind the Talmud's judgment that "it is permissible for a man to deviate [from the truth] on account of peace."[18] This dictum has come to be interpreted as meaning that one may speak something other than the truth for the sake of peace or another ethical imperative (such as humility, modesty, and sensitivity).

In a Talmudic tale, Rabbi Yehoshua ben Chananiah tells a lie out of sensitivity for another's feelings: "I was once staying at an inn where the hostess served me beans," he relates. "On the first day I ate all of them, leaving nothing. On the second day, too, I left nothing. On the third day she overseasoned them with salt and, as soon as I tasted them, I withdrew my hand. 'My master,' she said to me, 'why do you not eat?' I replied, 'I have already eaten earlier in the day.'"[19]

The Judgment of Truth

The soul and society both require that we make a commitment to truth, but not in a rigid or naïve way. The Mussar tradition offers us more mature and down-to-earth guidance based on the recognition that in this complex life, different values can compete with one another in any situation, and literal truth isn't always meant to be the victor. It is given over to us, in our humanity, to use our judgment to define truth and to decide how to apply it.

I've already quoted Rabbi Shimon ben Gamliel's teaching that truth sustains the world. His proof-text is a verse from the prophets: "Speak every man the truth to his neighbor; execute the judgment of truth and peace in your gates."[20] The phrase "execute the judgment of truth" points out that truth demands judgment. Truth isn't outside us, but emerges within us, as an outcome of our acts of judgment.

Maybe that's what the psalmist meant when he wrote: "Truth shall spring from the earth."[21] You can bet that if the Nazis came to my door and asked where my children were, I'd tell the biggest lie I could think of, and by this set of teachings, I'd not be wrong to do so.

This seems right, but it leaves us with a major problem. While it makes sense that a person committed to spiritual life has to be sensitive to others and tactful in speech, and even to be prepared to bend the truth to a higher purpose, it's apparent that we have just entered an ethical minefield. Once we abandon the unyielding position that we will only tell the bare truth in every situation, we make ourselves dependent on our own judgment, and therein lies the danger. For surely our judgment is fallible. We are so easily misled and deceived, perhaps most of all by our own penchant for self-deception. Our judgment is a very narrow road with sheer drops on either side.

Yet we have no better road to follow. Despite the pitfalls, "executing the judgment of truth" is preferable to adhering to an ironclad loyalty to the facts. Rabbi Jonathan Sacks explains that this idea reflects the core Jewish view on truth: "Truth is not something we discover at one time.

That is how things are for God, but not for us. For Judaism, truth—as understood and internalized by humanity—is a developmental process. That is why so much of the Bible is narrative and so many of its books are works of history."[22]

We have to let truth emerge from our judgment and to accept that that puts the onus on us to maintain a very strong inner compass. Rabbi Eliyahu Dessler gives us hope here because he tells us that our human hearts come ready-equipped for the task. If we listen to our own heart of hearts with sensitive ears, we will receive guidance that directs us to "where the real truth lies."[23]

The Torah and the teachings of the rabbis give us all the guidance we need, but to follow the path that lies before us still calls for a discerning heart. This is the ultimate instrument for recognizing what is true and for guiding our speech and actions. It's the heart that calls you to go looking for guidance from tradition when that's available. And it is the wise heart that will show the way in the myriad situations for which there are no black-and-white answers.

We all have a discerning heart, though its voice may be quiet, or even muffled, or drowned out by other inner voices. We also may not be so familiar with its language. Mussar tells us that one of the primary tasks on the spiritual journey is to cultivate and exercise that implement of skillful discernment, the wise heart. Only then will we become the masters of truth, with all the judgment, discernment, fearlessness, and wisdom that mastery implies.

The Impact of Truth

One student's experience tells us how influential it is to recognize and pursue truth. She found herself at a gathering where a game was being played. A letter of the alphabet was announced, and then tables competed to see which one could come up with the most titles of songs beginning with that letter. A bell would ring to end the round. Despite the fact that there weren't even any prizes to be won, her table still cheated. The bell would ring and they kept adding to their list.

It struck this woman that this was a direct contradiction of the value of truth to which she was aspiring. She said so to her tablemates and, sheepishly, they agreed to play fairly. She wondered whether she had done the right thing. Would they still be her friends?

Later, she ran into a woman who had been sitting at an adjacent table. This woman told her that she had overheard her asking her teammates to honor truth in the game. She told her how inspired and grateful she had been to hear this woman speak up on behalf of higher values. And from there, the influence will have rippled out.

A story is told about Rabbi Yisrael Salanter that not only reinforces this point but also reveals the inner process that a master of truth goes through in "executing the judgment of truth" that is our guideline and goal.

Rabbi Salanter gave a regular Talmudic discourse. One day, a student asked a very sharp question that seemed to undermine the entire argument Rabbi Salanter was making. He paused for a moment, then he conceded the point and stepped down from the dais.

Later he told his students about what he had thought in the moment before he stepped down. In that instant at least five acceptable answers came to his mind to refute the question. Even though he could see that they were not ultimately true, he knew it was unlikely that anyone in the audience would see through them as he could. He was tempted to try them, even for positive reasons: his admission of failure might cause the Torah he represented to lose honor, and he himself might lose face, and that might negatively impact his ability to affect people positively.

After these thoughts, he chastised himself. "You study Mussar!" he said to himself. "Admit the truth." And he stepped down.

In the end, he explained, it was in serving the needs of his soul and the souls of others that he had to be truthful. Though difficult, this is the guideline we too must follow. Truth is not a thing that depends only on the scientific verifiability of the facts. Truth is also an exercise, a judgment, and a test. The goal is to live truth according to the guidance of your discerning heart, for the sake of the soul you are as well as the souls of others.

The signature of The Holy Blessed One is truth.

—*Shabbat* 55a

19

Moderation

SHEVIL HA'ZAHOV

With awareness I observe the pull of impulse, and wisdom guides my response.

> The path of the upright is one of moderation in every trait, so that each trait is equidistant from either extreme and not close to either. Therefore the early sages commanded that man should put his traits [before him] constantly and direct them to the middle road, so that he will be complete in his person.
>
> —Rambam (Maimonides),
> *Hilchot De'ot* (The Laws of Behavior)

THE TALMUD[1] reports on a wedding celebration arranged by a great sage for his son. The host noticed that the rabbis were going overboard in enjoying themselves. He then took a very valuable glass cup and smashed it in front of them. They saw what he did, and they became serious.[2]

We learn from this story that moderation is the way in everything, even of joy and celebration. We also learn that achieving moderation can require sacrifice.

The Middle Way

Most of us actually prefer a life of moderation.[3] We don't want to sleep all day or go without sleep; we don't want to eat until we feel we are going to burst, or starve; we don't want to work to exhaustion or be absolutely idle. Only fanatics would reject those values, and yet the fact is that most of us

173

have a tendency to swing toward extremes and away from the middle path to which we claim allegiance. Wherever we habitually run up against difficulty and repeatedly cause suffering in our lives—to ourselves and those around us—lack of moderation is often the culprit.

Many things are healthy in moderation but potentially damaging in either excess or abstention. Much research says that a moderate intake of alcohol can be good for your health, though we all know the sorts of diseases and problems born of alcoholism. The same is true for dieting, which can maintain a healthy weight and can also devolve into anorexia. At the other end of the scale, obesity is now a major public health issue. Self-esteem is a necessary spiritual strength, while self-debasement or arrogance veer away from the balanced middle range. So it is with many other things we do in our lives. Except for what is harmful in any measure, which ought to be totally avoided, in most other cases the ideal route is the middle one, neither abstaining in the absolute nor indulging to the hilt.

Ask yourself, in what area of my life am I not following the middle way?

One example I can offer is that I get a clear message on the need for moderation from my body. If I exercise too little, my body, my mind, and my emotions don't function optimally. And when I exercise too much, I hurt myself. The golden mean is the rule; enough but neither too much nor too little.

The Torah role model for the middle way is Jacob, who made a vow asking God to "give me bread to eat and a garment to wear."[4] By pointing out the seemingly obvious—that bread is to eat and clothing to wear—Jacob is telling us that the proper measure for food is enough to satiate hunger but not to the level of sumptuous feasting. Similarly, we should clothe ourselves, but only in simple, functional attire. There is no more virtue in starving our bodies (whether in fasting or in anorexia or bulimia) than there is in gorging endlessly on delicacies. Both extremes miss the mark. Similarly, not taking care to have proper clothing is as spiritually inappropriate as is flaunting costly and fashionable garments.

The Root Is Desire

Overindulgence drives us from the way of moderation. We also lose our way when we defy the natural level of desire that is healthy. In our affluent society, overindulgence is the more common pattern today.

The Jewish tradition is clear not only in accepting the reality of our desires but also in seeing that, at their root, desires are a force for the good. Those inner urges that compel us to eat and to sleep, to procreate and to grow, motivate us to participate in the processes of life, and as the Torah says, we are to "choose life."[5]

But like all sources of physical energy—fire, nuclear power, electricity—our desires need to be handled properly or the result is almost certain to be disaster. Desires arise like sparks, grow to become surging currents and, if not channeled or guided, can end up jolting our lives toward outcomes we would never choose. Desires can be like the charge that passes safely along the well-ordered and insulated wires that the licensed electrician installs in our home, or they can run more like the lightning bolts that flash across the night sky, wildly following their own course without predictable pattern, striking destructively wherever they will.

We gain the benefits of a life of moderation only when we govern our desires instead of being governed by them.

When an inner impulse first begins to move in us, it is hardly perceptible, as described by novelist Amoz Oz:

> Like sneezes, which start from nothing at all, a faint pinching sensation at the base of your nose, and then gradually take over so that there's no stopping them. Temptations generally start from a little patrol to check the terrain, tiny ripples of vague, undefined excitement, and, before you know what it wants of you, you start to feel a gradual glow inside, as you do when you switch on an electric fire and the element is still grey but it starts to make little popping noises and then it blushes very faintly and then more deeply and soon it is glowing angrily and you are full of reckless lightheadedness; so what, what the hell, why not, what harm can it do, like a very vague but wild, uninhibited sound deep inside you, coaxing and pleading with you: Come on, why not.[6]

If we give ourselves over to our desires without limit, the negative consequences are usually obvious to us because we suffer. The effects of overindulgence are often physical, showing up as high blood pressure and cholesterol and other "lifestyle" ailments. Workaholics do physical as well as psychological damage to their well-being, but damage their relationships as well. But less obvious is the way in which sworn allegiance to the reign of our desires sets off a chain of events that ultimately leads to spiritual ruin. Rabbi Moshe Chaim Luzzatto describes what happens when desires and excessive consumption rule our lives:

> You will eventually be forced to subject yourself to the clutches of the drive for livelihood and possessions so that your table could be set the way you would like it to be, which will lead you to wrong doings and thievery, which will themselves lead you to vain oaths and all sorts of transgressions that naturally follow these. Ultimately you will remove yourself from Divine service, Torah, and prayer.[7]

The Chafetz Chaim offers a variation on the same theme. He writes about spending money, but the message holds true for any sort of material excess we might pursue:

> One should behave when it comes to personal expenditures in the middle way, according to the individual and place. And even if God has been kind to him and given him great wealth, he should not wear very expensive embroidered clothing since that will damage his soul because it brings a person to arrogance and also incites the Evil Inclination. In addition, it causes others, who do not have the means, to look at him and desire to emulate him. In the end, they will borrow and not repay their loans or rob and cheat. And because of these extravagances, the expenses in our times for clothing for weddings have increased so that many of our daughters are humiliated when it comes time for them to get married. Fathers and mothers cry and wail and no one can help them.[8]

Both these sages of tradition emphasize that what begins in ungoverned desire goes through a chain of step-by-step stages until we bring down spiritual (and often also material) disaster upon ourselves and those around us. We need this caution to help us identify what is harmful in, for example, the hugely expensive, extravagant, blowout bar and bat mitzvahs and weddings that go on today. Our sages' intent is to sensitize us to the real consequences of living to excess, so we will appreciate and be motivated to follow the way of moderation.

Just because it is available, just because you can afford it, just because others do it, these are not reasons enough. In 1978 the Grand Rabbi of the Ger Chassidim issued a decree requiring his followers to limit the number of guests at their weddings to 120 people. A wealthy follower complained that he should be exempt from the decree because he was rich. The rebbe told him: "Then buy yourself a new rebbe."

The Way of Desires

The Mussar teachers tell us that the secret to becoming masters of moderation is to cultivate sensitivity to the inner processes of desire as they arise within us. They urge us to be aware of the interior course that an impulse runs, starting as a tiny sensation and eventually growing to a full-blown indulgence. This is what prompts Rabbi Yitzchok Isaac Sher to write that a person "cannot undertake to follow the mussar way of life until he fully understands the processes of thought formation and the modes of thought development."[9]

Thoughts and impulses seem to land on our minds, just like birds that have been hidden in the dense grass, until they unexpectedly flutter into the air before our eyes and alight on a limb of a tree. Once a thought or desire has perched in the mind like that, it has just begun to live. That's its most critical period. Will the impulse live or be stillborn? Will it run a course of its own, or will a higher sensibility guide it toward ends that coincide with our values and goals?

Left alone, desires develop a self-guided trajectory, and so the earlier we are able to become aware of the presence of a desire, the quicker we can act. Act to do what? To choose whether we want to let that newborn desire take root or not, and, if we are going to let it come to life, to what end and in what way. The ideal is to be as aware of our desires as early as possible, in order to give ourselves as much freedom of choice as we can possibly muster. The Mussar masters refer to this as becoming aware of the thread of hair that can grow into a great mountain.

If the thought or impulse does go to the next step, whether because we unconsciously allow it to proceed or because we agree to give it life, it takes flight. Now the idea or desire is on its way to becoming fully formed. It will carry on developing and will draw in resources as it makes its way toward fulfillment.

Finally, the thought or desire moves right out of the mental realm and into speech or action. If it has been guided through filters of wisdom and choice, it is likely to express itself in a way that matches up with your values and goals. But if not, chances are that you will suddenly wake up to find that a rampant notion has tossed a rope around your life and is now dragging you away to some unknown and not too inviting destination. Too often, we become aware of the desire only when we discover ourselves already living out circumstances of which we are unquestionably the author, and which we have to deal with, even though we didn't consciously choose them.

When things go that far, it's almost certain that we will suffer. I can attest from my own rough experience that I have brought big misery on myself and others by allowing myself to drift into unfortunate and avoidable life circumstances.

A student tells a similar tale. He pursued undergraduate and graduate studies with the goal of serving the public as a health care administrator, but the job he got was in the private sector. "I ultimately found myself as a lay partner in a physician group." That was the first step down a long road. Along the way, he reports, "I pursued my job with great zeal, perfecting the delivery of the 'product,' expanding the 'marketplace' for those services, being as much 'hands-on' as possible." As the years went by, "I found myself devoting phenomenal hours to the enterprise. The financial rewards were substantial, but they were coming at a cost I either failed to appreciate, or more probably chose to ignore. I neglected my family. I made decisions that were, at best, shading into falsehood. Spiritual life? No time or interest."

Standing outside the flow of events, it isn't hard for us to imagine where this story might be headed: "Ultimately my own greed, great as it was, couldn't surpass that of my partners. In short order everything imploded and when the dust had settled, I was left with nothing in a material way, and less in my emotional life."

And in hindsight, this man could see it, too. "My contribution to the crisis was not insignificant. By shading truths, treating others as faceless competitors or envious pretenders to my throne, more significantly by ignoring my family, I brought it all on."

This is the picture of desires taking the reins out of our control. Wherever you have desire—food, sex, possessions, ego gratification, states of mind, and so on—lack of moderation is almost always a staircase that ultimately descends to an unimagined level of pain and loss.

The distress that comes from being immoderate contains a message waiting to be decoded. This student said, "The loud 'crash' in my life was actually an alarm clock going off for me." Pain can be a bright red flag marking out just the sort of imbalance that exists in our lives, telling us that we have strayed too far from the middle way. If we don't pay attention to these signals when they first come to us, and don't impose enough of a guiding hand on our thoughts, we may drift away from moderation and will pay a heavy price for our excess.

I want to reinforce that the issue is not the desires themselves. They are natural and implanted in us all. And even indulging our desires has its place, as in the enjoyments that are meant to be part of Shabbat, the drinking that is condoned on Purim, and the eating we are meant to do on various feast days. The issue is mastery: whether you have it or it is given over to the desires. The sages of the Talmud convey this message with a play on words. One who drinks in proper measure becomes a leader (*rosh*) while the one who overindulges becomes a pauper (*rash*).[10]

Self-Denial

As familiar as some of us are with overindulgence, others know its opposite, which is self-denial. The Jewish tradition has been very consistent in raising as much opposition to asceticism as it does to self-indulgence.[11] Neither is seen to be a positive value or a spiritual practice. Hence we find that there is no tradition of monasticism or celibacy in the Jewish world.

The closest we come is the tradition of the *nazir*,[12] which is the name given to people who take a temporary vow of abstinence from wine, hair-cutting, and contact with the dead (of whom Samson is the most famous example). But the abstinence of the *nazir* is more permitted than it is condoned, as we learn from the fact that the Torah demands a sacrifice of atonement for one who takes on Nazirite behavior: "And make atonement for him, for he sinned regarding the soul."[13]

The Talmudic sage Rabbi Elazar Ha'Kappar extends what we learn from this requirement for atonement: "If one who afflicted himself only with respect to wine is called a sinner, how much more so is one who

ascetically refrains from everything considered a sinner!"[14] Similarly, the
law states that whoever fasts excessively is called a sinner,[15] and the Jerusalem
Talmud asks: "Is it not sufficient what the Torah has forbidden you, that
you seek to prohibit from yourself other things?"[16]

Though not condoning asceticism, the Mussar teachers do speak of a
kind of abstinence that is good and valuable. The ability to restrain ourselves is a necessary soul-trait and the very one that is often invoked to guide
a person who seeks to counter the tendency to overindulge.[17] But this capacity to hold ourselves back is distinguished from asceticism. Abstinence
can maintain or restore the middle way, whereas asceticism rejects it.

The Rambam, who preached the golden mean,[18] warns: "A person may
say, 'Since envy, desire, [the pursuit of] honor, and the like are an evil path
and drive a person from the world, I should separate myself from them
and move entirely to the other extreme' and as a result he will not eat
meat, drink wine, marry, live in a fine home, or wear proper clothes, but
rather wears sackcloth and coarse wool and the like, as the pagan priests
do. This too is a bad path and it is forbidden to follow such a way. Whoever goes in this path is called a sinner."[19]

Rambam concludes: "A person should not prohibit from himself
through vows and oaths the use of permitted things. . . . Our Rabbis for-
bade that one afflict himself by fasting. Concerning this and similar matters, Solomon commanded us (Ecclesiastes/*Kohelet* 7:16): 'Be not overly
righteous, nor excessively wise. Why should you be so desolate?'"[20]

What's the problem with asceticism? One is that the ascetic (consciously or unconsciously) is rejecting the gifts he or she has received in
life, all of which ultimately derive from God. Judaism does not condone
the extreme rejection of desire and pleasure because it views this physical-
material realm where we find ourselves as true, valuable, and spiritual—
not an illusion to be transcended, as some other religious traditions suggest.
The Mussar teachers tell us that it is within this world, rather than in rejection of it, that we can elevate our spiritual natures.

So strong is this notion within Judaism that we are told in the
Jerusalem Talmud[21] that we will be held accountable in the afterlife for
every pleasure of the world we failed to enjoy during our sojourn on
earth: "Rabbi Hezkiah and Rabbi Kohen said in the name of Rav: 'In the
future each person will have to give an accounting for everything that he
has seen with his eye and not eaten.'"

Another problem with asceticism is that the rejection of the physical can reflect or give rise to a preoccupation with the very realm that is being rejected. Pushing away bodily needs easily develops into preoccupation with the body. Denial of the sensual fosters obsession with the sensual. In the effort to become spiritually elevated, the person succumbs to being overly concerned with the material.

Even though the goal may be lofty, less is not always better. Consider the motive. If a person is forgoing desires and pleasures as a way to earn something for himself or herself, then that may be just another form of self-service. It is entirely possible for people to be seduced into serving their lower nature in the guise of their higher nature.

The Role of the Evil Inclination

One person abandons moderation in favor of overindulgence, while another denies him- or herself any pleasures at all. This human reality is aptly described in the sixteenth-century Mussar classic *Orchot Tzaddikim*:

> One man is lustful, his lust never being satiated, and another exceedingly pure-hearted and not desiring even the few things that the body needs. One man is expansive of temperament, unsatisfied with all the wealth in the world, and another is of constricted spirit, for whom even a bit suffices and he does not rush to obtain all of his needs. One man afflicts himself with hunger and goes begging, consuming not even a penny's worth of his own without dire distress, and another deliberately wastes his money.

In either case, the culprit who strives to lead you away from the moderate middle (in either direction) is the *yetzer ha'ra*, that implanted adversary who challenges you by making doing good and acting in the interests of the soul so difficult. What Amos Oz describes so well that I quoted earlier in this chapter is nothing but the voice of the *yetzer ha'ra* as it cajoles you to do something even you know you shouldn't.

Because the *yetzer ha'ra* is the master of disguise, it cleverly scripts its appeals in precise fit to the unique (actual or potential) imbalances of your soul-traits. While you might well hear that voice whispering within you temptingly, "Come on, why not?" someone else will hear, "No, don't. You can't. You'll fail. Don't even try." The deceiving and seductive lines will differ, but the process is the same for all of us. That voice whispers enticement, promising fulfillment it never delivers in order that we not be moderate. When we obey its call, trouble ensues.

The person who indulges exhibits weak will, while the one who abstains is overly developed in the same faculty. As a result, living by the golden mean might seem to turn life into a dangerous tightrope act, with dire consequences on either side. But that image is far too narrow, and living a life of moderation is not nearly so precarious as that. Even on the middle course there's room to stretch a little from side to side without harm, and, in fact, a degree of flexibility helps us avoid making an obsessive habit of rigidly consistent behavior.

Rabbi Yisrael Salanter[22] writes:

Now, the Rambam writes that a person must conduct himself according to the middle path. Yet, is there anyone who can fathom this, and is there a seer who can declare, "Here is the mid-point"? This matter cannot be proven by syllogism, nor even by deductive reasoning. Rather, it can only be determined by a wise man using his faculty of common sense, each according to his place and time. The Athenian sages asked, "Where is the center of the world?" meaning, "What is the way to determine the middle path?" Rebbe Yehoshua replied, "Here," meaning, "According to the judgment of your intellect."

In the end, despite our best efforts, we still might find that we sometimes do slide off the central beam. The fall from moderation is not always a plunge to the circus floor. Life is surprisingly elastic. In that case, there might be a price to pay and amends to make. But as for how to approach ourselves once we've had that sort of skid, the most constructive thing to do is to have soft-hearted compassion toward ourselves for our humanity, and to seek out and strongly reaffirm whatever traces we can still detect within us of the motivation to make the best of our lives. Then it's time to pick ourselves up and resume our good efforts.

There is no lasting satisfaction in a life given over to desires. Excess yields up injury and suffering. At the other extreme, abstinence from what is permitted and not intrinsically harmful denies some aspect of life, and thereby reduces vitality, joy, and gratitude. Either extreme constitutes a stumbling block on the spiritual path. Moderation requires choice and strength. Its fruit is the strength to make even greater choices. It reduces harm and minimizes suffering. It is the companion of wisdom and stability.

> The luxuries we indulge in eventually come to seem
> to be necessities, as if we could not live without them.
>
> —Rabbi Yisrael Salanter

20

Loving-Kindness

CHESED

Do justice, love loving-kindness, walk humbly with God.[1]

> The cornerstone of Rabbi Nosson Zvi's[2] service of God was *chesed*. This, to him, meant being careful of another's honor and dignity, helping others, having one's heart overflow with love and kindness, utilizing every opportunity to benefit others. It meant that older students should learn with younger ones. . . . Above all, it meant that one should greet his fellow with a pleasant countenance, because it makes the other feel good and binds people together in friendship.
>
> —Rabbi Chaim Zaitchik, *Sparks of Mussar*

A PUBLIC DEFENDER in the American federal court system was also a student of Mussar. There came a point when his Mussar practice focused on cultivating the soul-trait of *chesed* (which we can provisionally translate as "loving-kindness"). At the end of one extremely long and demanding day, as you can imagine a public defender might face, he received a phone call from a client, who was calling from jail. She needed to talk to him and, what's more, she really needed to see him. His first response was to say (in his mind), "Get lost! I have a life, too!"

But in the very next instant another thought emerged: "*Chesed*," he reminded himself. He recalled the task he had set himself, which was to bring to life the psalm, "Surely goodness and *chesed* shall follow me all the days of my life."[3]

He went home, had dinner, then went to the prison to see his client.

"How was your interaction with her?" I asked.

"Very good," he answered.

This world is a vale of tears, no doubt about it. At the drop of a simple "How are you?" anyone can open their book of loss, disappointment, and pain. It's true for all of us, though we have to acknowledge more for some than others. Still, black threads are woven into the very fabric of every life.

No wonder, then, that the Jewish tradition elevates deeds of loving-kindness to the highest possible ranking among soul-traits. Only some problems have solutions, while all of them are alleviated by the loving response of those around us.

In *Pirkei Avot*[4] we learn that "the world stands on three things: on the Torah, on the service of God, and upon acts of lovingkindness." The fact that loving-kindness is one of the three pillars on which the world stands underlines how very important this soul-trait must be. *Chesed* is also one of the ten kabbalistic *sefirot* (emanations) that are the primary strands that are woven together to create our universe.

We need to be cautious, however, around the almost universal translation of the word *chesed* as "loving-kindness." To my ear, and maybe to yours, too, loving-kindness suggests being *nice*. Perhaps that's precisely what the world does stand on, and the very simplicity and innocence of being nice is the strength we can find in *chesed*. Most of us are vulnerable to being seduced by visions of ourselves and our potential that are dressed up with drama and importance, while it is undeniable that this entire world would be transformed beyond recognition if we were suddenly to just be nicer to one another.

Still, it's possible that the Jewish tradition and its wise teachers had something else in mind in the notion of *chesed* than just kind niceness. For now, until we come up with another maybe more accurate translation, let's stick to the Hebrew, *chesed*.

Defining Chesed

We start to build a picture of *chesed* by looking at how this quality is associated with God. *Chesed* is one of the primary attributes of the divine, and so the references are many. In fact, of the whopping 245 times this word appears in the Torah (telling you something right there), about two-thirds of these instances speak of God's character and actions. For example:

- "The world is built with *chesed*" says Psalm 89:2.
- In Psalm 136, which is also recited as a prayer, the congregation responds to every description of the wondrous deeds of the divine by saying aloud: "*Ki l'olam chasdo*"—His *chesed* endures forever.[5]
- When Moses descends from Mount Sinai with the tablets, God proclaims thirty-two words that have become known in Jewish tradition as the Thirteen Attributes of God's compassion. One of these attributes is "*v'rav chesed*"—abundant in *chesed*.[6]
- Jeremiah[7] records: "'I am God Who does *chesed*, justice and righteousness on the earth, because in these I delight,' says God."

And so on. In fact, God is the master of *chesed*, because, as the psalm states, "The world is built with *chesed*."[8] It was nothing but an act of *chesed* for God to have created the world at all. Then, to add to our amazement, God is constantly engaged in sustaining all of creation through acts of *chesed*.

We might well wonder, if this world is actually so infused with divine *chesed*, where is that quality to be found in the suffering and tears that plague our lives? Tradition answers that great *chesed* is extended to us at every moment, though it may be hard to see. We are weak, and we all fumble, stumble, and fall. We transgress against others, against ourselves, and against God. And yet why is it that we are not snuffed out like a feeble candle, as well we might be? We persist in breathing and our hearts go on beating because God sustains us. That's God's *chesed*.

An aspect of *chesed* that goes beyond merely being nice is already starting to surface. *Chesed* involves acts that *sustain* the other. This is a dimension of the notion that doesn't come through so clearly when all we think of is loving-kindness. In the Jewish view, it isn't enough to hold warm thoughts in our heart or to wish each other well. We are meant to offer real sustenance to one another, and the ways in which we can do that are innumerable: we can offer our money,[9] time, love, empathy, service, an open ear, manual assistance, a letter written, a call made, and on and on.

Mussar tells us that action is the key to opening the heart. It is too easy to think good thoughts and say the right things but then just continue to be stuck in the same old ways. We're too easy to deceive, especially self-deceive. Action is required. Then, through experience, the heart learns and opens, setting off a chain reaction of hearts opening and connecting, leading right up to openness and connection to God.

Yet not all acts that sustain constitute *chesed*. Some things we might do out of obligation—like paying taxes, which sustains the government and in turn sustains programs that sustain people. But it would be a big stretch to call paying taxes an act of *chesed*.

We might also act to repay goodness done to us, or to offer sustenance with a plan of getting something back for ourselves. Those motives aren't reflective of *chesed*, either.

Here the notion of kindness comes back into the picture. *Chesed* must be some sort of sustaining action, but to qualify as *chesed*, these actions need to come out of kindness and no other motive. This means that in acts of *chesed*, a spirit of generosity motivates our sustaining action. You are not obligated to do it, you aren't repaying an act done for you, you don't hope to get anything in return—you are generously reaching beyond those limited acts to give of yourself in a spirit of honest and selfless generosity. True *chesed* involves offering without any expectation of return, even of gratitude. Any hint of a payback undermines the very essence of *chesed*.

I can hear somebody saying, yes, but what of the inner feeling people get when they know they are doing something good? Isn't that a "reward" of sorts? The Mussar masters tell us that unless you do the act specifically to get that feeling, being joyful in *chesed* does not invalidate the act, if in giving you had to stretch yourself beyond the boundaries of the usual and the comfortable to offer benevolent sustenance to another. Do that and you have surely entered the territory of *chesed*.

It's the quality of generosity in *chesed* that makes it sensible why the Jewish tradition accords service done to the dead as *chesed shel emet*, which translates as "true *chesed*." Only with a dead body can we have absolutely no hope or chance of a payback for our generosity. I'd add, too, from my own experience, that kindness done for nonhuman creatures is similar. People who free whales trapped in fishing nets, nurse injured birds back to health, or work to protect animal rights are not doing it because the bears and the beavers are going to send them a basket of cookies and a thank-you card.

With these additional considerations in mind, I'd now venture to re-translate *chesed* as "generous sustaining benevolence." That's surely more clumsy than the already clumsy "loving-kindness," but it conveys so much more than just being nice and wishing well in your heart.

Giving and Receiving

Generous sustaining benevolence is how Rabbi Eliyahu Dessler understands the trait of *chesed* (which he sees as a primary root of spiritual life).
He writes at the beginning of his *Discourse on Lovingkindness*:[10]

> When God created man, He made him a giver and a taker. The
> power of giving is a higher power of the traits of the Creator of all,
> blessed be He, who has mercy, does good, and gives without receiv-
> ing anything in exchange. . . . Thus He made man, as it is written,
> "In the image of God He made man," for he [man] is able to have
> mercy, do good, and give.
>
> But the power of taking is man's desire to pull to himself every
> thing that comes within his domain. This power is what people
> refer to as "selfish love," and it is the source of all evil.

There is a lot to explore in these few lines, but I want to keep the focus
on the sustaining benevolence that Rabbi Dessler helps us see comes from
the soul-trait of generosity. Man is made in the image of God, which
means that we all have the power to be givers because God, our template,
is a giver. Practicing *chesed* means being a giver. Whenever the equation is
calculated to work out for our benefit, or even if it comes out square, that
can't be *chesed*. Giving in the way of *chesed* requires that we go beyond the
boundaries that are familiar and comfortable to us. We have to stretch
into *chesed* or else it simply isn't *chesed*.

I once heard Rabbi Abraham Yachnes clarify the extent of the stretch
that is necessary to have an action qualify as *chesed*. He said that if you are
walking down the street and someone is walking beside you carrying a
large box, and you offer to help the person carry the box, that's not *chesed*.
You'd simply be a terrible person not to help someone in that situation.
What counts as *chesed* is when you are walking the opposite way from
someone carrying a burden and you turn around to help carry that load
in the direction he or she is going. That's *chesed*.

It is, of course, true that no one would be able to give in this way if there
wasn't also someone there ready to receive their giving. Aren't those all
"takers"? Here Rabbi Dessler makes a useful distinction. We all have the
dual potential to be givers as well as those on the other end of the giving,

but he points to a big difference between those who take gifts into their hands as "receivers" and those who are "takers."

Takers view everything that others do for them as if it were their right and so have no qualms about being the recipient of others' giving. Receivers, in contrast, expect nothing and are filled with gratitude for the slightest benefit conferred upon them. Something comes into the hands of both, but their attitudes are so different that receiving and taking have to be seen as actions that are entirely distinct from each other.

Acts of Loving-Kindness and the Chesed Personality

People who do acts of generous sustaining benevolence are not all the same. The Mussar tradition points out that some people are moved to acts of *chesed* whenever they are confronted by someone who is in need of their help. Others, however, don't wait for that sort of opportunity to arrive on their doorstep, but rather search out any chance to act generously in ways that sustain others. This is what the sages meant when they wrote that the way of those who do *chesed* is to run after the poor.[11]

Abraham was the paragon of what it means to pursue *chesed* because the Torah tells us that he actually ran to do kind acts for others. When three strangers happened by his tent, he invited them to stay. He offered them bread, water, and a little rest, and then

> Abraham rushed to Sarah's tent and said, "Hurry! Three measures
> of the finest flour! Knead it and make rolls."
>   Abraham ran to the cattle and chose a tender, choice calf. He gave
> it to a young man who rushed to prepare it.[12]

The Torah uses verbs meaning "run" and "hurry" a total of four times in relating this brief story. Abraham didn't sit passively waiting for a chance to do good but charged after the opportunity to render kindness to others.

Abraham was not someone who just did *deeds* of *chesed*, but rather he was a soul who was so infused with the *spirit* of *chesed* that this quality defined his very outlook on the world. This distinction helps us understand the deep significance of the quote from the prophet Micah:

He has told you, O man, what is good! What does HaShem your
God ask of you, that you do justice, love *chesed,* and walk humbly
with HaShem your God.

This is all we need to know to fulfill the Creator's vision for our lives on
earth, and what it says about *chesed* isn't what we might ordinarily think.
We are not told that we accomplish our spiritual destiny just by filling up
a scorecard with acts of generous sustaining benevolence, but rather we
are told that we need to *love* those acts. Of course if we love them, we will
surely do them, so the doing is still covered, but really only as a spin-off.
The focus is not on the doing but on the quality of the heart that lives
within us. Love loving-kindness: what a profound demand.

We find out here that it is central to our spiritual job description to
stretch ourselves to sustain one another, and the most important dimension of that behavior is to awaken your heart to love the very act of caring
for the other. Done for any other motive and the act is not *chesed.* It does
not sustain the world, which is the outer mandate of *chesed,* nor does it
move us closer to realizing the purpose of our souls, which is its inner
mandate. But when we get it right, our perfected *chesed* sustains the other
and makes us pious and righteous people. The Hebrew term for "piety" is
chasidut, from the same root as *chesed.*

It's with attaining this outlook in mind that the students in the Mussar
yeshiva of Rabbi Eliyahu Lopian[13] pledged to perform three acts of loving-
kindness in a day. Having a goal like that sent them off searching for kind
deeds they could do and helped them overcome the habitual behavior and the
resistance that stood in the way. Rabbi Lopian joined them in this practice.

Walk after the Eternal Your God

Our instincts for self-preservation run deep, as do our anxieties about
having enough for ourselves, and so our hearts need to be trained to do
chesed, in order that our lives reflect our higher selves more than our
lower. The rabbis understood our resistance and so offer us practical
guidance on how to do acts of *chesed.* They took as their starting point the
biblical instruction to "Walk after the Eternal your God."[14] Then they

asked how we could possibly do such a thing as "walk after God"? We read their conclusion in the Talmud:[15]

> Rabbi Hama son of Rabbi Hanina further said: "What does the text mean: 'Walk after the Eternal your God'? [The meaning is] to walk after the attributes of the Holy One of Blessing. Just as God clothes the naked, so should you clothe the naked, as it is written [Genesis/ *Bereshit* 3:21]: And the Eternal God made garments of skins for Adam and his wife and clothed them. Just as the Holy One of Blessing visited the sick, so should you also visit the sick, as it is written [Genesis/*Bereshit* 18:1]: And the Eternal appeared to him by the terebinths of Mamre.[16] Just as the Holy One of Blessing comforted mourners, so should you also comfort mourners, as it is written [Genesis/*Bereshit* 25:11]: After the death of Abraham, God blessed his son Isaac. Just as the Holy One of Blessing buried the dead, so should you also bury the dead, as it is written [Deuteronomy/ *Devarim* 34:6]: God buried him [Moses] in the valley."

Rabbi Hama's view is that we walk after God by imitating God's deeds of loving-kindness in our own lives. What we have here is a primary guideline for spiritual living, sometimes called *imitatio dei,* meaning that we take on certain very concrete acts of loving-kindness in conscious imitation of the ways of the divine.

When we imitate God's great traits in our own life, this doesn't make us more divine, it just elevates who we already are to the highest potential. Although the Torah tells us that we are made in the image of God, some rabbis see this not as a statement of our present condition but of our potential. Rabbi Shlomo Wolbe, for example, helps us identify just where we can locate that image of God in which we are made: "The image of God is His character traits. When you love kindness, you become the image of God."[17]

Chassidic thought also guides us to adopt the attributes of God in our lives. Chassidism seeks the experience of direct and personal experiential connection to God, and the issue that Rebbe Menachem Nachum of Chernobyl[18] confronts is the difficulty of figuring out how we can cleave to God when we are rooted in this material world, while God is ultimately formless, boundless, and endless:[19]

Boundless God is cloaked within the attributes. When a person holds to the attributes of HaShem, "As he is Merciful . . ." and so on, then he is cleaving to Boundless God, Blessed is He, *Himself*, because Boundless God, Blessed is He, resides within the attributes. Therefore the Sages said, "Cling to His qualities," and thus it is as if he clings to God Himself.

This means that when you bring out a divine quality like *chesed* in your own life, then that is cleaving to God Himself, because God resides within our soul-traits. And so when we act with *chesed*, we find our way to God and draw close to Him.

Signposts for Loving-Kindness

We need to know how God does *chesed* in order to discover the signposts we are to follow in our lives. In the Torah, where thirteen attributes of God's compassion are listed,[20] among them is "abundant in kindness."[21] The medieval commentator Rashi explains that the phrase "abundant in kindness" tells us that God shows kindness to all those who are in need of sustenance, even those who are not deserving of this help. Here we find our model for *chesed*. When we act with sustaining generosity to others not because they deserve it but because we are being kind, beyond any calculation of what they have earned from us or what we can get in return, then we are doing kindness in emulation of God's way of loving-kindness.

Don't worry about loving the poor; your job is to clothe them.

If people you know are ailing in any way, don't just think or even pray for them—take your time to go visit them.

Offer your comfort to the bereaved in a house of mourning.

And burying the dead is the example of active loving-kindness par excellence; since a corpse has no capacity to reciprocate, caring for its needs is purely generous kindness.

This same theme is explored in the sixteenth-century kabbalistic Mussar text *Tomer Devorah* (The Palm Tree of Deborah).[22] The writer, Rabbi Moshe Cordovero, is also concerned with showing us how to bring the qualities of the divine into our lives, though he takes a different biblical text as his starting point. In the Book of Micah we find another verse that lists the attributes of the divine, and among them is the description of God as "He is the one who desires *chesed*."[23]

Rabbi Cordovero brings this lofty teaching down to our level by giving us instructions on how to implement it. He tells us to look beyond what a person might deserve so that our kindness extends into the realm of *chesed*:

> A person should emulate this attribute [*chesed*] in his own conduct. Even if one is aware that another person is doing him evil, and this angers him, if that person has some redeeming quality, for example, he is kind to others, or he possesses some other virtue, this should be sufficient cause for one to dissipate his anger and find the other person pleasing, that is, to delight in the kindness he does. One should say, "It is enough for me that he has this good quality." ... A person should say to himself with regard to every man, "It is enough that he has been good to me or to someone else in such-and-such a way, or that he has such-and-such a positive quality." In this way, one should delight in kindness.

Rabbi Cordovero hands us an extreme situation in which to do *chesed*, when a person is actually doing us evil. Even in that case, however, we are not given dispensation to avoid sustaining the other, but rather instruction on how to overcome our predictable resistance. The rabbis understood that *chesed* represents so primary a force of the soul that it needs to be cultivated regardless of logic and circumstance.

Even in more ordinary situations, we are likely to find resistance to doing deeds of generous benevolence that sustain others. If you give in to that resistance, you will stop short of acting with loving-kindness, with negative results for both inner and outer life. If you overcome it, you will have made the world a better place for someone while strengthening the place of your higher self in your own life.

The Test of Loving-Kindness

Overcoming resistance to doing generous sustaining acts is a primary spiritual test. To help you appreciate the reality of the struggle to bring higher self to the forefront, let's consider the four situations where we ought to do *chesed* that the Talmud identifies for us. Consider what comes up for you when you actually imagine doing what we are told to do in these cases.

Clothing the Naked

If you saw a naked person in the street, would you run to clothe them, or would you more likely shy away, thinking to yourself, "crazy"? Perhaps you have other ways of resisting the poor and the needy. Right now, what (if anything) is stopping you from sorting through your drawers and cupboards to empty out all the unworn old clothing to give away?

Clothing the naked can mean taking care of people's material requirements in whatever ways they have needs.

Visiting the Sick

Visiting the sick means offering care and companionship to anyone who is not feeling whole, whether in body, soul, or mind. Is there anything preventing you from picking up the phone to call and volunteer some of your time in a local hospital or seniors' home? Perhaps you are familiar with some (or all) of the following rationalizations that keep you from offering your support to those who are ailing:

- "I just hate hospitals."
- "What good would it do?"
- "I'm not such a close friend."
- "They probably have hundreds of visitors and I'll just be in the way."

Or do you have your own special favorite?

Comforting the Bereaved

Do you know someone who recently lost a person who was dear to them? Could you visit, or at least phone? Many people feel resistance to visiting a house of mourning because contact with death, even indirectly, can make people feel nervous or even frightened. Jewish tradition helps us deal with this resistance by giving us guidelines for comforting mourners. One is to enter the house of mourning quietly. The mourners are not hosts and so are not expected to greet the visitors, rise for them, offer them hospitality (like food or drink), or see them out. Most important, one who has come to comfort a mourner should sit close to them without speaking first. Our nervousness or our own needs can make us babble, but we are guided to let the mourners speak first, if they so desire. That way, too, they get to choose the subject about which they want to speak.

Bereavement arises from loss, and comfort is a great salve for all sorts of losses, not just death. Do you know someone who lost their job, or who had to move to a new house, or whose pet died, or who suffered any other sort of loss, and can you find a way to offer your comfort to them?

Burying the Dead

Few of us have any responsibilities for burying bodies because that task has been handed to undertakers and funeral directors. We live cut off from the reality of death, hoping to still its influence by looking the other way. It doesn't work. People die and bodies still need to be dealt with. In the Jewish community, volunteer committees care for the bodies of the dead.[24] Would you consider doing a stint in such a group?

What dead do you have to bury? What relationships need to be ended, finally? What tasks need to be done and concluded? What unfinished business needs to be wrapped up?

If I Am Only for Myself, What Am I?

You can do any and all of these deeds, and you will do them, if you can get over any inner resistance that may be holding you back. You are to ask your heart to enter joyfully into the love of generously sustaining the other. It's typical of Mussar teaching to urge you to step into just those situations where you are inured to feeling, where your behavior has sunk into the habitual, where you have built walls of defense, where your fears lurk. When you put yourself into action, habits and fears are likely to come to the surface, where they can be confronted and dispelled. Even the thought of taking these actions can bring up old fears, and once exposed to the light, they can be seen, acknowledged, and ultimately banished. The heart and the world are then called into connection. The results register in the outer world, which will be sustained by your kindness, as well as in your inner world, where your higher self will have gained more strength and dominion.

You will then be liberated from the grasp of your resistance, and grow.

This is an especially important message for members of our generation, the me-generation, founded on the antithesis of *chesed*, whom the poet Adrienne Rich identifies so painfully well:

> In those years, people will say, we lost track
> of the meaning of we, of you
> we found ourselves
> reduced to I
> and the whole thing became
> silly, ironic, terrible

Tradition echoes this reminder that life is not about every man for himself. Hillel puts it, "If I am only for myself, what am I?"[25] To be someone is also to be for the other and the expression of that virtue is *chesed*.

Hillel's statement ends with a challenge: "If not now, when?"

> A day should not pass without acts of lovingkindness,
> either with one's body, money, or soul.
>
> —Rabbi Yeshayahu Segal Horowitz,
> *Sh'nei Luchot ha'Brit*

21

Responsibility

ACHRAYUT

I am your guarantor; you are my guarantor.[1]

This world is like the eve of the Sabbath
and the World-to-Come is like the Sabbath.
One who prepares on the eve of the Sabbath
will have food to eat on the Sabbath.

—*Tamid 7*

A FRIEND'S SON confessed to his grandfather that he felt guilty because
he didn't go to synagogue very often. "Good enough!" said his grandfather, hitting right on the nose the unfortunate connection that is too often
made between guilt and matters of religion or spirit. As we open the discussion of the soul-trait of responsibility, it is important to look for a way
to embrace responsibility that is wholesome, positive, and nurturing to
the soul—and not with guilt, because guilt is none of those things.

It is unquestionable that we are all responsible and we are held responsible. Rob a bank, be indifferent in a relationship, or just sink into laziness,
and you can count on there being consequences because it is a fact of life
that you are responsible. Even if you happen to "get away with it," there is
your conscience to contend with. Some of us have very lively consciences
that prick us over every little misdemeanor, while others seem to be quite
content to evade, deny, and rationalize. But those denials are superficial.
Somewhere deeper within, the denied conscience goes about its corrosive
(and restorative) work. The Hebrew word for conscience—*matzpun*—is
from the same root as the word for "north," no doubt because conscience
sets the navigational compass for life.

The Hebrew term consistently translated into English as "responsibility" is *achrayut*, or *achrayus*. We can learn a lot about the intrinsically

Jewish concept behind a soul-trait by investigating the root of the word, and in the case of *achrayut,* there is disagreement—and this disagreement itself is instructive.

Some say the root of *achrayut* is *achar,* which means "after."[2] Others say it is *acher,* meaning "other."[3] These two different sources reveal different aspects of the soul-trait of responsibility. Ultimately, though, they both come to point at the same issue in living.

When we establish the notion of responsibility in the realm of *time*— that is, finding the root of this soul-trait in the concept "after"—we are drawn toward recognizing that every single thought, word, or deed has its "after"—its antecedent and its consequence, connecting up in a great chain of cause and effect that spreads over time. We humans are unique among creatures in being able to anticipate consequences to the extent that we can, and as a result, we bear responsibility for our actions.

"Who is wise?" asks *Pirkei Avot,*[4] and Rabbi Shimon ben Netanel answers, "One who sees what is born [i.e., the outcome]."

And because we are able to foresee the future and we are wise to do so, the principle is established in the Mishnah[5] that human beings are always responsible for the consequences of their actions, whether what occurred was the result of action that was voluntary or involuntary, deliberate or inadvertent. We'll soon modify this all-encompassing view of our responsibility, but the message here is clear that each of us is called upon to take responsibility now for what we will cause to happen *after.*

Jewish thought about the future and our responsibility for it is tied into notions of the two worlds—this one in which we live now, and the one "to come."[6] We are guided to be concerned about damages we might cause in this world and also in the future world where spiritual eternity plays out. If we have a sense that we ought to care for the world we live in, how much more for the aeons of time that make up eternity?

The spiritual dimension of earthly responsibility is brought out in a discussion that takes place in the Talmud[7] in response to the question of what a person should do to develop personal piety and to become more saintly. One opinion says we should study *Pirkei Avot,* which contains so much wisdom for living. Another is to study the laws of blessings, which reveal how a person should utter blessings in the many contexts in which you go about your daily activities, such as upon waking in the morning, washing, going to the bathroom, eating, praying, studying, and so on. The third, and often considered winning, opinion is that of Rav Yehuda, who says, "Someone who wants to be saintly should fulfill matters of civil torts." That is, a person who wants to be more pious should know and fulfill the laws of damages as laid out in the Talmudic tractate *Bava Kamma*.

It's challenging and, at first glance, very surprising to think that a legal tract on monetary losses would be the ideal focus for developing more personal piety, but that is exactly what this voice from the Jewish tradition tells us. What's the message?

It is fairly easy to see that taking responsibility for the consequences of damaging actions will help preserve the civil peace and keep relations among people harmonious. But recall that the initial question was about steps to take to become a Chasid, a pious one. It is mysterious how learning the laws that cover such situations like my ox goring your cow could make me a more spiritual person, to the point of even being called pious. But there is a very particular logic here that gives us a valuable insight about how to cultivate the soul-trait of responsibility.

The Talmud in *Bava Kamma* seems to focus on civil litigation, but its real concern is a person's relationships with other people. Everything taught there has the implicit purpose of revealing to us how to be more considerate to our fellow human beings, not in some abstract sense but in the very real and practical places where we interact with them, especially in the areas that are prone to conflict. How can we be helpful to others even when they do not reciprocate? How can we act so as not to cause harm? What can we do to make amends when we do cause damage? We must always see that the other person also has a valid point of view.

These concerns reflect the Mussar principle that our personal spiritual advancement takes place not separate from but rather right in the midst of our relations with other people. It was Rabbi Yisrael Salanter himself who stated that the foundation of a spiritual life lies between a person and his friend.[8] To my knowledge, Mussar is unique among major spiritual paths in handing us the challenge of making our human relationships into the primary focus for our spiritual efforts. We know that it is relatively easy to feel spiritually top-drawer in a synagogue or on a meditation cushion or in a mountaintop cave, where we have effectively insulated ourselves from the sorts of provocations that really test us, as well as from the people who are close to us, who can provoke us and test us like nothing else. Mussar doesn't let you off the hook by encouraging transcendence of this world, but instead takes you by the shoulders and turns you around so that you face squarely all the (real or potential) messes, breakage, or offenses you might have had a role in causing. Take responsibility, it says. If you made that mess, clean it up. Better still, foresee the mess and take responsibility *before* it happens, so there won't even be a mess for you to have to clean up afterward. Any spiritual undertaking that sidesteps or minimizes the importance of this sort of responsibility is purveying fantasy of one kind or another.

We are talking here about foreseeing (and perhaps avoiding) consequences for which we will be responsible. It's important to qualify this by saying that this applies only to matters over which we have choice. We are considered to be most liable when we have had the freedom and ability to have chosen otherwise—and yet didn't. Rabbi Eliyahu Dessler tells us as much:

> No one is held responsible for the evil to which he is accustomed from birth and as a result of his environment, never having learned any better. In this respect he has the halachic status of "a child taken captive and brought up among idolaters." He will be held responsible only for that which he could and should have learnt.[9]

To elevate your soul in the direction of holiness, you have to become more skilled at anticipating the consequences of your actions and taking responsibility for the details in all areas where you make choices, even in the most practical and mundane sorts of ways—or, more accurately, *specifically* in the practical and mundane matters you might tend to overlook or to consider other than spiritual. Rabbi Yissocher Frand, eulogizing Rabbi Naftoli Neuberger of the Ner Israel Yeshiva in Baltimore, said: "When someone was starting a new synagogue and asked Rav Neuberger for advice, Reb Naftoli even went with him to the bank to help fill out the paperwork to open an account. Had he nothing better to do? But he had to see it taken care of, he took responsibility."

The court report section of the daily newspaper reveals what an uncommonly elevated way of being this is. We human beings far prefer to put on blinders and adopt all sorts of rationalizations that permit us to avoid shouldering responsibility and even to do all kinds of harm. When confronted with the damage we have caused, we are prone to taking refuge in denial. But when we elevate responsibility for even the details into personal spiritual practice, we deny ourselves all opportunity for self-imposed blindness and rationalization, and thus do ourselves an enormous spiritual favor.

This, then, is how we can understand responsibility in terms of what comes "after" in this world. You are responsible to do good and will be held responsible for doing wrong, so it is best to foresee outcomes and choose now to do good. The soul will thrive.

If Not in This Life

Some Mussar teachers extend this concept and dwell not on the outcomes of our actions in this world but rather on the eternal consequences of what we do, that is, what will happen to us in the World-to-Come. Jewish sources don't agree on the nature of this eternal world, and it is truly beyond my capacity to imagine this realm, but throughout the Jewish tradition since after the time of the Bible we find affirmation that the soul survives the physical death of the body and, at that point, is rewarded for the good that was done in life and punished for the bad. Taking together this world and that world, we find that we are not only responsible for the car accidents we cause and the hearts we break, but we also reap for all eternity the fruits of our behavior. This is the next level of "after" for which we need to realize that we are held responsible.

Rabbi Yisrael Salanter, and especially his disciple, Rabbi Itzele Peterburger (Blazer), were graphic in their depiction of the consequences of transgression, though the roots of the notion of "reward and punishment" run deep in Jewish thought. The Talmud puts it as succinctly as can be: "The wicked deepen hell[10] for themselves."[11]

Rabbi Salanter provides details of what to expect in the World-to-Come and links those predictable rewards and punishments directly back to our own choices and actions, for which we are responsible:

The pain is frightening and terrible, while the pleasure is wondrous and supreme. [The pain and pleasure of the Next World] far exceeds that which one is capable of feeling in this world, while still connected to the body. This future pain and pleasure is dependent

on a person's actions—how the self conducts itself in this world. By
observing and fulfilling the Almighty's commandments, a person—the self—will attain sublime delight. Conversely, if one transgresses the commandments, he will be subjected to terrible pain
and suffering.[12]

No denying that this sort of concern for reward and punishment is
there in the tradition, but I confess that it does not have much impact on
me personally as a motivator for responsibility. I am therefore grateful
(and happy to report) that from at least the eighteenth century we hear
voices from within the tradition saying that fear of punishment for our
actions—and hence the reason to take responsibility—isn't the highest of
spiritual motivations. In *The Path of the Just*, Rabbi Moshe Chaim Luzzatto
considers punishment to be the lowest of three possibilities. He doesn't
deny it, however, and neither should we, since accentuating fear of punishment may serve you well as an effective motivator to take responsibility and make change now. If it does, you have many spiritual ancestors to
support you in this.

More recent Mussar teachers have been leading us away from this particular image of the afterlife. Rabbi Shlomo Wolbe, for example, writes
that today, rather than being a motivator, threat of punishment is likely to
incite more rebellion than compliance. He doesn't dispute that we will
each face an ultimate reckoning, but he plays down fear of punishment as
not being well suited to this generation that has been raised on democ-
racy, rights, and personal freedoms.

The influential religious leader and mystic Rabbi Abraham Isaac Kook[13]
goes even further, asserting that fear of punishment is not a worthy motivation for a religious and spiritual life. It is, he says, "the product of a weak
personality; it is not a beneficial trait that should be emulated."[14] Of
course he would be aware that there are voices in the Jewish tradition that
for centuries have been saying the opposite.

Although we have here Jewish guides who are sensitive to modern sen-
sibilities as they steer us away from leaning our soul-trait of responsibility
on fear of punishment, they certainly would not deny the existence of the
World-to-Come nor of the personal reckoning that will have to be given by
each of us. But what exactly might that mean? In Rabbi Wolbe's view, there
is certainly a World-to-Come, but he doesn't identify it as some heavenly

realm that awaits beyond death: "The World to Come is the most internal of internal worlds! God is deep inside the World to Come. To get to the World to Come you have to build your own internal world during your life, and it is with that internal world that you will enter the World to Come."[15]

Though Rabbi Wolbe's perspective is different, the difference is not all that significant in relation to the subject of responsibility. He, too, sees responsibility arising out of the concept of "after," meaning concern for what lies ahead. We are reminded forcefully of the fact that our actions have real consequences for which we are responsible and for which we are urged to take responsibility now, before it is too late. He tells us that where we take responsibility and where we reap the fruit is in our interior world, the world of consciousness and spirit that is there for us to cultivate right now. As well, if your cosmology includes an afterlife in the way of the earlier Jewish mainstream, your sense of personal responsibility takes on much more weight when you realize that your actions will have an impact on the journey your soul will take for all eternity.

Bearing the Burden of the Other

But the soul-trait of responsibility—*achrayut*—has another possible root besides the notion of "after." The other candidate that offers to help us understand what lies at the heart of the notion of responsibility is the word *acher,* meaning "other." This shift seems to take us in a radically different direction. The core idea here is that something beyond us is calling on us to fulfill an obligation. What could that "other" be, and what is the nature of our responsibility to it?

Rabbi Simcha Zissel Ziv, the Alter of Kelm, developed the notion of responsibility to others to its highest form. "Bearing the burden of the other" is how he put it. This concept became the basis not only of his thought but also of the practices he embraced to guide his students on a level-by-level spiritual progression.

The source he draws on to root his spiritual teaching in tradition is explicit. He cites it right in the first line of his book *Chochmah u'Mussar* [Wisdom and Mussar],[16] where he writes, "Our sages taught: One of the methods by which the Torah is acquired is by carrying the burden of our fellow [neighbor]."

He is referring to the sixth chapter of *Pirkei Avot*, which says: "The Torah is acquired in forty-eight ways. These are . . ." and then it lists point by point the qualities and actions that lead to the acquisition of the Torah and the elevation of spiritual life (which are synonymous). Number 39 on the list is "sharing his friend's burden." Rabbi Simcha Zissel interprets this to mean "to diligently seek the benefit of the other in every possible way."

Of course, it's possible and even good to interpret this as guidance to do good deeds, help out around the house, be a contributing member of society. This would be an interpretation consistent with the notion of responsibility. Rabbi Simcha Zissel aims deeper within us, however, taking as his working premise that life is about developing the qualities of the soul. In his view, bearing the burden of the other becomes not just good social behavior but the central practice he taught to bring about a profound realization of the soul's destiny. In acts of caring for the other, he saw one focus that encompassed all others and a route to the development of both mind and heart.

> This is the reason why our ancestors occupied themselves as shepherds like Jacob, peace be upon him, and David. Moses our teacher was also a shepherd because he wanted to accustom himself to bear the burden even of the simple creatures and all the more so of fellow human beings. . . . David would bring out the young sheep first to pasture in order that they could graze the best grass. Afterward, he would take out the old ones in order to give them ordinary grass. Finally, he would bring out the strong ones who could graze on the tough grass. . . . As our Rabbis said: "When Moses our teacher, peace be upon him, was the shepherd of Yitro, one of my lambs fled and Moses ran after it until it reached a watering hole where the lamb had stopped to drink. When Moses arrived he said: 'I did not know that you fled on account of thirst. You must be tired.' He lifted him on his shoulders and walked."

The contrary case is of a man who was not a shepherd and who asked famously, "Am I my brother's keeper?"[17] Cain's words have come to symbolize people's unwillingness to accept responsibility for the welfare of the other. The Alter of Kelm identifies this tendency in all of us and urges us to recognize that, yes, we are our brothers' keepers, and not just for our brothers' sake. Rabbi Ira Stone, translator of Rabbi Simcha Zissel's words, sums up his spiritual teaching by saying, "The ego develops as the object of love, the soul as its subject." In other words, bearing the burden of the other is action that cultivates the soul of the doer. The ego wants everything for me, cares only for me, and it is by learning and struggling to bear the burden of the other that one is enabled to overcome the insistent voice of the ego as the guiding source in life. Taking responsibility for others in their physical and emotion needs is nothing less than the method to free ourselves from the grip of ego that is always clamoring to be satisfied and yet never is.

Rabbi Simcha Zissel's teacher was Rabbi Yisrael Salanter, and Rabbi Salanter provides us with a succinct statement to remind us how the work we do for others feeds the soul: "Spiritual needs are more elevated than material needs," he said. "But the material needs of another are an obligation of my spiritual life." My soul cannot develop, refine, and ascend except through caring for the needs of others. Why? The logic is not obscure. An elevated soul must be a sensitive soul, and you couldn't possibly be sensitive without feeling the pain and suffering endured by others. And if you were (and hopefully are) a sensitive soul like this and so you did feel the burden that others bear, you couldn't possibly hold yourself back from taking a role in helping them out.

This chain of connections provides the practice you can take on in life to bring the soul to its higher state. Making the effort to bear the burdens of others—as a conscious, deliberate practice—diminishes the power of ego to commandeer your life and also instills sensitivity in the soul that might otherwise not be there. Each act of support you undertake is an opportunity to develop finer sensitivity and to elevate the soul you are.

That Rabbi Simcha Zissel gave more than lip service to this insight is revealed in the fact that there were almost no employees in the large yeshiva he ran. Every task was performed by the students themselves. The more menial the task, the more highly it was valued, with the most menial tasks going only to the senior students. One of the mottos of the small groups within his yeshiva to which students were assigned was: "Do not go a single day without doing something for someone else, whether directly or by money or by speech."

That this idea and guidance is a central principle of Jewish living is revealed in a fundamental difference between civil and Jewish law. Under common law a person who merely sees the lost property of another person is under no obligation to take possession of the object and to arrange its return. Jewish law, by contrast, says that one who sees lost property is fully obligated to involve himself in that property and to assist in its return. Three verses in the Torah[18] provide the basis for this obligation, including: "When you see your brother's ox or sheep going astray, do not ignore them; you must return them to him."[19]

Jewish law is based on an encompassing worldview that, in this case, reveals the responsibility we have to others. Corroboration for this notion comes from a perhaps unlikely source. It is Elie Wiesel who warns us:

> Consideration for others must precede scholarship. Abstract erudition may turn into a futile game of the intellect. Words are links not only between words but also between human beings. The emphasis on the *other* is paramount in Judaism: *Achrayut,* responsibility, contains the word *Akher* [*acher*], the Other. We are responsible for the other.[20]

Caring for the other is essential to our own spiritual lives. As the sage Hillel says in *Pirkei Avot:* "If I am not for myself, who will be for me? But if I am only for myself, what am I?" He questions: "If I am only for myself, what am I?" The answer is that I am an ego, nothing more. Mussar sees connecting oneself to others as a great antidote to the selfishness that lies at the root of every negative soul-trait. Only by stretching to bear the burden of the other do I extend my being beyond ego and come to live in the realm of soul that is my potential and my highest destiny.

We can find examples of people who were very diligent in bearing the burden of the other because they understood this to be a central pathway on the way of the soul they were committed to walking.

In the biography of Rabbi Aryeh Levin,[21] called *A Tzaddik in Our Time,* we read that Reb Aryeh dug into his own funds to support a young Torah scholar who was learned and devout but very poor. At some point, the young man found out that Reb Aryeh was friendly with a rabbi who did not share the young man's viewpoint on certain things. He then refused to take any more funding from Reb Aryeh. Instead of being insulted and maybe even vindictive, as would be understandable, Reb Aryeh undertook to continue supporting him. He found an intermediary and continued to channel funds to the man, though the young scholar never knew from whom the money really came. Such was his determination to shoulder responsibility to bear the burden of other.

That we can draw meaning and inspiration to be responsible by rooting *achrayut* in *acher*—other—has, I hope, been made clear. This is both a primary spiritual value of Mussar and a practice as well. When we consider bearing the burden of the other as a practice, however, one more important consideration needs to be explained. It is relatively easy to say and explain the spiritual value of carrying others, but this is very difficult to do. As noted, one of the spiritual benefits of this practice is the effect it has on de-centering ego in your life. Can you guess where resistance comes from?

Resistance to Responsibility

The more a person tries to take on supporting others, the more the ego will protest, at least until the new pathways are well established and the ego is made to realize that it is not threatened by this way of living. If the ego is already feeling strong and self-esteem runs high, then it is not likely to feel as threatened when we open our hearts and extend our hands to others, and here we find many Mussar voices chiming in to say yes, a healthy ego is very important to spiritual life.

Rabbi Elyakim Krumbein points out what might not, at first glance, be obvious: "Praiseworthy humility is always associated with healthy self-esteem. Lack of self-esteem leads to the damaging feeling of worthlessness."[22] Focusing on the soul-trait that most commonly supplants humility—arrogance—Rabbi Krumbein links that state not with being full of oneself, as if to say with an overblown ego, but rather (surprisingly and counterintuitively) the opposite:

> We diagnosed *gaava* [arrogance] as stemming from lack of self-esteem—the wallowing preoccupation with one's past achievements, which is needed to compensate for the missing conviction of self-worth.

Since humility is considered by *all* Mussar teachers to be the essential trait on which to build all other traits, the entire structure of inner life can be seen to stand on healthy self-esteem.

It appears to me (and I hope to you as well) that we have now come full circle. I opened my discussion in this chapter by stating that a healthy sense of responsibility does not arise from guilt, and now I am saying that the soul-trait of responsibility rests squarely on a quality quite the opposite to guilt, which is positive self-esteem. Guilt is all about "should." In the two approaches in which I have explored responsibility, I have come to two very different sources of motivation.

When we think of responsibility as deriving from awareness of "after" (*achar*), contemplating and including in your calculations the possible consequences of your actions requires that you overcome the urge to satisfy your ego and your desires right now.

In regard to the second derivation of *achrayut*—from *acher,* meaning "other"—to live a life in which you actively reach out to bear the burden of your neighbor requires that you quiet the demanding voice of desire and ego in order that you can hear the voice and feel the need of the other and respond.

Though these roots may be different, they both connect up to the same stalk. The message is clear. We are capable of being responsible, and indeed we are inclined to be responsible. There is also undeniable benefit both practically and spiritually to being responsible. But we face a major obstacle to being responsible, which is our tendency to slavishly feed our selves in this moment. This is a force as strong as gravity for us to overcome. Responsibility, then, takes on even greater importance because it stands for and reflects a central thrust of spiritual growth, which is to rise up and beyond living in our small self who is interested only in gratification in the present, to evolve into the larger self who, from its elevated vantage point, can see and take in both the larger sweep of time and the living presence of others. Responsibility is both the means and the fruit of that evolution.

> First a person should put his house together, then his
> town, then the world.
>
> —Rabbi Yisrael Salanter

22

Trust

BITACHON

Blessed be the one who trusts in the Lord and the Lord shall be his source of trust.

—Jeremiah 17:7

A person who tries to practice trust in God while leaving himself a backup plan is like a person who tries to learn how to swim but insists on keeping one foot on the ground.

—Rabbi Yosef Yozel Hurwitz, Alter of Novarodok

THIS WORLD CAN APPEAR so unpredictable sometimes. Hurricanes, earthquakes, tsunamis, wildfires, and other natural disasters can and do strike at any moment. Your life can suddenly be overturned by illness or accident or financial setback. And most of all, there is the unaccountable cruelty, incompetence, and stupidity of people. A level-headed view of life seems to offer us every justification to be worried and anxious.

Yet the soul yearns to trust. No one wants to live with anxiety and worry. When I am in the place where trust runs strong, life is manageable, and when trust has slipped away, life is a difficult, daunting struggle.

The soul-trait of "trust"[1] actually doesn't just mean trust, it means "trust in God." Including God in the definition may offer you some help, or it may bring on an additional challenge, depending on the role faith plays in your life. Growing in *bitachon* (trust) is a very different proposition for a person who already has a strong relationship to the divine as opposed to someone who has no active sense of Who/What he or she is being asked to trust.

God has a big role in this soul-trait, though in reality God is integral to all of Mussar. Including the divine in our reflections on our inner life is what elevates this tradition above and beyond psychology and self-help.

The Ramban[2] unambiguously stands trust on the foundation of faith:

> Faith and trust are two separate concepts. The latter is dependent on the former, while the former is independent of the latter. Faith precedes trust, and can exist in a believer's heart even when he lacks trust, for faith can exist without trust. Trust, however, denotes the existence of faith, for it is impossible for trust to precede it or to endure independently.[3]

But even assuming that you do have a sense of a relationship with HaShem, how could you possibly lean trustingly on a God who allows a million children to be killed in the Holocaust, who sweeps 150,000 people to their deaths in a tsunami, who permits AIDS and smallpox and ALS, who rains fire on the innocent and allows the guilty to die comfortable and secure in their beds? If this is what our omniscient, omnipotent divinity does, then it seems you'd have to be crazy to trust that God. And perhaps you'd conclude that the sum total of the suffering, evil, and madness in the world is just sure proof that there really is no God at all.

In a discussion in which I participated, a woman kept objecting to the idea of developing an inner sense of trust, and finally came out with her reason: "Are you telling me that I should feel trust in a God that allowed my ex-husband to sexually abuse our daughter?" And until you have stood in her shoes, you can't possibly know what you would think or feel in that situation, yet the startling answer from tradition is: yes, you should trust God.

This Difficult World

This world is so riddled with disasters and wars, moral failures and gross indifference, lies, betrayals, and violations, and that just begins the catalog of affronts. Arguments against the existence of God—all of which double as reasons not to trust God—often rest on the long list of undeniably terrible circumstances that disturb our enjoyment and deny us satisfaction in life. If the plan is that we are supposed to live happy and fulfilled lives, it doesn't seem to make a shred of sense for God to run the world the way God does.

Surely God would have had no trouble making a world that was free of all the terrible things that make us suffer and so undercut our trust. But have you ever wondered what it would be like to live in a perfect world, where everyone greeted you with a sincere smile, where the dictionary definition of *lock* was only "strand of hair," and in which there were no such words as *cheat* or *jail*? That Pleasantville world would be so boring and pointless that after a very short while, it would feel more intolerable than the terribly flawed world we already have.

More important, however, is the truth that we humans couldn't possibly manage in a world that went along without terrible events. If we lived in a safe and comfortable world and knew with certainty that there was no chance of a negative consequence to our actions, then we would have no reason not to act recklessly. Don't feel like rushing? Don't worry, God will divert the train. Too lazy to shop or cook? That's God's problem, too. Life would make even less sense than it does today.

So we're caught between this familiar world of pain and loss on the one hand and the alternative of mind-numbing predictability on the other. Of course, we really don't have that choice, because the world is as the world is. But where you do have a choice is over how you evaluate and respond to this world. It is up to you whether you see this world as a very botched creation, for which God is to blame, or whether you accept that this apparently flawed life is actually just as it should be, created in God's wisdom, and act accordingly.

I'll tell you why I think it makes sense that God created this world the way it is, replete with all its difficulties. It's because it's not our job description to become happy and fulfilled. The head-on pursuit of happiness and satisfaction is very unlikely to succeed in a world like ours. If celebrity were the answer, movie stars would not be the addiction-prone, suicide-prone casualties of our culture that they are. If the answer to life was wealth, the rich would be happy. You name it (whatever "it" is), if that were the key to life, then the people who had "it" would not suffer the way the rest of us do. But the truth is that everyone who is alive is subject to "the slings and arrows of outrageous fortune."[4]

Yet it is only when you are running after the elusive goal of being happy that this world seems so terrible. If you think that you are supposed to be the master of your life—as if that were possible—the terrible happenings that inevitably come your way in this imperfect world are defeats. They make happiness impossible. But the Jewish tradition actually gives us a different job description, one that fits much better with this world just as it is. It advises us not to seek happiness but to recognize instead that we are meant to be servants of God. From that vantage point, the world seems a rather fitting place to live, even with all its shocks and sorrows. As a servant of God, the challenges of life are just the stuff of a day's labor in the fields of the Lord. Though the direct pursuit of happiness is a sure-fire recipe for suffering, living your life as a servant of God paradoxically makes happiness possible. This may be the irony of ironies, or just the secret we need to uncover to make the whole puzzle work.

We know from experience that we can't rely on life to deliver everything we want, or even need, but it is certain that we can rely on life to give us the challenges that are fitting to the life of a servant.

It is given over to our free will to *opt* to be servants of God, and in so doing, we choose freely to align ourselves deferentially with God's will and order. Trust is not a philosophical principle; it is a practiced act. The result is foretold: "Fortunate are those who trust in Him."[5] Rabbi Ibn Pakuda fills in the detail: One who trusts in God "neither worries nor laments." She is "free of worldly cares" and "lives in perpetual repose, security and tranquility." He "is pleased with everything, even it if goes against his grain."[6]

Now we have come to the crux of the matter. When you accept that being a servant of God is your job description, then trust is warranted. And God can be trusted. And life works.

What exactly does it mean to trust God? *Bitachon* comes in two forms.

Under the Wing of God

There is the trust that God will look out for you. This is the trust that says God will deliver the providence you want and need. When you are on an airplane, you trust that God won't let it fall from the sky. If you have children in Israel, you trust that they will not be endangered by a terrorist attack. The classic image for this sort of *bitachon* is the story of the manna that fell from the sky every day, and each person could collect only what he or she needed for that day. The manna couldn't be accumulated or hoarded because it would rot overnight. So every day there was food for that day only, but no security about what would come tomorrow. The people had to go about their lives with clear awareness that they had no control over their sustenance. They could only trust, and they were provided for.

Rabbi Yosef Yozel Hurwitz, the Alter of Novarodok, understood *bitachon* in this way. He wrote:

> The man of *Bitachon* can turn away from all of life's problems for he knows that he will not want. What he must provide for the needs of the body, he does in peace and contentment for he knows that no one can take away what the Creator allotted to him. In times of danger he does not tremble. He walks securely and does not fear for tomorrow, for as long as he relies on the Almighty, he has everything.[7]

The Alter of Novarodok was radical in his pursuit of trust in God. He would send his students two hundred miles from the yeshiva on a one-way train ticket with instructions to find their way back—so they would learn to trust and not fear. So important was this trait to him that for years he would sign his letters just with the initials "B.B.," standing for "*ba'al bitachon*"—master of trust.

Nothing Happens by Chance

There is another more reasonable, less radical version of trust based on an attitude of acceptance. You don't expect that everything will turn out as you want, but instead accept whatever happens because you understand that there is reason and order behind the world—that nothing takes place without a reason, even if the reason is not apparent to you at the moment. So you still don't worry whether you will get food tomorrow, not because you feel assured that food will come, but because you accept whatever lies in store for you.

This sort of trust doesn't entitle you to walk through a dangerous neighborhood at night with assurance that you won't get mugged. It doesn't mean you can drive fast with no fear of having an accident. That's not trust—that's just unintelligent wishful thinking that actually runs counter to the guidance of tradition, which tells us that we have an obligation to guard ourselves from potential harm.[8] Exposing yourself to danger does not reflect trust in God, it reflects the trait of recklessness.

The Chazon Ish[9] argued for trust based on acceptance, defining this soul-trait as "total belief that nothing in this world happens by chance—Ha'Shem determines all that will happen."[10] This is not the trust that you will be safe, but rather that if you are hurt, there is real meaning and purpose to the pain. We are handicapped because we can only see part of the picture of life at any time, and often only a small part, and so we draw faulty conclusions about what something means.

In the Torah we find many individuals crying out to God for explanation. God always answers, though not necessarily before the petitioner has been brought to the edge of despair, and not necessarily in the form that we might expect. Consistently, the answers God gives are only partial or ambiguous and always need to be completed or interpreted. God never showed our ancestors the blueprint so they would understand, and there is no reason to hope that we are going to be given any more of a privileged insider's view on reality. Maybe that's because understanding how the universe works is ultimately beyond human comprehension. Beyond recognizing our limitations, we need to be able to learn from these models—and what they tell us is that our spiritual curriculum involves developing a free trust in God based on *ambiguous* signs.

The Chafetz Chaim told a story to make the point that we have to be careful about how we interpret the signs we see around us.

A man was once visiting a small town. As it was Shabbat morning, he went to the local synagogue, where everything was just as you might expect, until unusual things started happening. There were well-dressed, obviously prosperous people seated near the front, but all the honors for the Torah reading were given to scruffy men who stood clustered at the back of the room. When it came time for the rabbi to say a few words of wisdom, all he spoke about was the weather. After the prayers were finished, lovely food was spread on the table and nobody ate.

The man was flummoxed by all these incomprehensible goings-on. What kind of place was this? Was everyone crazy? Finally, he pulled aside one of the locals and asked, "What's going on here? The men who got the Torah honors, the rabbi's talk, the uneaten food ... nothing makes any sense!"

The man explained, "Those scruffy-looking men had been unjustly imprisoned and the community worked long and hard to ransom them to freedom. Isn't it wonderful that they are now free to come to bless the Torah? The rabbi spoke only about the weather because there has been an unusual drought this season and the farmers have nothing on their minds but their crops, and the rabbi knew and cared for their concerns. Why didn't anyone eat? One Shabbos every month the community prepares its usual lunch but instead of eating it, the food is donated to the local home for the elderly. I can see how it might have looked to you," the local man told the guest, "but when you can see only part of a picture, it's easy to put together the wrong impression of what is going on."

This is a parable for our own lives. Since at every moment you can see only part of the situation, then you can't possibly know what is really going on. That will be revealed only in the fullness of time. In the meantime, though, your task is to trust.

At times trusting can be an enormous challenge, when the burden of life itself is enormous. Try to put yourself in this student's shoes, if you can, and appreciate how far she got in processing her unimaginably difficult situation, emerging still to trust:

> Are you saying I should take the rape of my daughter by her father as "God's will"? Having moved through this particular abyss, I can no longer abide simple poetic words that tell me the past is God's will.
>
> I have arrived at a place where I trust that no matter what mess mankind makes, no matter what the devastation, God can bring good and right from it. I do not believe it was ever in God's plan for my child to be raped, or for the other one hundred atrocities I could name off the top of my head. Our free will to ignore God at any moment makes this earth. And earth is hard. However, I can now trust that God will be with me as I walk through my particular fires and will be there to provide the ways and means of healing.

Have you ever looked back over an episode in your life, or maybe your whole life itself, and only been able to see the story line in retrospect? Who in the moment could have seen the big picture? No one in the middle of a story is able to see how everything will work out, and so our reactions to what unfolds in life are either pure speculation or just our clinging to a story we ourselves unconsciously generated. Trust is the option that stands opposite to our reactivity. We call up trust to restore the correct perspective, which is that we do not write the script of our lives, nor do we direct the action, and so there is really nothing for us to worry about.

The students of the Novarodok yeshiva would sing this song about trust that was popular among them: "The past is gone, the future lies ahead, the present is like the blink of an eye—so why worry?"[11]

Rabbi Yehuda Leib Nekritz was a product of Novarodok. When he and his family were sent to Siberia,[12] and were thus spared the much worse fate of being in Poland when the Nazis invaded, he would be asked by the peasants in Siberia, "Why have you been sent here?" He would always answer, "To teach you *bitachon*."

No Fear

The Chazon Ish explains what it means to have trust of this sort by telling the following parable:

> In a small town, a man once opened a small grocery store directly across the street from another grocery. As soon as the old grocer saw the sign in the window announcing the opening, he went across the street and met the new merchant. He shook hands and welcomed him warmly, then sat down and taught him all the tricks of the trade—where to buy, how to buy, how to get good value. When he was asked why he had been so nice to a future competitor, the grocer answered with a well-known Talmudic saying: "All the sustenance of a person is determined for him from New Year to New Year. Only HaShem can take it away." In other words, there's nothing to worry about. What will be will be.

Bitachon gives us the capacity to act from a place of no fear. A heart cannot hold both fear and trust at the same time. When we cultivate trust, we inevitably loosen the grip fear holds on our heart. Fear stifles and censors, to the detriment of ourselves and the world. When we turn our soul to face the divine, we call on our higher nature and elevate ourselves away from animal instincts.

Love presupposes trust. You cannot love those whom you cannot trust. Cultivating trust, love becomes possible.

By activating trust in God, we transform ourselves into fearless, loving beings. *Bitachon* is the inner attitude that respects that whatever is happening in our lives is nothing more or less than the curriculum that God gives us, through any of the myriad channels God has available in the world. The stretching and pulling—by love as well as by blows—is what brings us to the threshold of growth that we would likely (almost certainly) never otherwise approach.

Trust in God gives rise to tranquillity and fearlessness that will make you a better friend, spouse, parent, worker, citizen, and just about every other role you play in your life. The ultimate gift of *bitachon*, however, is the help it gives you when it comes time to leave this world. Every sensible effort should be made to preserve life and restore health, but there will come a point when the right thing to do is to let go, because the time for crossing over has come. It's understandable that our animal survival instinct would have us clinging and fearful at that fateful moment, but a heart infused with *bitachon* offers no harbor to those feelings.

Not one of us can lay claim to creating him- or herself, and when there is recognition that dying means giving up what was really never our own, there is nothing to fear. "Dying," said Rabbi Yisrael Salanter, "is like taking off an old overcoat."

Trust and Effort

One more point needs to be clarified. Although trust requires acceptance, we aren't meant to be fatalistic. We are still obliged to make our own efforts.[13] We can see this as a paradox—our fate is in God's hands and yet we are still obliged to take action. But it isn't such a contradiction. To rely exclusively on *bitachon* is to imply that *all* capacity is on God's side and that we have absolutely nothing in hand to bring about change, when that is seldom the case. You do have some powers that are gifted to you, like the ability to think, to speak, to write, to lift objects, to move about, to care— and it makes sense that you should put these capabilities to work to bring about the outcomes you see to be the best, rather than relying totally on

God. God is the source of these capacities, so wouldn't it dishonor those gifts and especially their giver not to put them to use?

By making efforts to provide for our own needs and to help others, we are honoring the Creator by making use of the gifts God has given us. We have already received so much; isn't it a bit greedy to hold out for more? So it is that the Torah allows us to put in effort to accomplish our goals, and doing so is not considered a lack of reliance on God.

One student told a story that pushed the image of using God's gifts one step further. He had invested heavily in the development of a very worthy and potentially financially sound community project—a theater, actually—but when it first opened the operational losses were staggering. In place of trust in God, he worried and feared, and complained to his wife that all his life's savings were going up in smoke. She rebuked him gently, saying, "It's beautiful! It's incense being offered up to God!"

The theater eventually got on its feet and so both his efforts and his trust were warranted. The Chazon Ish writes of just this sort of situation, saying that the obligation to make an effort is limited to deeds that stand a chance of success. Acts of desperation, on the other hand, are unacceptable and are a contradiction to faith. In other words, reliance on miracles is taken to be contrary to a life of faith. And indeed, many commentators advise us that we are not to live our lives reliant on God's miracles, especially where our own capabilities are available to help.

It is right to put all your powers into taking action to better your own situation and that of the world because you understand and accept your real responsibility for yourself and the world. Do what is desirable or necessary under the circumstances, but do not succumb to anxiety and desperation. Your obligation is to act, not to determine the outcome. Once you have made all the efforts you can, don't torture yourself over the results. You can and you should take action, and then you hold in mind that the ultimate outcome is in the hands of HaShem, not you.

When the grandmother of the wife of Mussar teacher Rabbi Meir Chodosh was emigrating from Poland to Israel in the early twentieth century, the Jewish Agency in Warsaw had her fill out a questionnaire. One of the questions it asked was "What are you taking with you, and how do you plan to earn a living in Israel?" Rebbetzin Hutner looked at the form for a moment, and then in large letters wrote across all the questions: "*Bitachon.*" That's what she brought and that's what would sustain her.[14]

Cultivating Trust

Although I have been addressing anxiety and fear as if they are virtually the enemies of trust, in reality these sentiments can play a positive role in helping you develop this soul-trait. Every experience of fear or worry that strikes you is nothing but a signal calling on you to fan the inner sparks of your *bitachon*. Your task is to become aware of fear, anxiety, and clinging right as these experiences are occurring within you, and to respond to them inwardly by identifying them as signs of not trusting. These acts of bringing to awareness and naming should not be confused with self-recrimination, however. By simply being sensitive to whatever feelings you may experience that imply a lack of trust, you call yourself to self-awareness of the other option that lies before you—to trust.

Rabbi Ibn Pakuda ends "The Gate of Trust in God" with a prayer that is fitting for us as well: "May God in His mercy include us among those who trust Him and surrender themselves outwardly and inwardly to His judgment. Amen."

> Trust God with all your heart, and on your own understanding do not lean.
>
> —Proverbs/*Mishlei* 3:5

23

Faith

EMUNAH

The righteous live by faith.[1]

Ani ma'amin be'emunah sh'lemah—I believe with
complete faith.

— Rambam (Maimonides), *Thirteen Articles of Faith*

IN OUR YOUTH, questions come to us about space, time, and life that confound the human mind. No one has to introduce these questions to us. They arise unbidden when we are quiet under the night sky, or catch a glimpse of the structure and texture of a hand, or meet our first painful, unaccountable loss, or lie alone in bed shielded from the storm, and wonder.

Somehow, most of us reach an accommodation with the profound mystery of life that allows us to get on with living human lives. Some of us turn away from the large questions, which doesn't dispose of them but just tucks them into the back of life's closet. Others receive and accept answers that are really nothing but platitudes and hollow certainties about faith. A few reach their own understanding of the larger issues of life that seem satisfactory. However we may happen to first work out our relationship to the vast mysteries, there is a tendency to carry those answers into our mature years, where they fit no better than the clothes, toys, and books we left behind in childhood.

That may be one reason why so many people find the soul-trait of faith to be a challenge. There are other reasons as well. We are a generation still reeling from the horrors and excesses of the twentieth century that call into question not only the nature of this God of ours, but God's existence itself. Compelling evidence can be mustered to challenge any basis of faith, so much so that faith itself can seem to be not just the super-rational inner state that by definition it is, but fully irrational, an act that defies the empirical facts.

Yet people intent on answering the inner call to make the most of their lives unavoidably have faith on their spiritual curriculum. Even the most firmly atheistic person feels a deep and intense longing for an intimate connection to powers greater than himself or herself. To say "I don't believe in God" doesn't put an end to that yearning, though it may call into question what the person means by "God."

Faith is a challenge even to people who do feel some degree of resonance with the wellsprings of divinity, because too often that inner sensibility is corrupted by stories that have been internalized in the name of faith—because if faith means admiring a big white man with a long white beard enthroned in the sky, then this sort of faith is foolish or, in the view of Rav Kook, who was the first Ashkenazi Chief Rabbi of Israel, heretical.[2] He explains, taking as an example of faith the conviction that the Torah is of divine origin: "A person may believe that the Torah is from heaven, but his understanding of heaven may be so skewed that it allows for not a shred of true faith."

Even people who do have a well-established inner sense of God need to be challenged in their faith, because a fully resolved faith is a dead faith, since the facts of life challenge faith at every turn. Our understanding, like all our inner qualities, is meant to grow.

Faith is essential to the Torah-observant Jew, as the Rambam[3] emphasizes by making faith the very first positive commandment.

At this point, you might be asking me to define what I mean by *faith*, to help pin down the subject under discussion. I hesitate to offer a definition, and ask you to bear with me while I make the case that faith is not something to be understood intellectually but rather to be appreciated from experience.[4]

Tradition does provide some guidance through models for faith that are accurate to our own lives and with which we can identify. After the people of Israel had witnessed the ten plagues, for example, having seen God's power over nature, and having even experienced God's very presence (in the form of the Shechinah), and as they stood on the dry ground between the two walls of water of the Red Sea that had been split for them, the Talmud[5] tells us that the people worried whether God would destroy their Egyptian pursuers or whether they would be overtaken and killed. They said: "Just as we ascend on one side of the sea, so too, are the Egyptians ascending on the other side." As an aftereffect of the years they spent in oppression and bondage in Egypt, the people had little faith. It took seeing the Egyptians splayed out dead on the seashore for faith to become deeply implanted in their hearts,[6] as it says in the "Song at the Sea,"[7] which has been incorporated into the liturgy: "On that day HaShem saved Israel from the hand of Egypt, and Israel saw the Egyptians dead on the seashore . . . and they had faith[8] in HaShem and in Moses, His servant." That faith was strengthened by the revelation experienced at Mount Sinai. And then it crashed into the Golden Calf.

Here we have faith, in its strength and its fragility.

Faith must be a central concern of anyone who seeks the goals toward which Mussar directs. The target for a life well lived is summed up in the word *wholeness* (*sh'lemut*), about which Rabbi Shlomo Wolbe says: "We seek only our wholeness." Then he guides, "The foundation of wholeness is faith."[9] Without faith, wholeness will elude us.

Faith and Belief

One problem I see is that issues of faith are often misleadingly presented in terms of *belief.* The question that is presented as the heart of the matter then comes out as: do you or don't you believe in God? The problem here is the unexpressed assumption that God is some sort of entity that you might or might not think of as having an actual historical reality, like a Martian or the Yeti or, maybe more accurately, like arguments that take place over whether a certain species of animal is extinct or not.

The faith we need is not a simple matter of belief. Belief can be disproved by new facts. If I believed that the world was flat, pictures from space would rightly shake my belief. If I believed that maggots sprouted spontaneously in mud, a microscope would make me see differently. The Rambam conceives of faith not being about "belief" but about knowledge and understanding,[10] and this seems right to me. Rabbi Perr once said to me, "Everybody has faith, but only some people know it."

In a similar vein, the Lubavitcher Rebbe wrote a letter[11] to a skeptical student who claimed atheism:

I do not accept your assertion that you do not believe. For if you truly had no concept of a Supernal Being Who created the world with purpose, then what is all this outrage of yours against the injustice of life? The substance of the universe is not moral, and neither are the plants and animals. Why should it surprise you that whoever is bigger and more powerful swallows his fellow alive?

It is only due to an inner conviction in our hearts, shared by every human being, that there is a Judge, that there is right and there is wrong. And so, when we see wrong, we demand an explanation: Why is this not the way it is supposed to be?

That itself is belief in God.

The Lubavitcher Rebbe finds a basis for faith in the conviction that there is right and there is wrong.

I've brought up these sources to underline that, to my way of thinking, the primary question is not whether or not you believe in God, but rather a more empirical issue of where to look to find God. If you know where to look for God, then you have the potential to perceive a reality, and that is a far better foundation for faith than either blind belief or adherence to received opinions. The question of where to look for God is also primary because it helps us understand what it is that we are talking about when we speak of "God."

Where to Look for God

Let's dispose of the most obvious misconception first. God is indeed hidden, but that should not suggest that if you happen to pick the right bed to look under (even if that bed were as big as the sky), you would catch a glimpse of some sort of Big Boss who manipulates the levers of universal power. That's not the right place to look, because what we are looking for is not like a creature in space and time.

Thinking of God in creaturely terms gives rise to the classic question: if God is omnipotent, can God make an object so big that God cannot lift it? This question itself makes no sense because the God we are looking for need not be bound by the terms of that sort of question. It implies thinking about the universe from a creaturely perspective, which is a limitation that we have no right to apply to God.[12] As seems self-evident, if we acknowledge that there are limits to what the human mind can perceive and think, then why would we assume that all dimensions of reality need to be confined within those limits?

There have been many Jewish sages who have tried to use logic to prove this or that about God, including Rabbi Bachya ibn Pakuda, who devotes the first gate of *The Duties of the Heart* to "proving" logically the existence of one God. I find the chapter to be agonizing reading, and when I told Rabbi Perr that I was organizing a group to study this text but was worried that we would flounder right in this first section, he told me that whenever he leads a study of that book, he skips this section. As Rabbi Eliyahu Lopian teaches, the problem is that it just doesn't work to approach God through rational thought: "All philosophical speculations and explanations, even if true, can in no fashion bring man to cling to the living God."[13]

The Torah expresses this point by saying that God's "thoughts" are not like human thoughts.

Despite recognizing the limitations of human thinking, we are still able to find a logic to how God is placed in the world.

For example, if you imagine for a moment that you were given the assignment to design a universe in which there were to be creatures who had the potential to reach some sort of personal wholeness, how would you proceed? Wouldn't you want to create a world in which there were real pitfalls and detours so that the climb would be real and the consequences real as well? And wouldn't you want to make your role as "creator" neither fully revealed nor fully hidden? If you were fully revealed, that would put an end to the sense of independence of the creatures, who would then find it incontestable that they are created and would then give up on living and making effort. On the other hand, to be totally untraceable denies the creatures an all-important clue as to the nature of the universe in which they are living. The most useful and effective place to reveal your presence in creation would be only in glimpses, intuitions, and flashes.

And so it is.

To build a foundation of faith, then, we need to pay attention to the sorts of glimpses, intuitions, and flashes that are the only way in which we can hope to experience something of the presence of God. This is a point the Torah makes so beautifully when it describes Moses's request to see God, which is met only by a glimpse from behind. There is no reason to think that any of us ought to be able to see more, and every reason why we ought to be able to perceive so much less, than did a prophet of the stature of Moses.

Rav Kook[14] cautions us to remember that these flashes—glimpses from behind, so to speak—are all we get to see, and that the trouble with faith starts to arise when we impose images and language onto these perceptions:

> One must always cleanse one's thoughts about God to make sure they are free of the dross of deceptive fantasies, of groundless fear, of evil inclinations, of wants and deficiencies. . . . All the divine names, whether in Hebrew or in any other language, give us only a tiny and dull spark of the hidden light to which the soul aspires when it utters the word "God." Every definition of God brings about heresy, every definition is spiritual idolatry; even attributing to Him intellect and will, even the term *divine*, the term *God*, suffers from the limitations of definition. Except for the keen awareness that all these are but sparkling flashes of what cannot be defined—these, too, would engender heresy.

We are meant to pay attention to those sparkling flashes. They are how we experience the presence of God.

Transcendence versus Immanence

There are two different ways in which God is present in this world, often usefully summarized as the *transcendent* versus the *immanent*.

The transcendent aspect of God is represented by the notion of concealed light. This God is ineffable, inexpressible, and so thoroughly different in scope and concept from anything in creation that we can't fathom anything of the reality of this supreme reality. This is God without end, limitless in scope and limitless in purpose, whom the Jewish mystics call the *Ayn Sof*, literally "without end."

The immanent aspect of God refers to the ways God is present in the world. The transcendent God does not bless, but the immanent God does.

Having laid down these two traditional distinctions that concern God, we can approach them in the two ways in which we are enabled to know faith, which are by way of the intellect and through experience. In both cases, we can't hope to find certainty and proof, but only pointers for what you

yourself have to look for and investigate, since the world is created in such
a way as to offer only hints and no certainties of faith. These parameters
give rise to four permutations, each of which offers a doorway to God and
so is a pillar of faith:

- *Knowing the transcendent* is the least attainable of these permutations because, by definition, the transcendent aspect of God is remote and inaccessible from within human capabilities.
- *Experiencing the transcendent* is not easy, either, though we are more
  likely to have insight into the ineffability of God through nonintel-
  lectual perception than through the mind.
- *Knowing the immanent* is already true for all of us, though only some
  people associate their experience of the manifest world with God.
- *Experiencing the immanent* happens all the time.

The difference between knowing and experiencing is crucial, because
knowing alone has little bearing on faith. This point is made clearly by
Rabbi Eliyahu Lopian, who says that God is saying to us:

> For I have given you also great understanding and a powerful intel-
> lect in addition to your nature so that you are able to mate your in-
> tellectual knowledge with your emotive feeling and unite them in
> order to fulfill "And you shall know this day and lay it to heart that
> the Lord is God in heaven above and on the earth beneath; there is
> no other" (Deut. 4:39).[15]

Then elsewhere he elaborates on this same verse:

> The verse says, "Know this day, and lay it to your heart, that the Lord,
> He is God in heaven above and upon the earth beneath; there is
> none else" (Deut. 4:39). At first sight, if a man has attained convic-
> tion in his mind and brain—having perfect faith and true intellec-
> tual understanding—that the Lord is God, what more is required?
> Yet the verse contradicts this and says that is not so; if you lay your
> knowledge to your heart, all will be well, but if not, you hold a frag-
> ile piece of china in your hand. For unless the heart feels that the
> Lord, He is God, etc., his knowledge will not avail him at all to with-
> stand his impulse—however deep such knowledge might be.

I once heard Rabbi Itzele Blazer say: "Just as there is certainly a vast distance between one who does not know that the Lord is God and one who does know, so is there a very much greater distance between knowing without feeling that knowledge in one's heart and knowing and feeling it there.[16]

We stand before a doorway behind which we will not find belief, definition, idea, logical proof, or concept, but directly perceived experience.

Faith and Experience

Our teachers tell us that experience is the gateway to faith and this is guidance to any of us who seeks to plant the first seeds of faith or to nurture and foster its early sprouts. Rabbi Yosef Yozel Hurwitz, the Alter of Novarodok, is clear on this point:

But if he knows all this only with his mind and not with his senses, he will find that his mental effort yields only a mental [i.e., abstract] result, not a sensory [i.e., actual] one. . . . At the moment of trial he is like a blind man who never saw the light, because then the cloud covers the sun and he can see nothing. All his exalted knowledge exists either before the fact or after the fact, but when the [trying] situation is at hand, the distraction of the trial makes him like a different man.[17]

This is like the story of the actor who has only one line to deliver in the play. After the cannon goes off, he is to say, "Hark! The report of a distant cannon." He studies the script and memorizes his lines and is all ready. At his cue, he goes onstage and suddenly he hears a loud "Boom!" and he says, "What the heck was that!" All his preparation had been only intellectual.

The intellect is limited, its habit is skepticism, and so the foundation of faith must be rooted elsewhere.

Rabbis Ibn Pakuda, Lopian, and Hurwitz, among many others, have all been eloquent in telling us that the way to approach knowledge of God and hence to cultivate faith is to open our eyes to the experience of our senses. The world is the tableau of the divine, and in looking at it and experiencing its marvelous artifacts and ways, we can perceive the physical reality and the divinity that lies within it.

This is both the starting point and the key. It is the starting point because it is the most accessible domain for our investigation. And it is the key because the God we can know is hidden, and not only that—God has hidden that God is hidden. We can find our way to faith only by registering and trusting the glimpses, intuitions, and flashes that still come unbidden when we are quiet under the night sky, or catch a glimpse of the structure and texture of a hand, or meet a painful, unaccountable loss, or lie alone in bed shielded from the storm, and wonder.

To Grow in Faith

How can you grow in faith, or into faith?

The doorway to faith is not opened by rational thought. Only through elevated inner experience can one come to faith or strengthen the faith one has. Through reflection and learning, you may be convinced that there must be more to life than is apparent, but it is only through lived experience that this notion becomes implanted as faith.

Rabbi Yisrael Salanter taught in many places that emotional experience is more potent and convincing than intellectual knowledge—an idea that later generations of Mussar teachers adopted and expanded upon. Rabbi Zvi Miller writes: "In its natural state, the heart—which is the emotional core—is sealed, i.e., the knowledge attained by the mind does not penetrate the heart's barrier. [But] once the heart is awakened and electrified—it bolsters, stabilizes, and anchors the intellectual concepts.[18]

The Mussar teachers stress one sort of emotional experience in particular as effective in underpinning faith, and that is awe. We'll consider this quality more in the next chapter, because "awe" is one of the translations of the Hebrew word *yirah* that is our focus there. But of concern to us here is the way in which awe fosters faith more than any idea or concept could possibly do.

The expansive, impressive experience of awe is part of everyday life, though often only at its highest moments. The drama of the natural world brings it on when our breath is taken away by an encounter with a magnificent landscape, a strange and marvelous creature, or the order and intelligence of the natural world. Just to see a blue whale or a mother bear and her cubs or the flapping, honking precision drill of geese migrating is to know awe. Or human creations can bring on awe. Stand by the Western Wall (the Kotel) in Jerusalem, or in a great building, or in a cave inhabited by people for millennia, and then the calluses of the heart peel away to reveal a vibrant, sensitive core.

Awe is there to be had in any moment. When you walk outside, stop to look at a garden, watch or even hear children playing, observe an act of kindness, or feel an intimacy, then you can know with a certainty that bears no critique that there is more to this universe than the discriminative human mind can fathom. We all have those moments, often in nature, often in encounter with another soul, when we are visited by a sense of depths and levels of reality that we do not ordinarily perceive. To open ourselves to those moments without reservation—gently encouraging ego consciousness to step aside—makes it possible to gain more of the gift these moments hold for us. They will come more often as well.

The story is told about the great Chassidic Rebbe Zusya that whenever he would hear the Torah reading in synagogue begin with the words, "And God spoke to Moses, saying . . . ," as it frequently does, he would pass out cold. The thought that *God spoke to Moses directly*, face-to-face, was too awesome a notion for his mental circuits to handle, and he would just drop like a stone.

We are all familiar with the sorts of dramatic incidents that sweep us into a state of awe. In fact, the experiences of awe that come over us in nature, or in love, or upon hearing a profound idea are just the freebies that God provides as a sample of the wares of awe, like home-delivered advertising for God's existence. These moments of encounter bring us to the sublime dimension of lived reality without any effort on our part whatsoever. We just walk around the corner, run smack into the vista, and are struck dumb by awe as if shot in the heart with a flaming arrow.

But these sorts of grand encounters are certainly not the only way to know awe. When you choose to see the glory that lies within even the obvious and mundane, then that fly on the window, or simple cloud in the sky, or hand in your hand is as much an invitation to awe as the Grand Canyon or the pyramids.

What I am saying is that the choice is yours. Awe is right there at every moment, separated from ordinary consciousness by no more than a diaphanous curtain that can be pulled aside by an experience, or equally by an instance of will. Of course, I don't want to make it sound like entering awe is just as easy as flipping channels on your television remote control. There are obstacles and hindrances that keep us from even being aware that we can draw away the veil, and even more obstacles and hindrances that keep us from acting on this choice. These are the conditions that keep faith at a distance.

As each of us pursues our own spiritual curriculum, we are "graced" with our own personalized set of hindrances. These are the challenges that face us and that, when we overcome them, are rungs on the ladder of our ascent. As much as each of us has our own unique set of inner challenges, there do tend to be some that are generally problematic to most of us. They are like the spiritual illnesses of the age.

Among the spiritual disabilities that plague so many people today, one of the most common is busyness. Overcommitment of our time leaves little space for the simple experience of being, and awe (and, as we have learned, its child, faith) is much harder to find when we are moving at a speed of seventy miles an hour and our mind is taken up with all the items on the long and ever-replenished list that we can't possibly complete, today or ever.

I speak from my own experience. So much in my life is good, and I am deeply grateful for that, but there is just so much of it. There are so many needs, desires, ambitions, and commitments that I sometimes feel that a decade is really just a year. Every life has its challenges, and in mine, because I am free and not persecuted, because I am healthy and not sick, because I am alert and not disabled, because I love what I do and am not oppressed by it, my challenge is that my days are filled and overfilled. When I slip into that way of living, and overcommitment is my reality day in and day out, how can I ever find my way to the awe that precedes faith, that is the precondition and the gateway to faith? Awe can come only when there is space in which to welcome it. The moment needs to be made spacious, time a fertile ground and not an enemy.

That's why I treasure Shabbat. Shabbat is the corrective for me. It isn't just a day in the week on which I simply rest and recharge in order to reenter the fray, it's the reminder of what I so easily forget the other six days, and which I hope to remember so that some echo and trace of the spaciousness of the seventh can filter into the six as well. In my life, I am in danger of getting lost, deflected, and confused in the complex web of demands, responsibilities, and desires I carry with me. Shabbat is when and how I check the map.

You would be right to see the honoring of Shabbat as an act of faith, since the source of its observance is God. "God blessed the seventh day and sanctified it because He abstained from all His work that God created to make,"[19] and "It will be a sign between me and the people of Israel forever, for in six days God made the heavens and the earth, and on the seventh day God abstained from work and rested."[20]

To me, though, Shabbat observance is more the opposite, actually a pathway to faith. Although doing can arise out of faith, faith can also arise as a result of the doing. If I waited until God was more of a presence in my life to be convinced to observe the Sabbath, I would likely not get there. Because I observe Shabbat, my faith grows.

Although I am focusing here only on the spiritual hindrance that is busyness and its antidote, which is Shabbat, you need to ask yourself what it is that stands in the way of your opening to faith, and what you can do about it. There are many sorts of actions that can be undertaken as a result of faith, and that in the doing can also become a source of faith. This is true of the classic acts of loving-kindness, like giving charity, visiting the sick, clothing the naked, and burying the dead. The same is true of prayer. It is logical to think that living a life by the commandments would demand that faith be in place first; my experience is that living by the commandments fosters and nurtures faith as well.

In the end, what is important about faith is that you seek. The psalm says, "When You said, 'Seek My face,' my heart said to You, 'I will seek Your face, HaShem.'"[21] And the Torah reassures: "From there you will seek the Lord your God, and you will find Him," though there are conditions: "If you seek Him with all your heart and with all your soul."[22]

Rabbi Nacum Zev Broide, who was the son of Rabbi Simcha Zissel, the Alter of Kelm, asked before his death that he be eulogized by only one person, and that the eulogy consist of only one tribute—that "he had the desire to advance toward faith."[23] We learn from this to emphasize the search for faith over the fruits of that search, yearning over finding.

The body needs air. What is the air of the soul? Faith.

—Rabbi Eliyahu Lopian, *Lev Eliyahu*[24]

24

Yirah

In reverence is wisdom.

Man is weak and overwhelmed by his unending
workload. What is the strategy to end the raging war
of the evil inclination, and the secret to stop the spirit
of desire that roars unendingly like a churning sea?
Man's only hope is to fortify himself with the reverence of the Almighty God. This reverence is an im-
pregnable fortress that can deliver him from every
enemy and attack. It is mighty enough to bind his desires and prevent the evil intentions of his heart from
bursting into a destructive behavior. Only it can serve
as a valorous right arm to still the wild tempest of the
evil inclination and allow man to emerge victorious
in battle.

—Rabbi Yitzhak Blazer, *The Gates of Light*

EVERY OTHER CHAPTER in this book refers to its soul-trait by its English name, but that's not possible for this one. Merged within the word
yirah are two human experiences that are linked in the Hebrew but separated in English. One is fear. The other is awe. Experience shows us that
these can be two totally distinct inner qualities—you can be terrified of
the bear, and in awe at the sunset. But experience also justifies linking
them together. Imagine standing right at the lip of the Grand Canyon,
looking down into the vast and rainbow-colored cavern. Fear and awe
merge into one exuberant inner experience.

Though *yirah* can describe the unified fear/awe experience, the term can also be used for the singular experiences of fear and of awe. This shows up in Mussar thinking when the same word—*yirah*—is used to name *yirat ha'onesh,* which is fear of the ultimate punishment that will be meted out for wrongdoing, and *yirat ha'romemut,* which is awe at God's majesty and grandeur.

The Duties of the Heart makes this very point: "The fear of Heaven has two aspects: the fear of tribulations and Divine retribution, and the awe of His glory, majesty, and awesome power."[1]

When the discussion focuses on punishment, it is quite clear that *yirah* means fear. When it is the magnificence of the Source of Being, awe seems to be called for.[2] But when the word *yirah* is used without a qualifier, we are left to ponder what is being asked of us. How different is "And now, Israel, what does the Lord your God want of you? Only that you fear the Lord your God" from "And now, Israel, what does the Lord your God want of you? Only that you remain in awe of the Lord your God."[3]

We need to know what meaning to assign, because how else can we do what the rest of the verse directs: "So that you will follow all His paths and love Him, serving the Lord your God with all your heart and with all your soul"? Do we get there by cultivating fear or, alternatively, awe?

Similarly for the work of improving the soul-traits. Is fear the mechanism, or is it awe? Again, read the following quote from *Orchot Tzaddikim,*[4] and see how differently it comes across when you translate *yirah* first as "fear" and then as "awe":

And no deed is of much value without pure *yirah.* Therefore, all men must be informed that anyone who wishes to attain worthy character traits must intermix *yirah* of HaShem with each trait, for *yirah* of Ha'Shem is the common bond among all of the traits. This may be compared to a string which has been strung through the holes of pearls, with a knot tied at its end to hold the pearls. There is no question that if the knot is cut, all the pearls will fall. It is the same with *yirah* of HaShem. It is the knot which secures all of the good traits, and if you remove it, all of the good traits will depart from you.

Is fear the way, or do we follow the way of awe?

There Will Be a Reckoning

Jewish teachers, including many Mussar masters, have given much ink and voice to encouraging us to orient toward the side of fear, particularly of divine retribution for our transgressions. There is no question that they have meant fear and not awe or reverence because they describe all the symptoms of terror, like quaking and sweating, to make sure we get the point that they are talking about a fearful response to a terrifying reality.

Rabbi Yisrael Salanter himself wrote: "The belief that the Almighty is the True Judge Who recompenses each individual according to his deeds is the first step in the service of Hashem."[5] His disciple, Rabbi Yitzchak Blazer, wrote at length about the fear of punishment:

> Even when a person follows the whims of his heart and wallows in sin and iniquity, he still retains the capacity to fear punishment. Thus it is that this fear precedes the performance of the commandments, for it is the primary deterrent against iniquity and sin. This fear causes one to tremble before the Almighty and to fulfill the Torah and its commandments.[6]

Some people, particularly observant Jews, continue to respond to this message today. It has meaning and impact within a larger worldview and system of which it is a part.

Many people, including observant Jews as well, don't resonate with this message. I once attended a talk at an ultra-Orthodox learning center where the speaker was practically banging the lectern to get across his message of the fear we should feel right now over the consequences each of us can look forward to on the day we are called to give an accounting for our lives. A man sitting near me, black-hatted and bearded, leaned over to me and whispered, "It's a tough sell."

Why is that so? I have come upon many reasons that account for why many in our generation are not easily swayed by the promises and threats of what awaits us in the afterlife. I have heard most often that people relate to a loving God and find the punishment-wielding divinity an alien (and alienating) concept. Perhaps it's our comfort levels that inure us, or perhaps the inflated sense of the power of humanity, as demonstrated by our ever-more-potent technology and the extended lifespans we enjoy.

Maybe we have become such relativists that for us, even for all of eternity, "good enough" actually is good enough. Certainly many people simply do not believe that a reckoning awaits them, nor do they believe in the system of reward and punishment of which tradition speaks.

Whatever the reasons, the challenge of finding the spiritual value in fear of punishment isn't new to this generation. "Everything is in the hands of heaven except the fear of heaven,"[7] the Talmud says. It has always been up to us whether or not we choose to cultivate *yirah*, as it is not natural, or inborn, or self-evident that we should do so. Perhaps our teachers emphasized the long-term consequences of wrongdoing to ensure that we chose well in this regard. Rabbi Luzzatto says as much in his appreciation that "there's nothing more likely to keep you away from doing something harmful to yourself than the fear of injurious consequences."

The Chafetz Chaim cautions, however, that even though fear of punishment can be effective, especially in the short run, it is a faulty basis for spiritual endeavor compared to that other factor embedded in the notion of *yirah*, which is awe of divine majesty: "Whoever is unaware how exalted and praiseworthy is God, avoiding sin only out of fear of earthly or heavenly punishment, will seek ways to be legitimately exempt, without punishment, from mitzvah observance."[8] This is astute. If all you are afraid of is punishment, then any legitimate way to avoid responsibility serves you well. We see this all the time in situations where people hold themselves to be blameless, but only because they found a legitimate way to circumvent the rules.

Rabbi Blazer himself acknowledges that the experience associated with awe is the higher form of *yirah*:

> We have thus far noted that there are two types of reverence of Heaven—the fear of future accountability and the awe of Divine majesty. However, it must be stressed that the two are not equal. It is clear that the awe of God's majesty is on a more exalted plane than the fear of future accountability.[9]

What he says as well, however, is that, in his view, awe must stand on a foundation of fear that we will be punished for our sins. He is unequivocal: fear of retribution comes first and must be cultivated first, as an unavoidable level through which we gain the ability to enter into awe of the divine and then to live according to this awareness. The Malbim affirms

similarly: "The wise of heart have explained that it is impossible to immediately attain the exalted level of awe of heaven. Rather, one must first
come to fear His judgment, and only then ascend to the more elevated
level of *Yirat ha'Romemut* [awe of heaven]."[10] This then returns us to the
place of our problem, which is how to apply the Mussar teachers' exhor-
tation to fear what lies in store for us.

A Possible Resolution

I have struggled long and hard to try to understand what useful message I
can take from this piece of teaching and guidance. Despite the discomfort
the idea brings up, fear has been given prominence as a spiritual force by
our wise forebears. What can we learn?

For people who have a clear notion of the ultimate reckoning that will
be given after the day of death, there is no problem. That belief makes fear
of retribution a lively and significant factor in daily life.

But what of those who recoil from that idea, either because that isn't
the image of God they hold, or because they just don't believe it, or because it conjures up negative experiences with parents or teachers that
just don't inspire spiritual elevation? Could there still be a spiritual benefit from cultivating fear?

Fear is the deepest, oldest, and most intransigent aspect of our lower
selves. We are wired to be fearful as a basic mechanism for survival. As a
result, in the struggle to assert the dominion of higher self over lower,
there is no way fear can be simply ignored or overpowered. The question
is, since we are stuck with fear, can we put it to good use?

Rabbi Ephraim Becker, who is a psychologist and Mussar teacher, answers this question in somewhat more psychological terms, though still
focusing on the redirection of a person's "natural fear":[11]

> *Yirat ha'Onesh* [fear of punishment] takes advantage of a person's
> natural tendency for self-preservation, pain-reduction and pleasure-
> increase. This means that a person who has fear focuses his atten-
> tion on the fact that if he does not fulfill the Will of HaShem, he
> will pay a price in terms of pain, and that if he neglects a mitzvah
> he will pay a price in terms of loss of pleasure. The person must

apply his will to redirect his natural fear, which may draw him to take all sorts of other steps to insure his preservation and pleasure, to his awareness of HaShem's omnipotence, which will cause him to direct his fear toward HaShem.

Here we have one way in which the innate fear mechanism can be put to good spiritual use. The key phrase that I underline is "The person must apply his will to redirect his natural fear." This would be a conscious act and a choice. Fear may be natural and innate, but directing it to heaven is a deliberate and cultivated spiritual practice that has as its goal influencing behavior here in this world.

Rabbi Moshe Chaim Luzzatto[12] also encourages us to refocus our fear onto a different target. He is not calling on us to fear retribution, but rather to fear that we will misstep:

Fear of sin should be a constant thing. You should always be afraid of stumbling and doing something or some half of something that is against God's honor. That is why this trait is called "fear of sin," because its essence is the fear that sin might enter into or mix in with your actions due to some negligence, weakness, or one or another unconscious reason.

How different is that kind of attentive, cautious watchfulness from the cowering, quaking fear that God's wrath will flame us for our wrongdoing. In a similar vein, I have heard a Mussar teacher call on us not to fear punishment for our sins but rather to fear punishment for not living up to our full spiritual potential.

If the notion of reward and punishment strikes a visceral chord in you, these other ways of looking at how to bring fear into spiritual practice may be unimportant. Still, we can see that there are many other ways your natural inclination to fear can also validly be put to work. Though the concepts differ, the goal is always to harness a natural impulse in order to tap its strength to help you bring about change in this world. Fear is inescapable, so we are wise to try to put to work on behalf of our higher inclinations something that is firmly and intrinsically a part of our lower nature. Doing so assigns a positive role to what is, at root, a mere survival mechanism, the fuel that feeds the fight-or-flight reflex.

Take a moment to consider the role fear plays in your life. What do you fear? Is your fear tied to this world and material concerns, or to your spiritual life? Can you feel the motivating power that fear embodies? Can you direct and tie that fear to the highest purposes of your life?

Awesome Motivation

Fear has such power that it makes great sense to me to funnel that energy into spiritual endeavor. And yet I still join our generation in finding much more motivation for myself in the positive message that awe transforms the heart. Of awe, Rabbi Abraham Joshua Heschel says,[13] "Awe is more than an emotion; it is a way of understanding. Awe is itself an act of insight into a meaning greater than ourselves. Awe is a way of being in rapport with the mystery of all reality."

He goes on:

> The meaning of awe is to realize that life takes place under wide horizons, horizons that range beyond the span of an individual life or even the life of a nation, a generation, or an era. Awe enables us to perceive in the world intimations of the divine, to sense in small things the beginning of infinite significance, to sense the ultimate in the simple; to feel in the rush of the passing the stillness of the eternal.

These are lofty and enticing words, and they are undoubtedly true. They challenge us, though, because we need to know how to put the guidance into practice. We need to know the relationship between the experience of awe and doing good or bad so we can put that guidance to work in our own lives. Rabbis Luzzatto and Heschel come at this question from two different sides.

Rabbi Luzzatto says that the awe of God's grandeur "holds sway when you keep away from transgressions and do not commit them." In other words, awe is the goal, and keeping our actions pure and clean is the pathway that leads to that goal.

Rabbi Heschel sees awe differently, not as a goal but more specifically as a means to an end:

The question, therefore, *where shall wisdom be found?* is answered by the Psalmist: *the awe of God is the beginning of wisdom.*[14] The Bible does not preach awe as a form of intellectual resignation; it does not say, awe is the end of wisdom. Its intention seems to be that awe is a way to wisdom.[15]

Of course, there is no conflict between these two views of awe—they are just focused on different points along a pathway. Keeping away from sin is a precondition for awe, and awe is the gateway to wisdom. This gate is opened and closed by transgression, and it is because spiritual life depends on this passage that Rabbi Luzzatto emphasizes the "fear" of causing the gate to swing shut on us.

Our experience of living delivers up instances of awe without any effort on our part. It is the experiential reward that comes over us when we visit dramatic stands of trees, like redwoods, or closer to where I live, giant cedars, or seeing whales, or being in stillness while a great sunset unrolls its rich tapestry of shades, or hearing wonderful music. Awe arises when we encounter life and the world in ways that breach the ordinary. The ordinary can bring on awe as well—though only if we don't see it as ordinary.

Walt Whitman calls on us to have eyes to see "the glories strung like beads on my smallest sights and hearings." The title of his poem "Crossing Brooklyn Ferry" sets a mundane scene. Do you commute? Do you sometimes jump into the car and drive to the supermarket? Don't you walk under the sky a dozen times a day? But do you have the eyes to see the glories? Whitman sees deeply:

> I too many and many a time cross'd the river, the sun half an
> hour high;
> I watched the Twelfth-month sea-gulls—I saw them high in the
> air, floating with motionless wings, oscillating their bodies,
> I saw how the glistening yellow lit up parts of their bodies, and
> left the rest in strong shadow,
> I saw the slow-wheeling circles, and the gradual edging toward the
> south.

Do you have the eyes to see the glories? The answer, of course, is yes. We are all equipped to have this experience because it is one of the basic, built-in features of consciousness. We only need to turn and look and allow what we see to register, because "all truths wait in all things," or, in Blake's famous lines, the glory of the world is everywhere:

> To see a world in a grain of sand,
> And heaven in a wild flower,
> Hold infinity in the palm of your hand,
> And eternity in an hour.

The reality, however, is that we mostly allow ourselves to be so thick, crass, and dull that it requires the axe blade of a dazzling sunset or the drama of a birth or a death to cut through the callous rind of our hearts, so that we see and breathe once again as if for the first time. But it doesn't need to be so. The glory that triggers awe is everywhere.

In the Shabbat liturgy the words of Isaiah are paraphrased to have the angels asking, "Where is the place of God's glory?"[16] This question is repeated every week,[17] and it needs to be our constant question as well. Where is the place of God's glory? Even if you have no answer, even if you have no belief, or even if you do have faith, you must continue to ask the question, because certainty is the end of faith, and questioning is the pathway of spiritual ascent.

In that same prayer we get the answer (though, curiously, before the question is asked): "God's Glory fills the world."[18]

This is the vision of Isaiah:[19] "Holy, holy, holy is the Lord of Hosts; the whole world is full of His Glory."[20] This teaching is repeated over and over, day after day in the prayers, in the hopes that we will open and reopen our eyes to see that the entire world—in its infinite diversity, the great and the small—is filled with God's glory, majesty, and dignity.

A group of learned men once came to visit the Kotzker Rebbe. He asked them the question we have been considering: "What is the place of God's Glory?" The men responded by quoting the answer from liturgy: "The whole world is full of God's glory." Rabbi Menachem Mendel gave a different answer: "God's glory is found wherever we let God in."

This is the vision of the poet and the prophet. See the seagull and see more than the seagull. See the grass and perceive time. Look into the forest and know eternity.

Cultivating Awe

Our teachers have long recognized that, despite the most dramatic awakenings that can penetrate our hearts, left to our own devices, sooner or later we drift off to sleep once more. In a matter of time we stop seeing afresh and so lose contact with the awe-state of *yirah*. Rabbi Luzzatto wisely cautions, "This understanding imprints itself in a person's mind only through constant reflection and deep analysis."

Rabbi Luzzatto says (and we all know) that constant reflection is necessary if we are going to stay awake and be available to awe even a little more of the time.

In many synagogues there is the verse from Psalms inscribed over the ark that reads: "I place God before me always."[21] In the Talmud, Rav Chana bar Bizna cites the same verse and says that one who prays must picture the Shechinah—God's presence—in front of him.[22] Out of this idea has come a tradition of creating a type of artwork known as a *shiviti* (the first word of the line from the psalm). *Shivitis* are often complex and beautiful images that are drawn or painted as objects of meditative contemplation. In the eighteenth and nineteenth centuries, many elaborately decorated contemplative paintings were made to be hung on the eastern wall of synagogues, where they serve as a reminder that at every moment we are standing in the presence of God.[23]

Who has an imagination strong enough to see yourself as actually standing before God? The *shiviti* is an accessible reminder, and so the goal of contemplating a *shiviti* is to imprint on the imagination a deep impression like standing before HaShem, the King of kings, whose glory fills the world.

The great kabbalist Rabbi Isaac Luria helps us overcome the impossibility of imagining ourselves in the presence of the Holy One by telling us to hold the four-letter name of God—the Y-H-V-H—before our eyes always, and often *shivitis* do contain the four letters of the divine name.

The practice of contemplating a *shiviti* brings awareness of God's presence into consciousness. This is not something that can be explained or understood cognitively. It is an experience, and through that experience awe arises spontaneously. Contemplation of imagery also brings us to awareness of God's presence without calling on the discriminative intellect, which tends to be the faculty that gives us so much trouble with the notion of God. Only in the mind is God an issue.

Formal *shiviti* practice involves considering images in the imagination. Contemplating a painted *shiviti* obviously stresses the sense of sight. Rabbi Bachya ibn Pakuda, in *The Duties of the Heart*,[24] however, tells us that *shiviti* practice can be done orally as well:

> All this serves to reinforce what was said in the previous verse ("These words which I command you this day must be on your heart"): By keeping these words on one's lips continually, they are ever in one's consciousness, and one's thoughts are never empty of God. This is like what was said by King David: "I have placed God always before me" (*Tehillim* [Psalms] 16:8).

The last and encompassing word on the importance of keeping God in consciousness at all times goes to the Chafetz Chaim.[25] He pulls together the notion we looked at earlier—the whole world being filled with God's glory—with the instruction to keep continual awareness of God:

> It is the duty of conscientious people to constantly reflect that God's glory fills the whole world: we are ever in His presence and must fulfill His will. This is the meaning of the verse: "I set HaShem before me always."

Our teachers are offering us choices in how we walk the path, but they are united on the goal. It's up to us whether we choose to look at the imagery of a *shiviti*, or envision the letters of the divine name in the mind's eye, or repeat words that emphasize the presence of God, but these are just variations on the single notion that we need to do practices that will make us conscious of the divine plane of reality. The Mussar student seeks to develop the ability to look inside every object to find the soul, in which HaShem is represented. In this light, Rabbi Abraham Joshua Heschel taught that every human being is also a *shiviti*, who stands before us as a reminder of God's presence.

God's presence is often not accessible to us, unless we make a practice of cultivating that awareness. That's how we let God in, in the Kotzker's words. And then we know *yirah*.

The Need to Concentrate

You can vary the object or objects that you contemplate according to which work best for you. Experience will tell you which open doorways inspire your awe at the deep reality of divine presence. But whatever object you choose, you will gain the vision you seek only if you bring a power of concentration to the task. Rabbi Luzzatto acknowledges this by noting that "all inattentiveness nullifies constancy of *yirah*." As important as it is to have an object or words to focus on as a reminder of God's presence, we also need techniques that will help foster uninterrupted concentration.

It's for that very reason that I wear a *kippah*. The Torah does not call for a head covering and so wearing a *kippah* is not a commandment, which explains why there is no blessing recited when putting it on the head. The Talmud puts it this way: "Cover your head so that awe of heaven will be upon you."[26] Another word for *kippah* is "yarmulke," which has been explained as being derived from *yireh melekh* ("awe of the King"). The Talmudic sage Rav Huna[27] never walked even a short distance with his head uncovered. When asked why, he replied, "Because the Shechinah rests above my head." From this, we derive that wearing a *kippah* acknowledges that in every moment, I am in the divine presence, to which I show respect by covering my head. In fact, the practice really works in the opposite direction for me: by covering my head, I remind myself that "the whole world is full of God's glory."

The Rambam offers another way to counter our tendency to be distracted and so forget that we are always in the presence of HaShem. He explains that one method the sages employed was to recite many blessings "in order that we should constantly remember HaShem."[28] Jewish practice attaches blessings to so many of the ordinary events of every day—awaking, washing, eating, drinking, going to the bathroom, going to bed—to remind us that God is in every moment, if only we would be open to that presence.

There are requirements for how a blessing is done properly. You may know these, or you may want to find them out. Or you may want simply to make a practice of saying "thank you" for the myriad things that happen in your day that you want to mark in consciousness as signs of the benevolence that is directed your way.

In a formal blessing practice, we are meant to say "You are God"[29] a hundred times a day. Each time we call to HaShem, we remind ourselves that in every moment we are in the midst of a cosmic rendezvous with the divine source, from which we cannot be separated, even for an instant, and live.

In the Presence

Yirah is fear and *yirah* is awe and *yirah* can be an emotion blended of the two.

Whichever flavor you have experienced, the key ingredient is that you who experience *yirah* of heaven—the one who is called a *yirei shamayim*—have a keenly felt sense of the presence of God and of being called to be in the divine presence. The book of Ecclesiastes/*Kohelet* ends with the words: "The end of the matter, everything having been heard, is: fear God and keep His commandments, for this is the whole of man."[30]

The "You" that we call God in our blessings, and whom we fear, and whose presence infuses our hearts with awe, is the "You" whom Rabbi Levi Yitzchak of Berditchev[31] calls out to in the song that he sang, to "*Dudele*," which in Yiddish does not just mean "you" (*du*) but is the intimate, affectionate diminutive form, sung softly to one dearly beloved and close:

> *Ribbono shel Olam*—Lord of the world,
> I shall sing you a *dudele*.
> Where can I find you,
> and where can I not find you?
> For where I go, there You are,
> and where I stand, there You are.
> You, only You and You again.
> If life is good, it is You,
> and if it is bad, it is also You. You . . .
> You are, You have been, and You will be.
> You did reign, You reign, and You will reign.
> You . . .
> Heavens—You,
> earth—You,
> the high—You,
> low—You.

Wherever I turn from,
wherever I turn to: You!
You.

To the east Du,
to the west Du,
to the north Du,
to the south Du,
in front Du,
behind Du
Du, Du Du Du.

The beginning of wisdom is the *yirah* [fear/awe] of God.

—Psalms/ *Tehillim* 111:10

PART THREE

The Route

25

Doing Mussar

THE PURPOSE OF MUSSAR is to help you identify your spiritual curriculum, and then to give you the tools that will help you consciously and effectively engage with the inner work that lies before you. Mussar is summarized in the phrase *tikkun middot ha'nefesh*—improving or remedying the traits of the soul—and it takes some focused effort over a period of time to bring about this rectification. Put simply, practice is how you work on and master your spiritual curriculum.

Mussar aims to help you close the gap between your ideals and the life you actually lead. This convergence is brought about one small step at a time, through practice. Practice doesn't involve seeking some sort of spiritual generator to fill you with light, because all the holiness you need already lives within. Instead, practice focuses on recalibrating specific soul-traits that are obstructing your soul's light from shining into your life.

Life comes with tests, and usually the tests we face are right in line with the state of our personal soul-traits. If your tendency is to lie, you will be tested by situations that call for truth. If you are tightfisted, the tests will be of your generosity.

It is said that Abraham faced ten tests in his life. Abraham is acknowledged as the master of the soul-trait of loving-kindness (*chesed*), and yet none of his tests focused on loving-kindness. Rather, he was tested on the soul-trait of strength (*gevurah*), which is traditionally set opposite and complementary to *chesed*.

Each test we face is a rung on the ladder of spiritual life, and as you pass or fail your tests, you rise or descend spiritually. I call the moment a test arises in the midst of real life "Mussar work." Mussar practice is how we prepare for our inevitable encounters with Mussar work.

The Kelm Yeshiva stressed the value of practice. The Alter of Kelm as-signed the task of cleaning the yeshiva building to the "best" students, and explained why with a pun on the Yiddish verb *kert,* which means both "to sweep" and "to overturn": "*Ver es kert do kert die velt*"—"Whoever sweeps here overturns the world." Sweeping is considered to be a practice that lib-erates us from selfish desires: sweep away the obstacles and your world will be transformed.

It will take a lot of words to explain Mussar practice clearly and to an-swer questions that I know frequently come up, but be assured that once you have digested all these words, what you will have in hand is a simple daily and weekly practice that takes a total of only two to three hours per week.

The Personal Nature of Mussar Practice

No two people are spiritually identical. In consequence, Mussar practice is always geared to the uniqueness of the individual. Because we all have a different set of soul-traits to contend with, the practices that will have the most effect on us will also vary, from person to person and even for the same person at different points in life. This reality is acknowledged in the story I told in chapter 5 about the Mussar students who complained about the other students who were contemplating a decaying fish. "Does it work?" was their teacher's response. That is the bottom line on Mussar practice: is it effective in bringing about deep and lasting spiritual change?

I recognize that we each have our own spiritual curriculum and that different practices will work better for some and not others, so I must state an important caution right here at the beginning. It is entirely true that you may need to focus on a trait that I have in perfect balance, while your greatest trait will elude me. It is also true that you will find that my favorite practice just doesn't work for you. You will reach those conclu-sions through experimentation and self-analysis, and that's what necessi-tates this caution. When you hear an inner voice saying, "That trait is just not important to me," or "That practice has no effect," or "This is boring," I caution you to be very skeptical about who is speaking those whispered words. It could be the voice of good, sensible judgment. It could also be the voice of that adversary to growth and change, your own *yetzer ha'ra.*

Although you are right to seek a customized practice that works just for you, at the same time, Mussar practice requires a degree of submission to the form and a trust that change will happen. If you give heed to every doubt, criticism, and even mocking notion that comes up from within, your practice will be subverted. That is precisely the challenge that the *yetzer ha'ra* sets for you.

Mussar practice requires that you balance watching, learning, and adjusting with being steadfast and persistent. That attitude of persistence will help you overcome the momentary objections the *yetzer ha'ra* throws your way, which are nothing but attempts to see if you can be deflected from the course. You should expect that you will be susceptible to deflection. One reason for this is that, after you have taken on and engaged in some serious Mussar practice, no change will be visible to your inner eye.

You do your practice and it does leave its trace on your soul, but your mind looks around within the field of its limited light and sees no visible change. That makes sense, since the whole point is to bring about change at a much deeper, unconscious level. Still, your *yetzer ha'ra* will whisper, or maybe even shout, "See, this isn't working! Do you see any change? What a waste of time! You could be doing this or that instead!" And so on.

But you persist with your practice, and then one day, you find yourself in a situation to which you would typically, habitually, and predictably respond in a certain way, and suddenly you are aware that you have a different option. Where did that new thought come from? Or maybe it is not even a thought, but you respond spontaneously in an atypical way, and a way that comes closer to the values you have been striving for. What opened up that new possibility for you? It did not come from your conscious mind but from deeper within, where your Mussar practice has been making its mark, in a domain where the light of intellect simply does not shine.

As a practitioner, you have to trust Mussar practice, and trust that it is doing its work. As you will see, the practices themselves are benign, nothing radical or extreme. As well, these practices have been with us for generations. If they were ineffective, or if they had negative effects, we'd know by now. Instead, what we have are reports as well as direct experience of people who have elevated and strengthened their higher selves through practicing Mussar. People used to say about Rabbi Yehuda Leib Nekritz, who was Rabbi Perr's father-in-law, that when he did Mussar, he wasn't a person but an angel. They also said that when he was born, he was smooth as silk, meaning that his inborn character was very good. "But after Mussar . . . ," they would say, and they would never complete the sentence. If silk was the starting point, there were no words to describe where he went from there.

Traditionally, Mussar has been practiced under the direct supervision of a teacher in a community of fellow seekers, usually a yeshiva. The name given to the role of Mussar guide is *mashgiach,* which in Hebrew means, literally, "supervisor." Often the title is qualified as *mashgiach ruchanit,* "spiritual supervisor." Doing Mussar is meant to be a powerful experience that penetrates to the inner depths, and so supervision can be very important to ensuring that the seeker stays in safe and positive territory while still being challenged and moved along the path. As well, a community of seekers provides companionship and interaction to strengthen and guide the individual.

The Mussar practice that follows is based on the experience I have had guiding people who are not in intimate contact with a *mashgiach* or living in an intense, specialized spiritual/religious community. It is still best to do Mussar under the watchful eye of a *mashgiach* and in the company of fellow seekers, but when that is not possible, the next best thing is to cultivate an inner *mashgiach* of your own on whom you can rely. While I mention a few practices that do require supervision (like visualizations and chanting), the Mussar regimen described here has been practiced by hundreds of people and has proven itself to be feasible, effective, and safe without supervision.

26

The Stages of
Mussar Practice

RABBI YISRAEL SALANTER recognized and identified that there are three stages in the practice of Mussar. Understanding these three stages will make clear why the patterns of practice have developed as they have. These three stages form the backbone for everything that follows.

Stage 1: Sensitivity

You begin Mussar practice by becoming sensitive to the soul-traits that operate within you and seeing how they motivate you to think, say, and do the things you do. You seek to heighten your awareness of what is actual within yourself, both of things that are working favorably and things that are in need of attention. You can't go anywhere in your practice until you can identify your soul-traits and see clearly how they operate within you.

This opening stage is crucially important, as it sets the agenda for everything that might follow. Rabbi Yechezkel Levenstein, who was trained in the Mussar center of Kelm and went on to be a great influence in the last generation, underlines the importance of developing sensitivity in the context of Mussar practice:

> It was very often stated in the Beis HaTalmud of Kelm that in order for man to listen and understand *mussar,* he must first sensitize his feelings. Without that, he might listen and learn for an entire lifetime and not know at all what *mussar* is or what it demands of him. For *mussar* involves the most delicate sensitivity.[1]

Another teacher from that same generation, Rabbi Yitzchok Isaac Sher, clarifies exactly what sort of sensitivity we are after. He cites the teachings of the sages from the Talmud that report that when Shaul [Saul] heard David being praised, "he [Shaul] had a sinking feeling and he envied him."[2]

Based on this comment, Rabbi Sher identifies what we look for when we seek to be sensitive: "From their words we can see that the generation of envy is accompanied by a 'sinking feeling'—a fleeting, transitory thought to which man pays little attention." Rabbi Sher is teaching us a key lesson: only by being consciously aware of inner sensations as these occur in our interior world can we know what is happening moment to moment with respect to our soul-traits.

He goes on to underline what is important about this awareness of inner sensations: "One who is aware of how jealousy develops in the heart understands that if he experiences a sinking feeling when hearing his friend being praised, he had better fortify the musings of his heart with wisdom and knowledge."[3] First you have to be aware of what you feel when jealousy arises; those feelings are cues to take appropriate action. Without that awareness, jealousy will arise and flourish unexamined and uninhibited, and the consequences are likely to be destructive, as we read in the story of the first murder recorded in the Torah, when jealousy prompted Cain to kill Abel.

Rabbi Sher is discussing jealousy just as an illustration. What he says applies to all soul-traits. The goal he sets is to be "one who is sensitive to the images of his heart." These "images" are sensations that arrive prior to a thought even taking form. Are you able to see and notice the sparks of impatience before your foot starts tapping? Are you familiar with the inner stirrings that signal desire, before your hand has started to move? Can you be aware of the first tiny inner ripple that is headed toward building into a wave of self-glorification?

Sensitivity means being aware of the seed of a thought, word, feeling, or deed as early as possible in its cycle of germination and birth. The more acute your awareness of what moves within you, the earlier you will see what is arising, and the more you will have choice over the course that inner impulse will take.

So we enter into Mussar practice recognizing that it is vitally important to cultivate inner sensitivity. As well, we must be sensitive to the effect we have on others. This type of sensitivity may seem to be of a quite different sort, but actually it's not, because only your own inner sensors can register the effect your behavior has on others. You know from your own experience how people can anger or hurt you, and yet they can be completely oblivious to the impact their words or actions are having. That's not how we want to be. We should not always aim to please people, and sometimes quite the opposite, but the measure of how well our intentions are translating into reality can be gauged from the responses of others.

The importance of paying attention to life and the way your surroundings respond to you is emphasized in Proverbs: "The ear that hears the reproof of life will abide among the wise."[4] Hearing is a sense, and to practice Mussar means becoming delicately and perceptively sensitive.

Stage 2: Self-Restraint[5]

Though the ultimate goal of Mussar practice is the total transformation of a soul-trait, along the way, and after you become sensitive to the negative role a trait is playing in your life, you need to make a conscious effort to control the behavior that arises from that trait. Once you are aware of your behavioral patterns, you need to try to rein in potentially soul-damaging behavior or push yourself to engage in soul-nourishing behavior that is currently lacking.

In this stage of Mussar practice, informed by our sensitivity, we swing into action using the power of our will.

Let's look at what is meant by practicing self-restraint by taking the quality of truth as a case study.

Let's say that you are at a point in your Mussar practice where you have become sensitive to the role truth and untruth is playing in your life, and you realize that you have a tendency to tell white lies. You are actually aware that telling the truth generates different inner sensations from telling an untruth, and you know which is which.

Once you have come to a heightened awareness of what is going on, the next task for a Mussar practitioner is to exercise self-restraint. I'd go so far as to say that you are obliged to do so, because the excuse that you are unconscious of your behavior is no longer available to you. Farther down the road, you will want to look at the trait or traits that may be motivating the tendency to lie (which could be honor, love, pride, trust, or something else) but at this stage, all you are concerned about is restraining the loose lips themselves. You have to guard your tongue. This will mean holding to a very strict standard of truth, measuring your words on the scale of truth while they are still thoughts and before you say anything.

Proverbs is a good guide here, too, as well as an inspiration: "Whoever restrains his lips is wise."[6]

In this stage of Mussar practice, you do what you can to restrain and guide your words and deeds in regard to those soul-traits that are on your spiritual curriculum. If you are aware that you are impatient, you strive to be more patient. If you have a tendency to lust, you consciously direct your eyes the other way. If you are rather stingy, it is your will that tells your hand to reach into your pocket or purse. I recall an incident when I walked by a plate of cookies. I wasn't hungry, but they appealed to my greed. I asked myself if it was within my capacity not to reach out my hand. It was and I didn't.

Exercising your will to do some things and not to do others is a great and necessary practice. This sort of action will bring your outer life more in line with your inner life, which is itself a Torah value.

In time, the Mussar teachers assure us, the efforts we make to steer our behavior through self-restraint will trigger internal change. The teachers saw great benefit in using personal behavior as a transformative tool, as illustrated by the thirteenth-century saying from *Sefer ha'Chinuch:* "One's heart is drawn after one's outer actions." As you do, so you become.

In *The Path of the Just*[7] Rabbi Luzzatto tells us: "External motions instigate internal motions." What he means is that actions you take that relate to a specific soul-trait can have the effect of changing that trait. You don't have to hold back from acting until the trait has changed; acting itself will generate the reworked inner way of being.

Our teachers assure us that consciously choosing to practice certain behaviors will, in time, cause something new to take root deep within, and our second nature will be transformed as a result of our actions. This principle applies to all soul-traits, as Rabbi Luzzatto says concerning the trait of enthusiasm:

> The best advice for the person in whom this desire does not burn is that he consciously enthuse himself so that enthusiasm might eventually become second nature to him. External movement arouses

the internal, and you certainly have more of a command over the external than the internal.[8]

If you know something about psychology, you may see a parallel here to ideas that would be called behavioristic. Behaviorism is a movement in psychology and philosophy that emphasizes the outward behavioral aspects of thought and tends to dismiss the inward experience, which is where it begins to distinguish itself from Mussar. Behaviorism is unconcerned with inward experiences or states of consciousness, whereas Mussar is deeply concerned with the inner life. Rabbi Shlomo Wolbe has defined Mussar as "building an interior world." But Mussar splits off even further from behaviorism because its concern is for the soul within the context of a spiritual universe with a God, and this is far from a behavioristic perspective. Though Mussar and behaviorism both recognize that actions have real impact, they differ in their understanding and appreciation for what that impact is, where it is registered, and why it should be stimulated.

Rabbi Luzzatto ends his comment on how external actions can create an internal legacy by saying: "Experience testifies to this." It's interesting to see him bring this source of confirmation, rather than relying on the proof texts of the Torah and Talmud. It seems that he wants to let us know that he directly experienced the internal changes that accompanied his behavioral changes. Of course, he can refer only to his own experience, but by doing so he encourages us to trust his experience and apply his teachings to our own lives.

Your will does have transformative potency, though that power is limited, which is why people so frequently break pledges and resolutions. "Quitting smoking is easy," the joke goes. "I've done it hundreds of times." Still, your will is a power with which you have been gifted, and once you are aware that something is clearly out of line, bringing your will into play will have some positive effect.

Stage 3: Transformation

The ultimate step of Mussar practice is to rework the problematic soul-trait so thoroughly at its root that it no longer stands as a barrier to the light of holiness and the connectivity of the soul. Rabbi Yisrael Salanter speaks about the self-restraint stage of Mussar practice we just considered, and contrasts it to this stage of transformation:

> The first is for one to overcome his nature so that he does not commit evil. The second is to change one's nature so that he performs good. The second aspect is more difficult than the first, for it is more difficult to transform one's nature than to overcome his nature. Therefore, man must develop stage by stage. Initially, he should strive to fulfill the precept "Turn from evil" (*Tehillim* [Psalms] 34:15); this is the first aspect of growth. Afterwards, he should strive to fulfill the imperative to "do good" (ibid.), which is the second and more advanced level.[9]

The Mussar masters have developed many techniques to transform soul-traits, as well as many variations on these methods. Three practices that illustrate what is involved in the transformation of soul-traits are visualizations, contemplations, and impassioned chanting (*hitpa'alut*). A visualization is a vivid image held in the mind, a contemplation is a deep idea that is wrestled with, and Mussar chanting involves the repetition of a phrase over and over with melody and emotion as well as meaning.

These sorts of practices are to be done while in retreat from the world of your daily life. None of these methods is analytical. Each in its own way is meant to generate felt experience, which the Alter of Novarodok designates "sensory learning." Visualizations, contemplation, and chanting all create experiences that leave their lasting trace at a deep inner level, far deeper and more effectively than an intellectual idea can penetrate. This is how they are transformative.

Mussar starts from the premise that the roots of our thoughts, words, feelings, and deeds are buried deep within the inner realm, beyond the range of the conscious mind. The unconscious sources from which your life flows are designed to be out of sight, and so no matter how hard you strain and stare, you aren't going to be able to catch even the slightest glimpse of what lives in those permanently shadowy depths.

As Rabbi Leffin writes in *Cheshbon ha'Nefesh* in the early nineteenth century, decades before the birth of psychology: "It is clear that a considerable number of the motions of the psyche are concealed in the hidden chambers of a man's heart every day, one within another, so that he no longer knows or recognizes them. But the more deeply they are hidden, the more strongly do they act within the psyche."[10] It follows, then, that a transformation in our thoughts, words, feelings, and actions requires practices that have an impact at that deep inner level as well.

To continue to illustrate with the example of truth, it should be clear that if you have become sensitized to the role untruth is playing in your life, you will next do what you can to swear off falsehood. That will mean consciously guarding your tongue so the impulse to lie is restrained and overcome. But it is much greater to transform yourself so that this impulse no longer exists. Instead of curbing the desire to tell a lie, the thought of lying simply does not arise in you.

The step to transformation involves focused practice not aimed at the soul-trait of truth itself, but rather at what it is that is motivating the lying. There will be an underlying trait that is being served by straying from truth. You may lie to gain honor or for financial advantage or some other perceived advantage. To be completely freed of the tendency to lie requires that this causal trait be reprogrammed, not with ideas but with the sorts of direct experiences that can wire new patterns of thought and feeling, from deep within. Do this, and it will not even occur to you to act in habitual negative ways, nor will it take any act of restraint to adhere to good and beneficial speech and deeds.

27

Identifying Your
Spiritual Curriculum

WITH THIS BACKGROUND of explanation and theory, I am now ready to outline a Mussar practice you can take on in your own life. As you have learned, the starting point is to become sensitive to the reality of what is true for you. Next, you need to take steps to restrain and avoid your negative patterns. Ultimately, your goal is to change yourself so profoundly that you will have reworked your impulses and intuitions.

I have been saying all along that the starting point to doing Mussar practice is identifying your personal spiritual curriculum. Now is the time to do so. You take your first step into this practice by setting out a list of the traits that you need to focus on because these are the ones that are obstructing the light of holiness from shining brightly in your life.

Traditionally, the norm has been to compose a list of thirteen soul-traits. This is the pattern given in the book *Cheshbon ha'Nefesh* and that was implicitly endorsed by Rabbi Yisrael Salanter, who made known a list of thirteen that he held to be of great importance. It is possible to work with a smaller number of traits, and complicated to go for more. I'll explain the logic to a list of thirteen.

In Mussar practice, we focus on the first soul-trait from your list for just one week, then move on to the second trait for the next week, and so on, through your full list. After you have focused for one week on each trait on your list, you then go back to the beginning and repeat the whole cycle.

This pattern of practice is based on the recognition that inner change happens most effectively when you exercise a single trait intensely for a limited period of time, after which you put it on the back burner until it comes around for another week once again. For any given week, you will be "majoring" in one trait, and you will also have a list of other traits that you are "minoring" in.

If you have a list of thirteen traits, it will take thirteen weeks to go through the full cycle, after which you go back to the beginning and start again. It works out neatly that if your list has thirteen traits, then you can fit four full cycles into one year, as four times thirteen equals fifty-two, the number of weeks in a year. Although it may seem like a period of one week focused on one trait is far too little time to accomplish a task like becoming more generous or less angry or more humble, in this pattern of practice you will actually spend a total of four weeks per trait per year. Doesn't it seem much more plausible that you will see a real effect after spending a month in a year cultivating each of your priority qualities?

Still, there is nothing magical about the number thirteen, and experience has taught me that some people can get completely paralyzed by having to come up with a list that long. It is fine to start with as few as five or six identified soul-traits. As time goes on, your own observations of yourself may cause you to add to your list.

Thirteen qualities and a whole year might also seem like a big bite to chew, but as you'll soon see, all the steps are actually small and manageable.

To prepare you to go through the task of identifying your own spiritual curriculum, I will describe some steps you can take that will help you know whether a trait ought to be on your list or not.

Using an "Accounting of the Soul" Diary

Some traits that are all too well-known to you will leap onto your list. Or perhaps in reading or reviewing the chapters in part 2 of this book, something you need to work on became clear to you. There will likely be other qualities that need to be discovered.

When asked how a person could become familiar with his or her own character traits, Rabbi Shlomo Wolbe answered, "If one would keep a daily accounting of the traits that arise in every given situation, after a few weeks he will be able to tell which trait manifests itself most often."[1]

Rabbi Wolbe is referring to the practice known as "Accounting of the Soul."[2] This practice embodies a systematic process of self-observation—the "accounting"—that provides you with clear knowledge of the forces and contours of your own inner landscape. Like an accountant doing an audit, when you do the Accounting of the Soul you observe your life and sort out a balance sheet of your inner being. The conscious mind now gains access to features of the unconscious and becomes aware of the soul-traits that shape your everyday existence. This new awareness is crucial to the journey of transformation and ascent.

Accounting of the Soul practice involves keeping a journal. Starting that journal in the right way is the first concrete step in Mussar practice and can help you compose your list of traits. Later, you will use your journal in a different way, once your practice begins to focus on the traits on your list.

Equip yourself with a notebook. I've found that a nothing-fancy, lined, coil notebook from the local drugstore works just fine for the job. More recently, I have used bound blank books and even sketching books. The only rule I suggest is not getting a very small notebook because it may disappear too easily. Place the notebook beside your bed, along with a pen, and prepare to make some notes every evening.

The norm is to make an entry as you are retiring for the night. Some people are so tired by the time they get to bed that this isn't the ideal time for them, and if that is true for you, then look for another point in your day that works for you. One student found that it worked well to keep her journal by her coffeepot.

At this stage, what you are to record in your journal is any experience you had in the last twenty-four hours that tells you something about one of your soul-traits. With your journal open and pen in hand, take a moment to cast your mind back over the day. Did anything take place that in any way reflects any of the eighteen soul-traits described in this book? You can use the table of contents as a prompt. Mentally run through your day, looking to see if any of the listed traits made an appearance in your experiences. These traits may show up in something you did or said, or in thoughts you had or sensations you experienced, even if you didn't speak or act on those notions.

A quality may leap right out at you—you lost your temper with your kids or you got coerced into saying yes to something you know you shouldn't have taken on. Did you have an opportunity to give charity that you let pass by? Are you aware that you spoke falsely, gossiped, or, at the other end of the spectrum, told the truth when it was difficult to do so?

to put your efforts, without waiting to learn those lessons from a massive earthquake.

Whatever you see, record. Note in your notebook any incident that reveals one of your soul-traits. Your task is to make a brief note of the thought, feeling, words, or acts within which you can identify the play of a soul-trait. Objectivity is what you seek here, avoiding self-judgment of any kind.

One student relates how he let his diary work for him in this way: "I just watch myself, and when something happens that upsets me, that makes me want to lash out at people or hurts me or makes me want to turn from them altogether, I try to identify what quality in me that is. Sometimes the answer is surprising. I go from very real and concrete events and emotions to identify general and foundational character traits."

Your journal will begin to reveal traits that you can place on your list. Does arrogance show up, because you can detect incidents that reveal a tendency to puff up your ego like a peacock? Or do you maybe see the opposite tendency, allowing yourself too readily to be walked all over? Many of us lead isolated lives, spending too much time in a one-to-one relationship to electronic media, or working in cubicles, or driving alone in cars, and so on. Those of us afflicted with emotional isolation might place the soul-trait of compassion or loving-kindness on our lists, since these two traits bring us into intimate relationship with others.

As you observe your behavior, record incidents, and identify the relevant soul-traits, try to find your list of thirteen soul-traits from the eighteen covered in part 2. These eighteen chapters address general topics that cover much of what goes on in our inner lives, as it relates to our soul-traits. I have seen students get lost and confused by trying to invent categories, some of which turned out not even to be inner qualities at all, like "money" or "abundance." So use these chapters to help you identify soul-traits that truly do need your attention.

There is a common tendency to be fascinated with the new and different, of which we need to be wary. While it may be entirely justified to add to your list a quality that isn't among the ones I've presented in this book, do so only if you feel clearly and strongly compelled to pinpoint that particular additional trait. In most cases, you'll find that if you think about it a bit, the "something else" that you want to work on can find a place under

Or you may have to think and probe a bit to uncover the imprint on your soul as it shaped your day. But I assure you the imprint is there.

One thing to pay particular attention to is something I discussed in chapter 4, the concept of *bechirah*-points. Recall that what Rabbi Dessler named as *bechirah*-points are those particular inner places where issues of choice are very lively in you. He was describing the front line where, when put to the test, good and evil turn out to be well-balanced and so any decision you make could go either way. On one side is the *yetzer ha'tov* (good inclination), and on the other the *yetzer ha'ra* (evil inclination). The place where they meet and contend are your *bechirah*-points.

You can identify soul-traits that ought to be noted in your journal by paying close attention to the struggles you wage on the front line in your inner life. Ask yourself, "Which *bechirah*-points are my challenges?" Think of and be alert to those situations where you can feel yourself teetering on the brink of a choice between one option you know to be good and another that, while it is bound to be attractive, isn't in the best interests of the soul. Whenever you find yourself to be struggling in that unconfirmed no-man's-land between that which elevates and that which doesn't, try to name the territory where the struggle takes place. The name you assign will be that of the relevant soul-trait.

If you pass a homeless person and you feel inclined to give money, but you hold back and your hand goes into your pocket but it doesn't quickly come out holding anything, that wavering is the sign of a *bechirah*-point in the soul-trait of generosity. Or if you feel grateful for something and you think of expressing your thanks, but you worry that you won't say the right thing or find the right moment, so you stay silent, but that doesn't feel right either, so you look at it again . . . , this is all happening in the territory of gratitude. And so on with all the soul-traits. The question is, where are the front lines in your own battles to choose and decide?

These examples I just gave tell you that the challenges that take place at your *bechirah*-points need not be monumental. In fact, what you are really looking to detect are the little tremors that take place in everyday life that are important not because they are large but because they reveal the fault lines that run beneath the surface of your life. By becoming aware of the habits, patterns, and tendencies that are revealed in the hundreds of choices you make every day, especially in the areas that have the ripest potential for growth (which are your *bechirah*-points), you will know where one of the eighteen traits already listed. Students have often asked me if there is a complete list of soul-traits, and I have not come across such a resource. In response, I have created a list culled from various Mussar sources. You'll find that long list in the appendix.

There is nothing wrong with recording incidents that reveal strong or balanced traits. The real quarry, however, is traits that appear to you as sources of suffering, confusion, conflict, or any other negative outcome. You might be able to identify that you feel you've got too much of a trait, like anger, for example, or it could be too little, like calmness. Too little anger (expressed as passion and vitality) is also a possibility.

As you keep your daily diary, whenever a single quality shows up more than once, add that one to your list. Any quality that could benefit from some measure of change belongs on your list. And if you already feel you are adequately generous, for example, you've identified one trait you don't need on your list.

You may get your thirteen right away, quite easily. If so, you can jump into the next phase of practice. But it may take you a week or two to come up with your list. If it takes more than a month to identify the full thirteen, start with what you have and keep an eye out for what else you could add later.

Don't fall into obsessing over the choice of your thirteen qualities, because it is actually hard to go seriously "wrong." Even if you put a quality on your list that turns out not be such an important one for you, it won't do you any harm to keep paying attention to that one, too. For example, just because you don't make a habit of lying doesn't mean that you won't be able to get some benefit out of having "truth" on your list.

And if you happen to miss out on a quality that really ought to be on your list, don't worry about that, either. You can pick it up on the next round, and in the meantime you will be surprised to find yourself doing good work on that quality anyway, because the Mussar practice has the effect of making you more aware and more committed to yourself in general, even if you are working on one individual quality at a time.

We learn from Rabbi Eliyahu Dessler that initially, a person should always look for positive traits to focus on. He means that the best way to reduce a negative trait is to try to build up another counterbalancing trait. If you see yourself as too angry, look for a trait that embodies the opposite of anger. You would then put calmness or humility on your list, not anger.

If you are judgmental and jealous, the corresponding positive trait might be "honor." If you come to see yourself as overly concerned with material possessions, put "simplicity" on your list. Maybe the clearest example is stinginess: don't try to be less of a miser—practice generosity. And so on. Wherever you identify behavior that is damaging and does not reflect Torah values, seek to name a positive counterpart and add that one to your list, not the negative one.

Rabbi Meir Chodosh[3] once discussed the trait of anger and pointed out that "it is not the trait of anger that needs working on, but the trait of goodwill. Once a person's anger is aroused it is too late to work on it. However, if one maintains goodwill and sees things in a positive light, one will never reach the point of getting angry."[4] It was said about Rabbi Chodosh that in general, he "did not deal with bad character traits. He preferred to deal with the positive to develop themes that exalt the personality and raise it higher and higher. Through this, a person will naturally keep his distance from the ugly and the degraded."[5]

There are several reasons for always choosing a positive trait as the focus for your Mussar practice. One is that it avoids a major pitfall of any discipline of self-improvement, which is that you develop negative feelings about yourself because you aren't perfect. I have had students become aware of a truth about themselves that was very hard to bear. Others have suddenly seen flaws in the world at large and so have become very judgmental of other people. Working on positive traits makes this negativity less likely.

There is also a spin-off effect to be gained from strengthening a positive trait. Even a small success in an area of strength will generate successes in weaker areas as well.

But the most important reason to stay focused on positive traits is the Mussar axiom that efforts to reduce negative traits are almost always doomed to failure. If you became sensitive to your own excessive anger, for example, and you then tried to reduce your anger, that would be like trying to get a fire to cool down. You are no more likely to be able to reduce anger directly than you are to get a fire to lose heat. Instead, what you need to do is to find whatever will serve as the "water" in the particular situation.

The guideline to stay with positive qualities, and to use a positive trait to work on a negative one, is very important to Mussar practice. Remembering this principle will save you a lot of potential grief along the way and, in the words of *Orchot Tzaddikim,* will "straighten the road to the great King's court."[6]

Calling on one soul-trait to affect another soul-trait relies heavily on your self-awareness, because you need to be able to identify not only your troublesome soul-trait, but also a positive one you can call on to strengthen.

It follows that the list you make up should only have positive traits on it.

As you identify the traits that belong on your list, write them on the first page or the inside front cover of your notebook, where you'll have easy reference to them.

Concerning your list, one question that comes up frequently is, what if a selected trait doesn't feel right or hold your interest? My advice is not to switch horses midstream. Each trait you work on is only a small part of the practice, so being a little bored or uncomfortable needn't undercut all the other good work you'll do. Just practice persistence. It's entirely possible that the resistance you feel may be pointing to something worthy of your attention. In time, the shell that you are bouncing off of will crack open to reveal something you didn't know about yourself.

And again (because you can't be cautioned too often), pay close attention to that little inner voice that complains and deflects you from the process in whatever creative ways it may crop up. As you think of your journal and making your list of traits, one night you might hear, "Not tonight," and another night, "That's a stupid quality," but if you stand in awareness as the witness to your inner dialogue, you may notice that the whispering you are hearing is very similar and maybe even strikingly familiar. You can test that voice by asking if it seems to be offering guidance that is likely to contribute to the well-being of your soul. Hear it, know it for what it is, and continue to place one foot in front of the other on your journey of ascent.

28

Daily Practice

DAILY MUSSAR PRACTICE is quite simple. Many of these practices were developed in the context of the nineteenth-century Orthodox Jewish community, where the unquestioned priority for spiritual/religious commitment was Torah study. Mussar techniques had to be effective without being time-consuming.

Daily Reminder Phrase

Soon after you have awakened in the morning, and before you begin the activities of your day, you need to remind yourself of the soul-trait you are currently working on from your list of thirteen. To do this, you need to equip yourself with a phrase that captures the essence of each soul-trait that is on your list. You'll find a statement of this sort at the head of every chapter in part 2 of this book. You can write out these statements on index cards or slips of paper for easy reference.

You can put your cards beside your bed or at another place where you will be sure to see them as soon as you start your day. I have my cards set up on the little table in the room where I pray and meditate. I place the card that applies to the soul-trait I am working on for that week at the front of the pile. My wife prefers to write her phrase on a small piece of paper that she tapes to the mirror in the bathroom, where she is sure to see it every morning. I know people who have programmed the screensaver on their computer to flash their weekly phrase.

The phrases that I have given often derive from traditional sources, but there is nothing magical in the words as I've written them. If you find that you want to change your phrase to be closer to your own understanding of the quality as it plays out in you, do so. Also, if you have on your list a quality that isn't covered in this book, you will have to find a reminder phrase of your own. Look in a dictionary, the Bible, or any other wisdom source, or just make up a phrase, so long as what you end up with accurately captures the essence of the ideal for that particular quality. The reminder phrase must always be short and pithy.

Every morning, read over the phrase of the week slowly and with full concentration. Read it aloud. Read it several times. Or chant it to yourself. Go over this reminder in whatever way will cause it to be so clearly illuminated in your mind that it seems to have been written in neon. Once you've really heard the phrase in so penetrating a way, go on with your day.

Of course, during the day you try to live up to the ideal stated on your reminder card, but not with strain or by repressing tendencies. Just do your best.

Meditation

The best time to meditate, chant, or do visualizations or contemplations is also in the morning, around the same time that you are reviewing your phrase. It's not advisable to do Mussar chanting, visualizations, or contemplations without supervision, but you can undertake a meditation practice on your own.

Meditation helps develop qualities of awareness and concentration that are very helpful and supportive of Mussar practice. For example, we've noted that the first stage of Mussar practice is called "Sensitivity," but how sensitive can you be without a tuned and sharpened sense of awareness? Things will happen and you won't even register them on the screen of your consciousness. And in describing the *shiviti* contemplation in chapter 24, we encountered the importance of concentration in this spiritual practice.

In chapter 5, I quoted a story from the book *Cheshbon ha'Nefesh* that describes a meditation practice. This description is the basis for the meditation I do and teach.

Sit in a quiet spot and close your eyes. You can meditate for as little as four minutes and then, as your concentration deepens, you can lengthen the time period, just as described in *Cheshbon ha'Nefesh*. You can estimate the time or set a timer (even a microwave timer will do).

Come to a quiet place within and pay attention to the flow of the breath coming in and going out. Just observe. Then, after a few breaths, direct your mind to hold in awareness the word *sh'ma,* which in Hebrew means "listen." This is a useful object to meditate on, since "listen" implies a certain sensitivity and receptiveness. It doesn't matter whether you say the word to yourself or visualize it. The point is to practice developing strong concentration, and some people are more aural and others more visual.

Your awareness is likely to wander away from that single word—*sh'ma*—and off into thinking and planning and wondering and judging. As soon as you become aware that your attention has wandered off, make note of that fact and gently let go of whatever it was that dragged awareness away from its focus. Return awareness to the word that is your object of concentration.

If it's a sound that has snagged you and dragged awareness toward it, note that "hearing" has taken place, and return your attention to the focus word *sh'ma.*

Or has a feeling in your leg drawn attention to your leg and away from your chosen focus? Here make a mental note of "feeling" and return your attention to the word-object.

Gently but insistently return to the single word *sh'ma.*

This meditation helps to develop your concentration and inner clarity. It also helps you to become more aware of the observer within.

Since distraction will commonly occur, meditation can be a way to identify the things that have the power to drag us away from our intentions. You can learn something important about your spiritual curriculum by becoming aware of what it is that distracts you from concentrating where you would like to. What distracts you won't be the same as what distracts me.

I have learned over the years that I myself am prone to planning when I am supposed to be meditating. I sit and clear my mind with the committed intention of meditating on a single word, and within a few seconds I fly off into thinking about what I have to do next, and what I have to get done that day, and what if this, and what if that. As soon as I catch myself doing that, I return my focus to the word-object. Later, though, when I reflect on my experience, I can see that having my mind steal away into planning reveals a soul-trait that is on my spiritual curriculum, which is trust (*bitachon*). I've told my mind to attend to the word *sh'ma,* but up bubbles concern about what will be coming in the future. With stronger trust, I could set aside any anxiety about future happenings. Now I am meditating; the future will be provided for.

You may be distracted by planning as well. Or maybe you sit to meditate and it's desire, or lust, or anger, or judgment, or jealousy that comes to pull your mind away from your meditation. When this happens, gently return your mind to the word-object. Later, you can reflect on what that distraction is telling you about the soul-traits on your spiritual curriculum.

Bedtime Practice

At bedtime, pull out your notebook and try to identify events in your day that might reveal the presence of the specific quality you are working on for that week. Record all relevant incidents, thoughts, and experiences that relate to that particular quality. This is a different use of the journal than when what you were recording anything that revealed a soul-trait so you could compose your list of traits. Now you are using the evening writing practice to gain insight and clarity on the one trait that is your focus for the week.

You may have assigned yourself exercises (*kabbalot*) regarding your trait of the week, a practice described in the next chapter. If so, your evening journal is where you record whether you did or did not do something that day to fulfill your *kabbalah*. If you are practicing generosity and you set yourself to do three generous acts a day, for example, you'll record in your journal whether or not you did those acts and what you did or didn't do. You can have a *kabbalah* for any soul-trait, and you will record in your diary how you did in fulfilling that exercise that day.

But you record more than just your fulfillment of *kabbalot*. Write down whatever you see in your day that touches on the soul-trait that is your focus for that week. Your notes should be brief, just an outline of the facts that reveal something of your characteristics. Focus especially on the role you played in events. Don't worry if what you write wouldn't pass as literature. No one but you ever need see this notebook.

It is crucially important that you not pass judgment on yourself in the retelling. You don't want to beat yourself up for your slipups or heap praise on yourself for your victories. You just want a factual and accurate picture of the play of your inner life as it shapes your thoughts, words, and deeds in action. The details contain the underlying patterns that recur in your life, and by examining them, you get nothing less than a readout on the contents of your unconscious, as these express themselves in the particulars of your life.

There is no need to write volumes. Brief notes will do. More important than the amount you write or the floweriness of the prose is the honesty you bring to your introspection. Shine a bright light on your day, see what there is to see about the quality that is your focus for that week, and write down just what you need to in order to record and clarify the facts of your motives, actions, and reactions.

It may not always be apparent which of the qualities was actually involved in a situation. In that case, reviewing a chapter or two from part 2 will help you to identify and understand which of the soul-traits may or may not have been present in that particular situation.

You may feel tempted to run over things mentally instead of troubling to write them out, but I can tell you from experience that it is important that notes be written. Just thinking about your day gives you no visible, tangible "practice" to hold on to, and that increases the likelihood that in time your "accounting" will slip away and, ultimately, be abandoned.

Also, most of us, me included, are often perfectly content to keep ideas all jumbled and fuzzy in our heads, even though we delude ourselves into thinking we have them all fully worked out. The act of writing forces us to get clearer than we otherwise would.

I ask my students to use their Accounting of the Soul journal to record the events of their daily lives. Some Mussar teachers forgo the recording of personal experience and instead have students check off whenever they fulfill a *kabbalah* or have just lived up to the ideal of the trait, and also when they did not come up to the mark. This is a more quantitative approach to Mussar, and while this is exactly how Rabbi Menachem Mendel Leffin presents the practice in *Cheshbon ha'Nefesh,* and despite the fact that some of my dearest colleagues in the Mussar world teach this method, I find this quantitative approach much less effective than recording (and thereby reliving) the details of the experiences themselves. In my experience and the experiences reported by my students, keeping a journal of daily incidents is very effective for raising the awareness that is the foundation for Mussar practice. I can't imagine that keeping a scorecard can be as effective in this way.

It is very important to commit to writing in your journal every day. Even if you don't feel like it, even if nothing much happened that day, even if you are tired, even if you get to bed late, even if . . . , just haul out your notebook and start to write. I have recommended to students that it is better to write the words "nothing in particular" in your diary than nothing at all. The only break I ever give myself is Friday evening, because I make a practice of not writing on the Sabbath, which begins at sunset on Friday.

The results of this practice reveal themselves very slowly, the way the outlines of a photo emerge on paper soaking in developing solution. When you miss a day, you delay that process. But worse still, missing one day can lead to missing another, until your notebook somehow gets buried beneath that dusty pile of books by your bedside, never to be touched again.

But here's my real warning to you on missing days: the little voice that says to you, "Not tonight" is very likely the same little voice that whispers in your ear at other times in your life, only to trip you up and send you crashing. This seductive, destructive little voice within you is actually the adversary you need to contend with. When you stick to your commitment to record your soul-trait experiences every night, you are already working to master those tendencies.

And if you do miss a night or two, or even a week, don't waste a moment in doubt or recrimination. The very next evening, pick up your pen and write again. And recommit.

This practice exposes to the conscious mind the forces and impulses that are firmly anchored in the unconscious, and when that picture clarifies, these shadowy influences begin to lose their power. The very act of becoming conscious of our inner life robs the unconscious sources of their might, and frees us to direct our lives closer to the values and ideals we hold for ourselves, that until now we have not been able to reach. In short, the dictatorship of habit is overthrown and replaced by true freedom of choice. The result is a clarity and strength you have never before experienced.

Your final daily activity is to read a small section from a Mussar text. The ideal is to read a few paragraphs that touch directly on the soul-trait you have in focus that week, such as from a chapter in part 2 of this book or from one of the other Mussar sources that focus on soul-traits such as *Cheshbon ha'Nefesh* or *Orchot Tzaddikim*. Mussar is also a perspective on life and on our journey through this world, and so it is also beneficial to read a Mussar text that doesn't focus on the soul-trait per se. Finally, a number of biographies of Mussar masters have been published.[1] These, too, make good reading because they embody the Mussar teachings and share the inspiring and instructive stories of our guides who went this way before us.

There is no set time to do this reading in your day. I prefer to do it in the evening, before I write in my journal. You might prefer to do it right after your morning recitation of your phrase. Or another time in your day might suit you. As with many good habits, the most important thing is to find a time that will work for you consistently, so you will be able to keep up the practice with minimum resistance.

An Illustration

Let's say that the first quality on your list is equanimity. On the day that you begin the practice, and for the next six days, every morning when you arise you will recite to yourself the phrase I've provided, or your own version of it: "Rise above events that are inconsequential—both bad and good—for they are not worth disturbing my peace of mind." You'll go over this phrase several times, perhaps in different ways, until its message is really imprinted on your mind. You want to absorb the message in a deep and penetrating way.

Then, every evening that same week, you'll record in your diary at bedtime those things that happened to you that day that reveal something about the presence or absence of equanimity in your experience. It may be big—"I got really upset when . . ."—or small—"I can recall the tiny twinge of disturbance that came up at . . ." Whatever it is, write it down.

Sometime during every day, you will read something from a Mussar source, preferably on the trait of "calmness of the soul," as the Mussar teachers name equanimity, though reading a selection from one of the classic Mussar sources or even the biography of a Mussar great will help your practice as well.

If you have a learning partnership, sometime during the week when equanimity is in focus you will meet to learn with your partner.

Then, at the end of seven days focused just on equanimity, you will have reached your changeover day. The second week is about to begin, and now you leave equanimity behind and refer to your list to see what your next quality is. You put the reminder card for that new soul-trait at the front of the pile, ready to recite every morning of that week, while in the evenings you'll record only those matters related to that next quality on your list.

So it goes, through the thirteen weeks, at which point you will again reach a changeover day that will return you right back to the first of the qualities on your list, in this example, back to equanimity. In the course of a year, you will go through that full set of thirteen qualities exactly four times.

29

Weekly Practice

YOU NOW HAVE YOUR LIST of traits. Congratulations! Now your practice begins in earnest.

You will focus on the first trait on your list for one week, then move to the next, on through the full cycle of traits on your list. It doesn't matter which day of the week you begin, but once you've chosen the day, that will be the day you change over to your next soul-trait. It's good to pick a day that is already in some way a "changeover" day for you, to make it easier to remember to make the switch from one quality to the next one on your list. I make the change on Saturday evening, which is when the Jewish week begins. If you work Monday to Friday, you might want to make Sunday evening your changeover day. Do whatever works for you that makes it easier to remember to make the switch.

We turn now to look at what you will actually do in your week of practice.

Text Study

Every week, you should read something from a Mussar source on the trait you have in focus. The chapters in part 2 of this book are written specifically for that purpose. You can also find reading material in the classic Mussar texts, like *The Duties of the Heart, Orchot Tzaddikim, The Palm Tree of Deborah, The Path of the Just, Cheshbon ha' Nefesh,* and *Ohr Yisrael* (all of which are available in both Hebrew and English versions). There are also more recent Mussar texts, like *Strive for Truth! Lev Eliyahu,* and *Musar for Moderns.* The Mussar talks of Rabbis Chaim Shmulevitz, Michal Barenboim, and Yechezkel Levenstein are available in both Hebrew and English.

Two extremely good Mussar books for study are currently available only in Hebrew: *Madregat ha'Adam* (The Levels of Man) and *Alei Shur.*

You will reap the greatest benefit by lining up your text learning with your soul-trait practice. I'm suggesting that, where possible, you focus your reading on the soul-trait that is your concern for that week. If your current focus is generosity, then you can make your reading chapter 17 of this book, and so on. On another cycle of traits, you might go over that chapter again. Or you might seek out the chapter on generosity in *Orchot Tzaddikim,* or Rabbi Dessler's discussion of "giving and taking" in *Strive for Truth!*

A certain amount of your selection should be read daily, as was explained in the section on daily practice.

It is very helpful to set up a learning partnership with someone else whom you meet with every week (or two) to learn a text. This is the traditional learning form called *chevruta,* which is traditional in large part because it is such a very effective way to learn. When you read something on your own, you don't get nearly as much from the text as you do when you discuss and even debate it with a partner. If nothing else, you will benefit from seeing the text through different eyes, with a different perspective. Ideally you should meet with your partner in person, though I have had very successful and satisfying telephone learning partnerships.

Learning with a partner can be focused on the reading you are doing about your soul-trait, or you may want to work your way through a Mussar text. At this writing I have two weekly partnerships, each of which is making its way slowly through a Mussar text.

Reading and learning a Mussar text are done in a specific way. You don't just read through the words as you would a novel or newspaper article. One partner reads a sentence aloud and then pauses. Either partner can then ask a question or give a reflection or illustration to support or even to challenge what the author says. When the point has been thoroughly considered and there seems to be no more to say, go on to the next sentence. The learning partners can alternate taking turns reading a paragraph or a page.

I can illustrate from my own experience. For over two years I met weekly with a partner[1] to study *The Palm Tree of Deborah,* a Mussar classic written by Rabbi Moshe Cordovero in the sixteenth century. My partner and I took turns reading a paragraph aloud, sometimes stopping after a sentence to clarify our own understanding of the meaning, and having a thorough discussion at the end of each paragraph. We made special effort to see how we could apply Rabbi Cordovero's wise counsel in our own lives. (Now this partner and I have gone on to learn *Alei Shur,* a more recent book on Mussar by Rabbi Shlomo Wolbe.)

I recall one paragraph in *The Palm Tree of Deborah* that made a big impression. It described how wisdom (*chochmah*) is distributed within the universe. The author then drew an analogy for how we ourselves should share our own wisdom in life. It didn't sound like much of a teaching. It simply said, "One should disseminate his wisdom to each person in the measure his intellect can grasp, according to what is proper for him and his needs." That's the whole of it, and had I just been reading on my own, I likely would have assumed I got the point right away and kept right on reading. But when my partner and I stopped to discuss this guidance, so many things came tumbling out.

We grasped that we were being told that wisdom, as good as it is, isn't necessarily better for being more. The analogy we came up with was of sunshine and rain, which are certainly good, though too much of one will create a desert and too much of the other, a flood. So it is with our wisdom—we surely have an obligation to share it, but for it to be helpful, before we pour our wisdom on someone, we have to exercise discernment to determine the level of that person's capacity and need. It's just not right to unleash our wisdom in excess of those levels, because if we do, we can cause harm, even with wisdom. This is so wise and practical, yet it took a careful reading and a lot of discussion to uncover this much value in the teaching.

Rabbi Yisrael Salanter gives a lovely insight into the nature of learning in partnership. The process begins, he says, "with a student passionately defending his own line of reasoning." Eventually, dispute gives way to the search for truth, which is characterized by "an unruffled and calm spirit, when a person accepts the validity of a conclusion regardless of whether he or his colleague was correct." He tells us that even the starting point is positive, as "the initial animosity is the aspect of learning with sharp analysis." But the end, he says, is love.[2]

Mussar involves study to support and guide the journey of transformation on the way of the soul. Intellectual activity is not the whole of the practice, of course. Other methods are needed to complement learning.

Kabbalot

We have encountered the Mussar principle that the external awakens the internal.[3] In short, the heart and mind of a human being are deeply affected by physical actions. As you can imagine, this reality has two sides: negative actions leave negative traces, while positive actions leave positive traces.

A diet of violent movies, political leaders repeatedly trying to achieve their aims by violence, or a home life punctuated by violence will generate a soul accustomed to violence. So too for other influences we might consider negative and damaging. Fortunately, the dynamic works in the opposite direction as well. The hard heart that does kindness in time becomes softened.

This teaching has given rise to the practice of *kabbalot,* a word that literally means "things received,"[4] but which can be understood more simply as Mussar exercises that a person takes upon himself or herself. Every week, you need to assign yourself *kabbalot* related to the soul-trait you have in focus during any given week.

For example, if you have the soul-trait of generosity on your list, you will want to cultivate a more open-handed way of being in the world. You look at your financial situation and determine that you can give away $100 in the week that generosity is the trait you have in focus. We have been taught that it is the act of opening the hand that leaves its impression on the soul,[5] and so it is the act of giving that stimulates the soul-trait of generosity. With that in mind, it follows that your *kabbalah* will be to give away $1 to one hundred people or causes rather than $100 to one person or organization. The act of extending your hand one hundred times is the external motion that will generate the internal motion you seek.

Rabbi Eliyahu Dessler looked at this very issue when he considered how we can develop the quality of generosity. For his starting point, Rabbi Dessler cites the same line from *Path of the Just:* "External motions instigate internal ones."[6] Rabbi Dessler concluded that the very act of giving is what makes us more charitable, merciful, and loving. "Love flows in the direction of giving," he said.

Giving $100 in $1 increments over the course of a week is a *kabbalah* for the soul-trait of generosity. So, too, is assigning yourself to greet other people. By "giving" your greeting, the trait of generosity will be implanted in your heart. I notice that when some people come to sit down after having received an honor in synagogue, they keep their heads down and beetle right back to their seats. Other people make eye contact and then a hand is extended and shaken. And there are some people who seem to want to shake every hand they can reach.

You could assign yourself the *kabbalah* to greet more people than you ordinarily do, or a certain category of people, or to greet people more enthusiastically.

Rabbi Shlomo Wolbe suggests a *kabbalah* for impatience. He suggests that we take on the practice in small doses, thirty minutes a day. Pick the time of day when your patience is most likely to be challenged. Is it when you first get to work in the morning? Or when you come home in the evening after a long and stressful day? Or when you, like me, slip behind the wheel of the car, late as usual? Now commit to being patient for a half-hour in just that period. If that is too long and you are likely to lose your patience before the time is up, start with fifteen minutes, or even ten. The point of this *kabbalah* is to begin to exercise some choice over how you react to situations and, like any training regime, start small and build up.

Rabbi Wolbe says that after doing this practice for a while, add thirty minutes some other time in your day. Like that, over the course of a whole year, you will have made patience a cornerstone of your daily life. "With so much experience with patience," he says, "you will respond patiently to whatever happens to you."

Another example of a *kabbalah* also comes from an assignment Rabbi Wolbe gave to a Mussar group. Drawing on the saying in *Pirkei Avot*— "Who is wise? One who learns from every person"—he deduces that there is literally something to learn from every person: some small behavior, some personality trait, or some bit of wisdom. His students were assigned the *kabbalah* of finding three things every day to learn from their friends. "We will continue for a number of weeks," he writes. "From this point it will be substantive learning, that we will pay attention to some good behavior of a friend and to say to ourselves, 'How nice is this behavior, and I will also act like him in this thing!'"[7]

Every week, assign yourself *kabbalot* that will give practical expression to the soul-trait that is your trait of the week. Your *kabbalot* should be custom designed to stretch you in just the way you need to exercise the soul-trait you want to strengthen.

Sample Kabbalot *for a Practice Week*

SOUL-TRAIT	KABBALAH
Generosity	Give $1 to one hundred people or causes.
Humility	Sit in the back of the room or hall.
Honor	Speak only positively about other people.
Gratitude	Express thanks to every inanimate thing that sustains you.
Simplicity	Acquire nothing nonessential.
Loving-Kindness	Greet everyone you meet before they greet you.

30

Further Practices

The Annual Cycle

When you have finally reached the end of a whole year of practice, there are several things for you to do.

By this time, you will have completed a tremendous amount of introspective work, more than many people do in their whole lives. You will see yourself and know yourself more fully and more deeply than ever before. In the deeds and thoughts that fill your diary, you will be able to discern a newly accurate picture of the forces that move your inner life.

At the end of the year, it is time to draw some conclusions. Basing your review on your bedside notebook, give yourself some time to compose a summary of what you've written night after night for a year. This is not to be a recapitulation of the details, but a summary, and especially a summary that pulls out the themes and the qualities in you that have come into high relief through the practice.

Again, no one but you is going to see this summary unless you choose to show it to others, so don't get hung up if your grammar or writing skills aren't buffed to a high polish. What is to go on the page is meant to be your honest truth, not creative writing or literature. You may want to write only in point form, or list summary points under each of the qualities. Do it your way, just as long as what you come out with is an honest assessment of yourself in regard to each of the qualities you've been following all year. Be as honest and direct as you can be about what there is to be seen in the record you've kept.

This year-end finale highlights to your mind in bold letters what you can see of your inner soul-traits as these have played out in your life over the year. You may want to begin under each quality by noting, "At the beginning of the year, I was . . ." And then go on to talk about what you came to see, and maybe even any change that you saw taking place. A lot of the statements may begin "I am . . .," and that's good. The following examples might give you ideas of where to start as you sit down to write for yourself:

- "At the beginning of the year I saw myself as a person who has no problem being decisive, and by the end of the year I had confirmed that view."
- "I conclude that I do not respect a firm line between what is true and what is false."
- "My equanimity is disturbed more than anything by events that trigger my greed."

And so on with whatever is true for you, as revealed in a full year of notebook accumulations.

It may seem to you now, reading this *before* even having begun the practice, that this essay will be hard to write, but I can tell you that when you do the practice, it almost writes itself.

Read over your summary, tuck it in the back of your notebook, and know that your year is done. You now have a sound foundation to identify the qualities you will want to have on your list as you carry on into the next year of practice.

All time-bound practices are enhanced by markers and celebrations. When you have finished a year, mark that passage in a way that is meaningful to you. At the very least, get yourself a new notebook for the new year coming up. You might want to do something more than that, and I suggest you consider ritual practices that are traditionally used to mark other sorts of closures and beginnings. For birthdays we have cakes and candles. The completion of a tractate of Talmud study is celebrated with friends and colleagues (and food and drink). Haircuts, new clothing, presents, special food—do whatever is meaningful to you as a marker to close an important period in your life. But please, do something to mark this completion. That marker gives the completion its finality, and it gives you the honor you deserve for having cared for yourself and your world enough to complete the process.

And lastly, at the end of the year, it is time to make a new list of thirteen qualities. There may be qualities you want to carry over from one year's list to the next. There may be new ones given in this book that you want to try out. You may have become aware of a particular quality of your own that you want to add. Select or compose your reminder phrases, and prepare the cards. Set your new notebook by your bed.

When does it end? I could answer by saying, "When you reach perfection," but it's better to ask, Why should there be an end? As my teacher has impressed on me, life is about growing and changing, not finishing. As long as you find this process is helping you to grow and develop, to get clearer and more effective, to become more radiant, it is of value and can be continued.

Partners and Groups

A final note. I've described all the preparations and practices for an individual practicing Mussar on his or her own. That isn't the only way. There is a lot to be said for working with a partner or even in a group. The main benefit of working with someone else is that you gain the strength of his or her support. You have someone to turn to when you feel your resolve slipping or you're stuck trying to get clarity about some aspect of yourself. We all know how much easier it is to see the consistent weaknesses in someone other than ourselves, and this faculty can be put to good use by working in partners.

Our ancestors caution us not to mistake our own strength. The Mussar teachers in nineteenth-century Lithuania developed methods of learning in partnerships and groups because they recognized how difficult it is to make the journey alone. The Mussar luminaries Rabbi Luzzatto (eighteenth century) and Rabbi Cordovero (sixteenth century) had their own learning circles. The fellowship of others offers not only companionship (though that is a great gift that should not be minimized either), it helps us to straighten our way. Spiritual friends are treasure, whether they are teachers or students or companions or all three in one.

But—and this is a big BUT—for a partnership or a group to work, there needs to be a tremendous amount of trust and safety. We get value from working together in direct proportion to the honesty and truth we bring to looking at ourselves. A partner may help us to be more honest, but we have to feel strong trust in that other person if we are going to reveal what we really think about and see in ourselves. I would recommend working in partnership only with someone with whom you already have a very sound pre-existing trust relationship, like a spouse, a close friend, or a clergy or family member.

This brings up the question, whether you are working solo, with a partner, or in a group, of how much of the results of this practice you should share with other people, even those very close to you. There's no absolute guideline about this. Some people gain even more insight by talking over their process and discoveries, while others prefer to keep it all private, like a personal diary. A lot depends on motive. If sharing increases your clarity, it would seem to be a positive thing. If you catch yourself gossiping or just going over and over old rants, silence would be the way to go.

> Do not be discouraged if your study of Mussar does not seem to produce results. If your study seems to make no impression at all on your soul, if your ways seem not to have changed at all, know with true faith that even if success is not revealed to the eyes of your body, it is revealed to the eyes of your mind. As you learn Mussar more and more, the hidden impressions it makes upon you gather together and have an effect.
>
> —Rabbi Yisrael Salanter

Conclusion
THE WAY IS OPEN

> Precious reader—I realize that you know as well as
> I that I have not exhausted all the requirements for
> piety in my book, and that I have not said all that can
> be said about the subject. But that is because there is
> no end to the matter, and we cannot fathom the ex-
> tent of it.
>
> —Rabbi Moshe Chaim Luzzatto,
> *The Path of the Just*

TRADITIONAL JEWISH BOOKS end with the statement, "It is finished and completed, praises to God, the Creator of All."[1] Those words express what I feel as I come to the conclusion of this book, and I hope you will join me in this prayer.

But what is true for this book is not so for the way of the soul. The soul's journey will continue as long as you are alive. As Rabbi Luzzatto says in closing *The Path of the Just*, "There is no end to the matter." There is no point at which you can say that you have learned all there is to know about your soul-traits and how they play out in your life. There is always more to learn. There are always new tests. There are higher levels of spiritual maturity that you can't imagine from where you stand and look today. There is no end to the potential for growth.

My Mussar teacher, Rabbi Perr, asked me why we should even want to come to the end of our learning. As he put it, the point is to read the book, not to finish the book; it's to be on the journey, not to reach the end of the journey. This notion has deep roots in tradition. The Maharal of Prague says much the same in a way that really defines the Jewish notion of the spiritual journey:

Man is not created in his final wholeness. Man was created to actualize his wholeness. That is the meaning of the verse "Man was born to toil." Man is born and exists for the aim of this toil, which is the actualization of his potential. He can, however, never attain the state of actualized being. He must toil forever, to actualize his wholeness. That is the essence of his final wholeness. Even when he attains a certain level of actualization, he still remains potential, and will forever have to go on actualizing himself.[2]

On the Jewish spiritual path, taking and keeping your place as a pilgrim on the way of ascent is much more important than reaching the peak. This is why students of Mussar have traditionally been called *b'nei aliyah,* those who ascend. Holiness in this world arises in the process of becoming whole (*hishtalmut*), not in the state of wholeness itself (*sh'lemut*). Becoming whole—*hishtalmut*—is a verb, while wholeness—*sh'lemut*—is a noun.

You are a soul. Yes, there is a body and a personality and a history, but fundamentally, at the root and core of your creation, you are a soul. Because this is the primary reality of your being, you should make the soul the prime consideration in charting your path through life. It is easy to lose track of your soulfulness, especially as we live in a culture that outright denies soul life, but don't be misled. Your spiritual nature is more profound than your physical, and no material attainments can compare to the spiritual.

The soul is not static: you are on a journey. Sometime it doesn't feel like it, just like it doesn't feel at this very moment that we are on a planet hurtling through space at an enormous speed. We can sometimes fall prey to the illusion that life has us in a stationary pattern, each day more or less the same as the one before or after. It isn't true. We are constantly in motion.

The journey I am speaking of does not take place through time and space but in living out your own personal soul curriculum. That's what you are here to do. You have already become familiar with your spiritual curriculum, and I encourage you to observe and learn even more, and then to embrace that curriculum willingly and energetically.

The fact is that none of us has any choice about having or not having a soul curriculum. Life is a soul curriculum, and in the course of living, you learn and grow. You do have a choice however, whether or not to engage consciously with your spiritual challenges. No one can compel you to wake up to the steps on the way you are walking, but you yourself can choose to do so. You can open to the guidance of the soul. In the words of Moshe ibn Ezra: "In my body he has kindled a lamp from his glory. It tells me of the paths of the wise." Are you listening?

As you continue to become sensitive to the soul-traits that make up your personal curriculum, the way will become clear. You will see with ever-increasing clarity exactly what you are bringing into your own life as well as the lives of others, and from that clarity will emerge both the motivation to change and a course of action. You will face tests, because life comes with tests, and when you see these tests through a Mussar lens, then the ones you pass will strengthen you, and the ones you don't will teach you.

When you let your path of growth unfold without any guidance from your wise self, you let God wring change from your heart, most often by applying a tourniquet of sorrows. The alternative is to enter consciously into a path of self-transformation through deliberate spiritual practice. That is the real choice that confronts us. Go through life blindfolded, banging and scraping along all the corners and edges, and finding your direction by what you bounce off. Or methodically work to lift the veils that obscure clear sight and wise guidance, so that the path of life is pursued with grace and wisdom.

Mussar offers you just that methodical path. Mussar has a positive (though lesser) effect when it is just learned as information, and a potentially enormous impact when it is taken on as a systematic practice. I was taught early on that Mussar is not something you learn, it is something you *do,* and that translates into reality as a discipline of personal practice.

The most important thing is to keep taking steps. The steps that are true and straight will bring their own reward. There is learning to be had in our stumbles, too. We can't help but regret our missteps, and they put upon us the obligation to do the work of making course corrections.[3] But why do they keep happening to us? Why, despite our best intentions to set our feet straight on the path of ascent, do we inevitably slip and fall?

It's part of the upward journey that we have to acquire new hearts, and before that can happen, our old hearts need to be broken and reformed (re-formed). There is abundant evidence that life is set up to crack open our hearts, whether through loss and disappointment or as a result of our conscious and deliberate spiritual practice. It's the cracks that let in the light.

The Torah advises us to "circumcise the foreskin of our hearts."[4] That's not an easy image, but if we start from the place of acknowledging that an obstructed, walled-off heart is an impediment, if not an ailment, then the breakthrough that the Torah speaks of seems entirely desirable. We have those times when our hearts re-form. Life seems so much more vibrant then, and our connections are so much more vital, even if there has been pain. We are made infinitely more present. The Kotzker Rebbe said it best: "There is nothing so whole as a broken heart."

But by small and imperceptible steps, we soon grow accustomed to our new situation, and the heart that was made so tender and accessible under the knife of experience once again begins to disappear behind a slowly emerging wall. And then at some point experience will intrude once again, starting the cycle anew.

There is something inevitable about the process I am describing. It happens to all of us, whether we self-identify as being on a spiritual journey, or whether that sort of language is completely alien. The soul is set in the factory to have its compass pointing toward wholeness, and yet there seems to be no way to get to wholeness without first breaking up the old formation in order that it can be put together anew.

The Torah uses the image of circumcision, and it seems to me that it invokes that covenantal rite of passage to teach us something additional and important. Circumcision is an initiation, consciously undertaken. It may be that our hearts grow through a natural process that is built right into the blueprint of our lives, but there comes a point where many of us realize that we can choose to put ourselves through the process of growth as a conscious, deliberate act, as we would an initiation. It's clear that none of us has any more choice over whether our hearts will be challenged to deepen and mature than we do over whether or not to grow older, but the precious choice that does lie in our hands is to decide whether or not to go through that spiritual growing as a conscious act in which the soul is given a guiding role in setting our course.

Mussar is dedicated to helping you take just such a conscious role in guiding your journey of growing. By becoming more sensitive to the soul-traits that are dynamic in your life, you will become familiar with your curriculum of growth. Every situation and interaction you encounter is a mirror for your soul-traits. I hope you will continue to stay awake to the reflections that appear to you there.

I also hope that you have come to a deeper recognition of the extent of your free will. While it may seem that the state of your soul-traits is unchanging, don't be deceived. Change is always taking place, and you do have choice. You can make a difference. All the great and little efforts you have made may have prepared the way so that the very next decision you make will be entirely uncharacteristic for you. The pattern might be just about to break. You can't know before you have made that choice, but along the way, you must believe that change is possible.

To return to the quote from Rabbi Luzzatto, he says another thing, too. Not only is there no end to our learning; there is also the reality that "we cannot fathom the extent of it." He is pointing here to the fact that the scope of Mussar work encompasses mystery, both the great mystery that permeates the farthest reaches of the universe, and the enshrouded dimensions of your own inner life, which are equally mysterious. The ordinary human mind like yours and mine is a wonderful thing, but it simply does not have the capacity to grasp all that is true of our world and ourselves.

The mind is the implement of knowing, and Rabbi Luzzatto is cautioning you not to set yourself up for disappointment by making your mind the sole judge of your progress on your journey of ascent. The mind just cannot see or fathom what is going on, especially at the most profound levels, within or without. Because of that, Mussar always engages your mind, but it addresses your heart as well. I have been guided by Rabbi Eliyahu Lopian's definition of Mussar: "Making the heart grasp what the mind knows."

Finally, you are not alone. You did not design the way of the soul, and the One who did is there to help. If you take steps, light will be shone on the path ahead. The Talmud assures us: "One who comes to purify himself is assisted from on High."[5] It continues: "When a man sanctifies himself a little here below, he is sanctified much Above, and when he sanctifies himself in this world, he is sanctified in the World-to-Come." Higher states, spiritual breakthroughs, and movement toward wholeness are gifts you can receive. These acts of grace are always possible, and yet are more likely when you take steps to help yourself along the way.

The learning you do on the way of the soul etches its message on the flesh of your heart. It becomes who you are. Those changes may be invisible to your mind, and so you may hear a discouraging inner voice telling you it hasn't made any difference. Don't believe it. The goal is not to be able to look and see a change, as if you were to be made taller, or change the color of your hair. The real point is to have made a change so deeply in the bowels of your soul that when a situation confronts you, you respond to it naturally and intuitively and yet differently from how you would have responded to exactly the same situation only a year ago.

I heard a story from a student that really makes clear how deeply the learning penetrates, and how little of what is really going on may be available to conscious thought. She told me that she had learned the word *nefesh* from my teaching, but actually she had forgotten it. Then, in the midst of a day of river rafting that was very therapeutic for her, the word *nefesh* suddenly popped into her mind. She couldn't remember where she knew the word from or even what it meant, but it didn't seem like a random occurrence, and so when she got home she looked up her notes, and there it was—"soul." Her conscious mind didn't remember a thing about the teaching, but the message had taken root much deeper down, in the soul that spoke up for itself just at the time she was nurturing it.

This is how Mussar works. I know that from my own experience, too. I hope you have or will see something of this at work in your life, as well, but even if not, it is just a matter of time.

I have tried to keep the focus in our work together on the positive. This isn't always the voice that you can hear in Mussar writings and teachings. Sometimes teachers have been relentless in urging us to focus on our weaknesses and flaws. I, too, want you to be honest with yourself about yourself, but I insist that the perspective you bring to seeing your overall situation be positive. If we are seeming to work on weaknesses, it is only in order that we can get beyond working on weaknesses. There is nothing but integrity in the notions of wholeness and holiness that are fixed points toward which we are orienting our steps.

And so, even if you feel that a soul-trait has you in its unyielding grip, step back for a moment and appreciate that it is only because of the gift of consciousness that you are able to perceive what you can, and the gift of the Torah that provides ideals for living, and those ideals that give you something to measure yourself against, and the gift of a conscience that makes you see where you can improve, and so on. Don't lose sight of your gifts. You should have "double vision" so that you can simultaneously see your curriculum *and* the gifts you have in hand that make it possible for you to walk that path. You need to see both.

Rabbi Simcha Zissel Ziv, the Alter of Kelm, encourages us in just this direction. "It is the work of a lifetime," he said, "and that is just why you have been given a lifetime in which to do it."

I will close with an expression of gratitude and a poem.

Many generations before us have walked this path. We are graced to have access to their precious wisdom, gleaned from centuries of acute observation. To them we must be grateful. Rabbi Elyah Lopian offers us a prayer: "Let us give thanks to our teachers, the guides of the community, who wrote at length on Mussar in order to cultivate and soften hearts of stone."[6]

The poem is from Shem Tov Ben Palquera,[7] a Jewish poet of thirteenth-century Spain whose words light the way and strengthen the heart, as I hope the way of the soul will be illuminated for you, and your heart will be strong:

> If fear is like a rock
> Then I am a hammer.
> If sorrow is a fire,
> Then I am the sea.
> When it comes, my heart
> Increases its strength,
> Like the moon that shines brighter
> When the darkness falls.

Appendix

A SOUL-TRAIT INVENTORY

THE FOLLOWING LIST of soul-traits is culled from many Mussar sources. It refers to many soul-traits in no particular order. A brief definition follows each name.

This list will help you identify the soul-traits that are part of your own spiritual curriculum. No list can be exhaustive, so if there is something that you feel you need to add to this list, you can do so.

The list is formatted so you can check off the traits where you see a personal need to learn, change, and grow. You may want to mark them with a date so that you can still use this inventory to create future versions of your list.

____ *awareness:* being awake to what is really present in the moment

____ *logic:* clear and orderly thinking

____ *humility:* an accurate recognition of self, neither too grand nor too diminished

____ *pride:* self-respect; self-love

____ *modesty:* retiring demeanor so as not to attract attention

____ *loving-kindness:* acting toward others from goodness of heart

____ *faith:* belief in a higher power

____ *anger:* heated emotion stirred by a real or supposed injury or insult

____ *zeal/passion:* fervor for a cause or service

____ *alacrity:* acting without delay

___ *generosity:* giving freely, without meanness or selfishness

___ *greed:* voracious appetite

___ *frugality:* honoring the value in physical possessions

___ *honor:* high respect; elevated reputation

___ *trust:* having confidence in others; lacking suspicion

___ *silence:* quiet; restrained speech

___ *love:* affectionate attachment and fondness of heart

___ *hate:* intense dislike

___ *jealousy:* resentment of another's status or possessions

___ *truth:* accurate speech

___ *lying:* untruthful speech

___ *honesty:* scrupulous uprightness in action; not stealing

___ *diligence:* persistent effort; industriousness

___ *empathy:* projecting yourself into another's shoes

___ *courage:* bravery; boldness

___ *timidity:* shyness; reactiveness

___ *fear:* apprehension of impending danger

___ *apathy:* disengagement; distance

___ *laziness:* apathy and inactivity in the face of a task or activity

___ *equanimity:* serenity; peacefulness; tranquillity

___ *patience:* ability to endure delay, trouble, pain, or hardship

___ *punctuality:* being on time

___ *gratitude:* being thankful

___ *compassion:* sympathy inclining one to help

___ *order:* everything in its proper place

___ *stubbornness:* inability to alter opinion

___ *purity:* cleanliness; liberation from physical or moral pollution

___ *concentration:* bringing all one's power to one point

___ *caution:* avoiding rashness; attention to prudence

___ *calmness:* freedom from mental agitation; serenity

___ *defiance:* bold resistance

___ *determination:* firmness of purpose

___ *devotion:* a great love or loyalty; enthusiastic zeal

___ *discretion:* being discrete in one's speech; keeping secrets

___ *flexibility:* adaptability; ability to change to suit circumstances

___ *forgiveness:* ability to let go of angry or bitter feelings toward a person or about an offense

___ *gentleness:* moderateness; mildness

___ *justice:* giving a deserved response; impartiality

___ *kindness:* friendliness; helpfulness

___ *obedience:* willingness to obey, to be controlled when necessary, to carry out orders

___ *openness:* readiness to be candid; receptivity

___ *prudence:* wisdom; care in conduct and planning

___ *responsibility:* having control over and accountability for appropriate events

___ *simplicity:* straightforwardness; authenticity

___ *sincerity:* freedom from pretense or deceit in manner or actions

___ *steadfastness:* firmness; resoluteness; determination

___ *strength:* forcefulness

___ *trustworthiness:* dependability; reliability

Notes

IN THE NOTES that follow I try to give as much information as I can so that you can get access to the sources to which I refer. Some are very easily found; others are more obscure. Most are in English, but a few are not yet translated from the Hebrew original.

When I cite a book of the Bible, I refer to it by both its English and Hebrew names, such as "Genesis/*Bereshit*" or "Deuteronomy/*Devarim*" or "Proverbs/*Mishlei.*"

I quote the Talmud a great deal because this collection of ancient rabbinic writings is a fundamental source for Mussar teachings. The Talmud consists of two interrelated parts—the Mishnah, which is the text of the Oral Law (in Hebrew) and the Gemara (written in Aramaic), which is a commentary and exploration of the Mishnah. The Talmud exists in two forms: one known as the Babylonian Talmud and the other as the Jerusalem Talmud, both of which were compiled and redacted between 200 and 500 C.E.

When I quote the Talmud, it is the Babylonian Talmud unless stated otherwise. There are sixty-three volumes of the Talmud, and I cite them in the traditional way: first the name, then the folio, then the side of the folio. So, for example, if a quotation can be found on the second side of the third folio of Tractate Yoma (which deals with matters concerning the holy day of Yom Kippur), the citation is *Yoma* 3b. There is no point in translating these titles into English, as they already provide adequate information to find the source, no matter which edition is consulted.

For books that have not been translated into English, I provide an English translation of the title in brackets so that a reader unfamiliar with Hebrew can still make reference to this source.

CHAPTER 1

1. Deuteronomy/*Devarim* 10:16.

2. In the narrow sense of the Torah as being the Five Books of Moses; the metaphor shows up as well in Jeremiah 4:4.

3. Deuteronomy/*Devarim* 30:6.

CHAPTER 2

1. And sometimes the even stronger "rebuke" or "reproof" or "reproach." It appears first in Deuteronomy/*Devarim* 11:2 and occurs many times in the Bible.

2. 1824–1898.

3. 1849–1927.

4. 1848–1919.

5. Also the title of a book by one of the scions of Slabodka, Rabbi Henoch Leibowitz: *The Majesty of Man* (New York: Mesorah Publications Ltd., 1992).

6. Rabbi Eliyahu Dessler (1891–1954) studied in the Kelm Yeshiva for eighteen years, yet when he began to teach Mussar himself in Israel in 1949, other Mussar teachers said of his teaching that it was not Mussar. "What am I to do?" he responded. "If I teach this generation as I learned in Kelm, they will run away from me."

7. The Mussar movement was born in Lithuania, in a world in which men and women had very different roles, especially with respect to participation in ritual life and study. Nonetheless, it was explicitly stated that Mussar was not only appropriate but incumbent on all. Rabbi Yitzchak Blazer, who was a prime disciple of Rabbi Salanter, quoted approvingly: "In his work *Ya'aros D'vash*, Rav Yehonasan Eybeshitz, author of the *Urim v'Tumim*, writes (section 1, exposition 5): 'The main thing is that everyone—Torah scholar and layman alike, both men and women—must study one page from a Mussar *sefer* [book] on a daily basis.'" Rabbi Yisrael Salanter, *Ohr Yisrael*, trans. Rabbi Zvi Miller (Southfield, Mich.: Targum, 2004), 98.

8. Leviticus/*Vayikra* 19:2; *kedoshim tihiyu* in Hebrew.

9. See, for example, Rambam's *Sefer ha'Mitzvot* [The Book of Mitzvot] (*Shoresh* 4), trans. Rabbi Shraga Silverstein (New York: Moznaim, 1993).

10. Genesis/*Bereshit* 2:17.

11. In *Madregat ha'Adam* [The Levels of Humanity] (Jerusalem: Yeshivat Ner Shmuel, 2002).

12. *Kedoshim;* elsewhere the Torah uses another plural in a similar way when it says, "*Anshei kodesh tihiyun li*"—you shall be holy people to me—where the word "people" refers not to a people but to a collection of individuals (Exodus/*Sh'mot* 22:30).

13. *Ohr Yisrael,* 399.

14. An acronym for Rabbi Sh'lomo Itzchaki, who lived in Troyes, France (1040–1105).

15. Rabbi Moshe ben Nachman, also known as Nachmanides (1194–1270).

16. The sixteenth-century kabbalist, Rabbi Chaim Vital, explains (*Sha'arei Kedusha,* part 1, gate 2):

> The inner traits were not included in the 613 commandments [*mitzvot*] yet they are integral to them since they are a prerequisite to the *mitzvot* themselves. Therefore, the one who possesses inferior inner traits is worse off than one who is only committing transgressions. Since the inner traits are such an important foundation, they were not included in the *mitzvot*. Good inner traits lead to *mitzvot*. One should be more concerned about his inner traits than his *mitzvot*.

17. Called the *mashgiach* in Hebrew. Rabbi Levenstein lived from 1885 to 1974. The quote is from his *Sichot Mussar,* ed. Yitzchok Kirzner (Lakewood, N.J.: Alter Yosef and Tzvi Gartenhaus, 2004), 12–13.

18. *Sh'lemut* comes from the same root as the word *shalom,* which is usually translated as "peace," though that definition lacks the connotation of wholeness that is prominent in *sh'lemut* and, we learn, implicit in peace.

19. Rabbi Moshe Chaim Luzzatto, "Siman Bet." In *Da'at T'vunot* (Jerusalem: Y. Goldblatt, 2001).

20. *Ohr Yisrael,* 38.

21. 1787–1859. He is commenting on the verse "Be holy people to me" (Exodus/ *Sh'mot* 22:30). In the Hebrew, the word "people" comes before "holy."

22. Rabbi Judah Loew, 1525–1609.

23. Rebbetzin Shulamit Ezrachi, *The Mashgiach,* trans. Libby Lazewnik (New York: Mesorah Publications, 2006), 377.

CHAPTER 3

1. *Sichos Mussar,* 16.

2. See Rabbi Hillel Goldberg, *Yisrael Salanter: Text, Structure, Idea: The Ethics and Theology of an Early Psychologist of the Unconscious* (New York: Ktav, 1982).

3. Noson Kamenetsky, *The Making of a Godol* (Jerusalem: Nathan Kamenetsky Publisher, 2002), 802. Rabbi Yaakov Kamenetsky was Rosh Yeshiva of Yeshiva Torah Voda'ath and lived from 1891 to 1986. His most famous work is *Emet l'Ya'akov* [Truth to Jacob].

4. The soul is sometimes said to be hewn from the *Kisei ha'Kavod,* the Throne of Glory on which God sits.

5. *The Eight Chapters,* in *Ethical Writings of Maimonides,* ed. Raymond L. Weiss with Charles E. Butterworth (New York: Dover, 1975), 81.

6. A description of the soul very similar to this can be found in Rabbi

Mordechai Miller, *The Sabbath Shiur,* vol. 3 (Jerusalem and New York: Feldheim Publishers, 2004), pp. 187–88:

> Although one can apply expressions of corruption and evil to the parts of our soul which are known as *nefesh* and *ruach,* these adjectives are never found in conjunction with the term *neshamah.* For the term *neshamah* denotes a part of the soul which is deeper, which constitutes part of the person's core and is impervious to evil. Negativity can besmirch both the *nefesh* and the *ruach,* but is unable to penetrate to the *neshamah,* one's essence. Thus we say each morning, "My God, the *neshamah* that you placed in me is pure." Despite the misdeeds of the previous day, despite how we stumbled and fell, we wake each morning and thank God for the pure soul that He gave us. Our sins are superficial, for the core of our soul remains pure.

7. Genesis/*Bereshit* 1:26.

8. The notion of the "veils" derives from the Rambam, Maimonides, who describes them in similar terms in his *Eight Chapters,* pp. 80–83.

9. The title given to a book by Rabbi Sh'lomo ibn Gabirol in eleventh-century Spain.

CHAPTER 4

1. Rabbi Eliyahu E. Dessler, *Strive for Truth!,* vol. 2, trans. Aryeh Carmell (Jerusalem and New York: Feldheim Publishers, 1978), 52–56.

2. *Yoma* 69a.

3. *Midrash Genesis Rabbah* 9:7. This is a book of midrash (literally, "explanation" or "interpretation"), part of the ancient collection of rabbinic commentary and explanatory notes, homilies, and stories that elaborate on scriptural passages, often from an ethical or devotional perspective.

4. *Pirkei Avot* 4:1. Literally "Chapters of the Fathers," this portion of the Mishnah deals with ethical behavior.

5. 1720–1797; in his commentary to Proverbs/*Mishlei* 7:13–14.

6. "Rabbi Ammi stated: 'He is called a renegade, because such is the art of the evil inclination: Today it incites man to do one wrong thing, and tomorrow it incites him to worship idols. And he proceeds to worship them'" (*Niddah* 13b).

7. *Madregat ha'Adam;* ibid.

8. *Sukkah* 52b.

CHAPTER 5

1. Rabbi Moshe Chaim Luzzatto, *The Path of the Just* [*Mesillat Yesharim*], trans. Yaakov Feldman (Northvale, N.J.: Jason Aronson, Inc., 1996).

2. He lived in Saragossa, Spain, in the first half of the eleventh century; his main work was written in Arabic and translated into Hebrew as *Hovot ha'Levavot* [*The Duties of the Heart*], published in 1040.

3. Also known as Ramchal; born in Padua, Italy, in 1707 and died in Acco, Israel, in 1746.

4. 1872–1970, a scion of Kelm Mussar who became Mussar supervisor (*mashgiach*) at Yeshivas Kfar Chassidim in Israel. His main work is *Lev Eliyahu,* trans. Rabbi B. D. Klein (Jerusalem: Eliezer Fisher Publishing, Ltd., 1989).

5. In his foreword to Rabbi M. M. Leffin, *Cheshbon ha'Nefesh*, trans. Rabbi Shraga Silverstein (Jerusalem and New York: Feldheim Publishers, 1995), 3. Rabbi Sher (1875–1952) was the last Rosh Yeshiva of the Slabodka Yeshiva before it was destroyed in the Holocaust. Just weeks before the outbreak of World War II, Rabbi Sher went to a spa in Switzerland and was there when the war began. As a result, he was spared the fate that befell the students and teachers of the yeshiva in Lithuania, all of whom perished.

6. *Cheshbon ha'Nefesh,* p. 47.

7. Spoken to his Mussar group (*va'ad*) on 16 Iyar 5761/May 9, 2001; Rabbi Wolbe (1916–2005) was Mussar *mashgiach* of Yeshivas Givat Shaul in Jerusalem and author of *Alei Shur*. He studied in the Mir Yeshiva, where he was taught by Rabbi Yerucham Levovitz and Rabbi Yechezkel Levenstein.

8. Dov Katz, *The Mussar Movement* [*Tenuat ha'Mussar*], vol. 1, trans. Leonard Oschry (Tel Aviv: Orly Press, 1975).

9. Or *hispailus,* in the Ashkenazi pronunciation of the yeshiva.

10. *Sichot Mussar,* 26.

11. Rabbi Eliyahu Dessler, *Strive for Truth!,* vol. 1, trans. Aryeh Carmell (Jerusalem and New York: Feldheim Publishers, 1978), 34–35.

12. Deuteronomy/*Devarim* 11:18.

13. *Madregat ha'Adam,* cited in Rabbi Elyakim Krumbein, *Musar for Moderns* (Jersey City, N.J.: Ktav, 2005), 90.

14. Heard from Rabbi Yochanan Zweig in a personal conversation. Rabbi Zweig is Rosh Yeshiva of the Talmudic University in Miami Beach.

15. Heard from Rabbi Yehoshua Wender of the Young Israel of Houston in a personal conversation at the Houston Mussar Kallah, 2004.

16. *Ohr Yisrael,* 210.

17. *Musar for Moderns,* 88.

18. Former Rosh Yeshiva in Beis Medrash l'Torah, Skokie, Illinois.

19. Rabbi Avrohom Chaim Feuer, *Tehillim Treasury* (New York: Mesorah Publications, 1993).

20. *Nefesh ha'behemah.*

21. Rabbi Joseph B. Soloveitchik, *The Lonely Man of Faith* (New York: Doubleday, 1992).

22. *B'rachot* 5a.

23. Rabbi Moshe Chaim Luzzatto, *The Way of God*, vol. 1, trans. Aryeh Kaplan (New York and Jerusalem: Feldheim Publishers, 1997), 45.

24. *Chochmah u'Mussar*, in *Me'orei Orot ha'Mussar* (Brooklyn: Rabbi Simcha Ziesel Levovitz, 1964), 9.

CHAPTER 6

1. Leviticus / *Vayikra* 19:18.

CHAPTER 7

1. Rabbi Bachya ibn Pakuda, *Duties of the Heart*, vol. 2, trans. Daniel Haberman (New York and Jerusalem: Feldheim Publishers, 1996), 589.

2. The Talmud (200–500 C.E.) is a remarkable document that, next to the Torah, is the definitive source of Jewish law. The Talmud doesn't only propound the law, it also preserves the intricate arguments of the various parties who reflect on the issues it considers. We gain access not only to the conclusions but also to all the thinking that lies behind them, as minority opinions are preserved along with the majority views.

3. Psalms/ *Tehillim* 51; *Sanhedrin* 43b.

4. Abraham Isaac Kook, *The Moral Principles*, trans. Ben Zion Bokser (New York and Toronto: Paulist Press, 1978), 176.

5. Numbers/ *Bamidbar* 12:3.

6. Psalms/ *Tehillim* 5:5.

7. A nineteenth-century Chassidic teacher from Europe.

8. *Gittin* 55b–56a.

9. *B'rachot* 6b.

10. *Sanhedrin* 37a.

11. Chapter 4 of *The Eight Chapters*, 67.

12. Genesis/ *Bereshit* 1:26.

13. Rashi, comment on Genesis/ *Bereshit* 1:26.

14. *Sotah* 5a–b.

15. Rabbi Elyakim Krumbein expands on the relationship of humility to self-esteem, developing the interplay to the point of offering the remarkable equation: "humility = self-esteem." See *Musar for Moderns*, 31.

16. Rabbi Yisrael Salanter about Rabbi Naftali Amsterdam.

CHAPTER 8

1. Deuteronomy/ *Devarim* 8:6, 19:9, 26:17.

2. *Sifre* 85a.

3. Rabbi Moshe Cordovero, *Tomer Devorah* [The Palm Tree of Deborah], trans. Rabbi Moshe Miller (Southfield, Mich.: Targum/Feldheim, 1993), 6–8.

4. Ibid., 8.

5. Published in the Ukraine in 1812.

6. Ibid., 121–23.

7. *Samekh-vet-lamed.*

8. *Cheshbon ha'Nefesh,* 29ff.

9. *Eruvin* 54b.

CHAPTER 9

1. *Pirkei Avot* 4:1. "Ben Zoma states, 'Who is wise? He who learns from all people. Who is strong? He who controls his passions. Who is rich? He who rejoices in his own lot. Who is honorable? He who honors others.'"

2. 1872–1970.

3. From Rabbi David Schlossberg, *Reb Elyah* (New York: Mesorah Publications, 1999), 121.

4. Genesis/*Bereshit* 29:35. The name Yehudah is the source of the Hebrew name of the Jewish people (*Yehudim*), revealing the very direct tie between Judaism and gratitude.

5. *Ha'tov v'ha'metiv.*

6. 135 C.E.

7. Rabbi Bachya ibn Pakuda, *Duties of the Heart,* trans. Yaakov Feldman, 68–70.

8. W. S. Merwin, "Thanks," *The Nation,* March 14, 1987.

9. *B'rachot* 60b.

10. *Mishnah B'rachot* 9:5a.

11. *B'rachot* 60a.

12. *Ta'anit* 21a.

13. Hence his name, *Nachum* (which has a sense of contentment) *Ish* (man) *Gamzu* (this, too—which is how he responded to everything that befell him).

14. *Ta'anit* 21a.

15. The *mashgiach ruchani* (spiritual guide) of the prewar Mir Yeshiva in Europe.

CHAPTER 10

1. Exodus/*Sh'mot* 34:6.

2. *Beitzah* 32b.

3. 1808–1888.

4. Commentary to Genesis/*Bereshit* 43:14. *The Pentateuch,* trans. Isaac Levy (London: I. Levy, 1963).

5. *Horeb* 17:125.

6. Words from this root occur 125 times in all books of the Torah. The root is also found in Assyrian, Ethiopic, and Aramaic.

7. Psalms/*Tehillim* 103:13.

8. Psalms/*Tehillim* 103:4.

9. *Baruch she'amar.*

10. *Adonai, Adonai, El rachum v'chanun, erech apayim, v'rav chesed v'emet, notzer chesed la'alafim; noseh avon va'fesha v'chata'ah v'nakeh*—(Lord, Lord, God, merciful and kind, slow to anger, with tremendous loving-kindness and truth. He remembers deeds of love for thousands [of generations], forgiving sin, rebellion and error). Exodus/*Sh'mot* 34:6–7.

11. *Din.*

12. As in Rashi's commentary on the first line of the Torah: "At first He intended to create it with the attribute of justice, but then saw that the world cannot exist and gave priority to the attribute of mercy and joined it with the attribute of justice. This [thought] is conveyed in the verse, "On the day when the Lord God made earth and heaven."

14. *Hagigah* 12a.

15. *Pesachim* 87b.

16. Anonymous, *Orchot Tzaddikim* (The Ways of the Tzaddikim), chap. 7 (New York and Jerusalem: Feldheim Publishers, 1995).

17. Deuteronomy/*Devarim* 10:19.

18. Writing about the kabbalistic quality of *tiferet,* which is identified as *rachamim;* in *Tomer Devorah,* chap. 7.

19. Benedict Carey, "In the Execution Chamber, the Moral Compass Wavers," *New York Times,* February 7, 2006.

20. *Alei Shur,* vol. 2 (Jerusalem: Hotsa'at Bet HaMussar, 1986), 40.

21. The Hebrew is unambiguous on this point: *makom ha'rachamim*—cause compassion to stand.

22. Genesis/*Bereshit* 43:14.

23. Deuteronomy/*Devarim* 13:18.

24. Philip P. Hallie, *Lest Innocent Blood Be Shed: The Story of Le Chambon and How Goodness Happened There* (New York: Harper Row, 1979).

25. Deuteronomy/*Devarim* 28:9.

26. *V'hatan l'cha rachamim v'richamecha;* Deuteronomy/*Devarim* 13:17.

27. What the Chassidic tradition calls *bitul ha'yesh,* reducing the sense of a substantial self.

28. D. N. Weinberger, ed., *Ha-Saba mi-Slobodka* (Brooklyn: D. Weinberger, 1986), 35; quoted in Yitzhak Buxbaum, *An Open Heart* (Flushing, N.Y.: Jewish Spirit Booklet Series, 1997), 32.

29. Ezekiel 20:7–8.

30. Exodus/*Sh'mot* 3.
31. Isaiah 63:9.
32. Jeremiah 32:21.

CHAPTER 11

1. *Seder* in Hebrew.

2. 1891–1954; he is best known as *mashgiach* (spiritual counselor) of the Ponovezh Yeshiva in Israel and the author of *Michtav me'Eliyahu*, which is translated into English under the title *Strive for Truth!*. See chapter 4, note 1.

3. 1824–1898.

4. The Kelm Yeshiva spawned the Slabodka Yeshiva, and the products of Slabodka have had a major influence on the Jewish world in the twentieth and twenty-first centuries, especially in Orthodox circles.

5. The yeshiva was destroyed when all the Jewish inhabitants of Kelm were massacred by the Nazis on one day in 1941.

6. Ritual bath.

7. Deuteronomy/*Devarim* 34:5.

8. Leviticus/*Vayikra* 25:55.

9. *Pirkei Avot* 2:4.

10. *Yismach Moshe bematnat chelko ki eved ne'eman karata lo.*

11. One of the most famous scions of Slabodka Mussar, who founded the Lakewood Yeshiva in New Jersey, where my own teacher, Rabbi Perr, was a student.

12. *Mesudar.*

13. The size of an olive, the measurement *k'zayit.*

14. The cup must hold at least a *revi'it* (3 fluid ounces), and at least a cheekful (1.6 fluid ounces) must be drunk.

15. According to the Ashkenazi custom.

16. Genesis/*Bereshit* 11:1–9; Rabbi Jonathan Sacks made the link of Babel to disorder in his book *To Heal a Fractured World* (London and New York: Continuum, 2005), 142–43.

17. Called *bal tashchit,* which literally means "do not destroy," a notion that extends easily to "do not waste," since wasting is a form of destruction.

18. Numbers/*Bamidbar* 2:1–2.

19. *Midrash Rabbah.*

20. *Ta'anit* 53a.

21. *Ner HaShem nishmat adam;* Proverbs/*Mishlei* 20:27

22. I have touched on only humility (*anavah*) and honor (*kavod*) as traits that counteract disorder. These are not the only ones. Reflect on your own life to identify the trait that might serve as a lever to have impact on your own sense of order. And experiment in practice.

23. He may have been adapting a metaphor found in the introduction to the sixteenth-century Mussar text, *Orchot Tzaddikim,* where the clasp on the necklace is referred to the trait of *yirah.* (See my discussion of *yirah* in chapter 24.)

CHAPTER 12

1. Immanuel Etkes, "Rabbi Yisrael Salanter and His Psychology of Mussar" in *Jewish Spirituality,* vol. 2, ed. Arthur Green (New York: Crossroads, 1986–87), 226.

2. 1872–1970.

3. Rabbi Adin Steinsaltz, *The Thirteen Petalled Rose,* trans. Yehuda Hanegbi (New York: Basic Books, 1980), 132.

4. The expression used by Rabbi Menachem Mendel Leffin in his book *Cheshbon ha'Nefesh.*

5. *Nisyonot* or *nisyonos* in Hebrew in the Mussar literature. No one goes through life without being tested. A person of faith sees God as the source of these tests, which are meant to help us grow.

6. Proverbs/*Mishlei* 17:3.

7. From *Kitvei ha'Ari,* "Gates of Holiness," chapter 4, gate 2, section 5, trans. Zecharia-Zvi Shemayim V'Aretz.

8. Also known as Nahmanides; and the Ramban (1194–1270).

9. In Hebrew: *l'hitrahek*—to distance.

10. Proverbs/*Mishlei* 1:15.

11. This is far from the only outcome of meditation. For more on Jewish meditation, the classic source is Rabbi Aryeh Kaplan's *Jewish Meditation* (New York: Schocken Books, 1995).

CHAPTER 13

1. *Kavod* in Hebrew. The word *kavod* has many shades of meaning in Hebrew. In personal and interpersonal contexts, it usually means "honor." Someone might do something as simple as open a door for another person out of *kavod* (or *koved,* as it might also be pronounced). A slight is a depreciation of *kavod.* Yet in the Bible, we find Moses asking God, *Hareini na et kovodecha,* "Please reveal to me Your *kavod*" (Exodus/*Sh'mot* 33:18). In this and other uses of the term in reference to God, it is almost always translated as "glory."

2. *Megillah* 3b.

3. Honoring others is referred to as *kevod ha'briyot* in Hebrew.

4. *Yoma* 9b.

5. 1749–1821; in his *Ruach Chaim* on *Pirkei Avot.*

6. *Ohr Yisrael,* 318.

7. Ibid., 316.

8. Rabbi Moshe Cordovero makes a similar point: that a person should "accus-

tom himself to flee honor as much as possible, for if he allows honor to be paid him he will become attuned to such matters of pride and his nature will find satisfaction in it and he will find it difficult to be cured." Quoted in *The Palm Tree of Deborah*, 60.

9. *Pirkei Avot* 4:28.

10. *Ketubot* 67b.

11. *The Mashgiach*, 627.

12. *Pirkei Avot* 4:1.

13. Jerusalem Talmud *Chagigah* 2:1.

14. *The Duties of the Heart*, trans. Yaakov Feldman, 291.

15. In Hebrew, to be *dan l'kaf z'chut*.

16. Rabbi Chaim Ephraim Zaitchik, *Sparks of Mussar* (Jerusalem: Feldheim Publishers, 1985), 12.

17. *Pirkei Avot* 4:15.

18. Founder of the major Lakewood Yeshiva in New Jersey.

19. "Ethics of the Fathers." See chapter 4, note 4.

20. *Pirkei Avot* 4:20.

21. *B'rachot* 17a.

22. The leading sage in the Land of Israel at the end of the Second Temple period.

23. *Ketubot* 111b.

24. *Shabbat* 127b.

25. Leviticus/*Vayikra* 19:18.

26. *Sifra, Kedoshim* 45. The *Sifra* is a collection of midrashic thought on the book of Leviticus/*Vayikra*. In this case, the commentary is to Parshat Kedoshim (19:1–20:27).

27. *Pirkei Avot* 3:14.

CHAPTER 14

1. Rabbi Israel Meir Ha'Cohen Kagan (1838–1933).

2. *The Way of God*, 65.

3. *Cheshbon ha'Nefesh*, 161.

4. *Yoma* 38b.

5. *Pirkei Avot* 2:8.

6. Genesis/*Bereshit* 2:7.

7. *Ohr Yisrael*, 115.

8. Kohelet Rabbah 1:13.

9. *Michtav me'Eliyahu* vol. 1 (Jerusalem: Chever Talmidar, 1963), 30.

10. The soul-trait of *histapkut*, sometimes *histapkut b'mu'at*.

11. Rabbi Shlomo ben Yehuda ibn Gabirol, *Mivchar Hapeninim* (Jerusalem: Vagshal, 1995), 155, 161.

12. The Mussar masters call desires *ta'ava* in Hebrew. They write much on the subject.

13. *V'lo taturu acharay l'vavchem v'acharay aynaychem* (Numbers/*BaMidbar* 15:39).

14. Sometimes credited as a soul-trait in itself, called *kimutz* in Hebrew.

15. Rabbi Eliyahu of Vilna (1720–1797) in his *Even Sh'lemah: The Vilna Ga'on Views Life, the Classic Collection of the Vilna Ga'on's Wisdom,* trans. Yaakov Singer and Chaim David Ackerman (Southfield, Mich.: Targum, 1994).

16. *Sukkah* 52b. The speaker is Rabbi Yochanan.

17. *Pirkei Avot* 4:1.

18. *Kohelet Rabbah* 1:34.

19. *Kohelet* 5:9.

20. *Yoma* 80a.

21. 1837–1907. Better known as Itzele Peterburger—*Itzele* as the diminutive of Yitzchak, and *Peterburger* because he served as the Chief Rabbi of Saint Petersburg.

22. *Ta'anit* 24b, stated by Rav Yehudah in the name of Rav.

23. In *Stars of Light,* a section of *Ohr Yisrael,* 604.

24. *Bitul hagashmiut.*

25. *Strive for Truth!* 1:194–95.

26. Psalm/*Tehillim* 100:2.

27. *Yevamot* 63b.

28. *Even Sh'lemah,* chapter 3, pt. 2.

CHAPTER 15

1. *Mashgiach.*

2. Or *hitorerut.*

3. 1871–1941, son-in-law of Rabbi Yosef Yozel Hurwitz, the Alter of Novarodok.

4. *Zerizut* or *z'rizus* in Hebrew.

5. In *Sha'arei Teshuvah* [The Gates of Repentance] 2:26, a primary Mussar text written by Rabbi Yonah of Gerondi (c.1200–1263). An English version is Yonah ben Avraham of Gerona, *Sha'arei Teshuvah: The Gates of Repentance,* trans. Shraga Silverstein (Jerusalem and New York: Feldheim Publishers, 1967).

6. Rabbi M. M. Leffin, *Cheshbon ha'Nefesh,* trans. D. Landesman (New York: Feldheim Publishers, 1995), 135–39.

7. Some see a common Hebrew root in the word *ratzon,* which means "will," and *ratz,* which means "run."

8. *Orchot Tzaddikim,* 285, 287.

9. *Mechilta Sh'mot* 12:17.

10. Psalms/*Tehillim* 119:60.

11. Genesis/*Bereshit* 19:27.

12. Genesis/*Bereshit* 21:14.

13. Genesis/*Bereshit* 22:3; *Pesachim* 4a.

14. *Kiddushin* 40a.

15. *Atzlut* in Hebrew.

16. My translation of what Rabbi Luzzatto writes in chapter 6 of *Mesillat Yesharim* (The Path of the Just).

17. Exodus/*Sh'mot* 7:14.

18. *Kaved.*

19. Proverbs/*Mishlei* 26:16.

20. "The Gate of Laziness," chapter 16 in *Orchot Tzaddikim* (The Ways of the Righteous), trans. Rabbi Shraga Silverstein (Jerusalem and New York: Feldheim Publishers, 1995), 297–99.

21. *Shabbat* 105b.

22. *Cheshbon ha'Nefesh*, 135–39.

23. Oscar Wilde, "Lord Arthur Savile's Crime," in *Fairy Tales and Other Stories* (London: Octopus, 1980), 4.

24. *Pesachim* 8b.

25. The soul-trait of trusting God is called *bitachon* in Hebrew; see chapter 22.

26. *Ohr Yisrael*, quoted in Immanuel Etkes, *Rabbi Yisrael Salanter and the Mussar Movement* (Philadelphia and Jerusalem: Jewish Publication Society, 1993), 294.

27. *B'chol et u'v'chol sha'ah.*

28. *Hakarat ha'tov*; see chapter 9.

29. Rabbi Moshe Chaim Luzzatto, *The Path of the Just*, trans. Shraga Silverstein (New York and Jerusalem: Feldheim Publishers, 1966), 89.

CHAPTER 16

1. The phrase for this trait is based on the saying in *Pirkei Avot* 1:17: "Rabbi Shimon ben Gamliel used to say: 'All my days I grew up among the sages, and I have found nothing better for a person than silence.'"

2. The same Rabbi Yitzchak Blazer, a close disciple of Rabbi Yisrael Salanter, whom we met in chapter 14.

3. Retold in Rabbi Paysach J. Krohn, *In the Footsteps of the Maggid* (New York: Mesorah Publications, 1992), 264–65.

4. Rabbi Meir Levin, *Novarodok* (Northvale, N.J.: Jason Aronson, 1996), 6–7. I wondered long about those two windows, until I discovered that one was for milk and one for meat, in keeping with Jewish dietary laws.

5. *Sh'tikah* in Hebrew.

6. *Orchot Tzaddikim*, 365.

7. Ecclesiastes/*Kohelet* 3:7.

8. Job 33:33.

9. *Pesachim* 99a.

10. *Bava Batra* 9b.

11. Proverbs/*Mishlei* 18:21.

12. *Sh'mirat ha'Lashon* [Guarding the Tongue], by the Chafetz Chaim, is the primary work that sets out guidelines for right speech. See Rabbi Shimon Finkelman and Rabbi Yitzchak Berkowitz, *Chofetz Chaim: A Lesson a Day* (Brooklyn: Artscroll, 1995).

13. Jewish law calls this "*avak lashon ha'ra*"—it isn't outright wrong speech, but it is speech that bears the "dust" (*avak*) of the evil tongue.

14. *Bava Batra* 164b; the speaker is Rav Yehuda.

15. *The Path of the Just,* trans. Feldman, 88.

16. *Hilchot De'ot* 7:3.

17. Ibid. 2:5-6.

18. Ecclesiastes/*Kohelet* 9:17.

19. *Alei Shur,* vol. 2, 36.

20. Vilna Ga'on, *Mussar Letter* [Iggeret ha'Mussar] (Lakewood, N.J.: Pirchei Shoshanim, 1995), 2.

21. *Chagigah* 5b.

22. *Erchin* 15b.

23. Simcha Raz, *A Tzaddik in Our Time* (Jerusalem and New York: Feldheim Publishers, 1989), 339.

24. 1518–1592.

25. Rabbi Eliyahu de Vidas, *The Beginnings of Wisdom* [*Reshit Chochmah*], trans. Simcha H. Benyosef (Hoboken, N.J.: Ktav Publishing House, Inc., 2002), 169.

26. The men of the Great Assembly—in Hebrew, *Anshei Knesset ha'Gedolah*—assumed leadership of the Jewish people between 410 and 310 B.C.E., following the destruction of the First Temple and including the initial building of the Second Temple, up until the invasion led by Alexander the Great.

27. *Mishna Tractate B'rachot* 5:1.

28. *Megillah* 18a.

29. *Pirkei Avot* 3:17.

30. *Megillah* 18a.

31. Though the name for the soul-trait of silence is conventionally *sh'tikah*, the extra depth in stillness is recognized by giving this profound state its own name, *d'mama* or *dumia.*

32. Or *hisbodedus,* in the Ashkenazi pronunciation of the yeshiva and Chassidic worlds.

33. The root of the word *hitbodedut* is *bada'ad*, which means "to be secluded."

34. 1543–1620.

35. Lived in Egypt from 1186 to 1237.

36. 1772–1810.

37. Nathan of Breslov, *Rabbi Nachman's Wisdom*, no. 7, trans. Aryeh Kaplan (Jerusalem: Breslov Research Institute, 1973).

38. *Tomer Devorah*, 68.

39. 1 Kings/*Melachim* 19:11–12.

40. Avraham Ben-Yitzhak, *Collected Poems*, trans. Peter Cole (Jerusalem: Ibis Editions, 2003), 19.

CHAPTER 17

1. The soul-trait of generosity is named *nedivut*. A generous person is a *nadiv*. In the Torah portion called *Terumah*, the commentator Rashi says that two types of donations are referred to as *terumah*. One is a specified amount of money. This goes against the plain sense of the verse, which reads: "Take My offering from everyone whose heart impels him to give" (Exodus/*Sh'mot* 25:2), which stresses the voluntary nature of the gift called *terumah*.

2. Related to generosity is the concept of *gemilut hasadim*, doing acts of loving-kindness.

3. Known as the Malbim (1809–1879).

4. Exodus/*Sh'mot* 25:8.

5. *A Tzaddik in Our Time*, 402.

6. Chapter 2. Translation by Rabbi Ira Stone (forthcoming).

7. Exodus/*Sh'mot* 2:11.

8. *Likutey Moharan* 2, 15:1.

9. Deuteronomy/*Devarim* 15:7–8.

10. Ian Parker, "The Gift," in *The New Yorker*, August 2, 2004.

11. *Midrash Tanchuma*, a midrashic interpretation written in the ninth century.

12. *Bava Batra* 9b.

13. In his *Discourse on Lovingkindness*.

14. *Strive for Truth!*, vol. 1, p. 119.

15. *Derech Eretz Zuta* 2.

16. *The Book of Instruction*, an anonymous work originating in Spain that comments on the 613 *mitzvot*.

17. Chapter 5; written in 1070 by Rabbi Bachya ibn Pakuda. There are several translations.

18. "The Gate of Magnanimity," chapter 17 in *Orchot Tzaddikim*, 311.

19. *Alei Shur*, vol. 2, 48.

CHAPTER 18

1. *Strive for Truth!*, vol. 1, p. 180. I have substituted "the desires of one's heart" for "the yetzer," which Carmell left untranslated.

2. 200–500 C.E.

3. Known as the Maharal (1525–1609).

4. *Emet* or *emes* in Hebrew. The phrase at the head of this chapter comes from the verse *Mi'dvar sheker tirachek*—from falsehood be distant—from *Orchot Chaim of the Rosh,* trans. Yaakov Petroff (New York: Mesorah Publications, 1992), 28.

5. 1910–1995.

6. University of Central Oklahoma study, quoted in Rod Liddle, "Truth Is, We're All Liars Now," *London Sunday Times,* July 31, 2005.

7. "*Sheker ain lo reglayim.*" From a Midrash called *Otiyot d'Rabbe Akiva,* as well as in *Tikkunei Zohar* 425; also *Shabbat* 104a in an Aramaic equivalent: "*shikra lo ka'in.*" This comment about falsehood plays on the fact that all the Hebrew letters of the Hebrew word for falsehood—*sheker*—have only one "foot"—as apposed to *emet* (truth), each of whose letters stands firmly on two feet. In the same vein, all the three letters that spell *sheker* are positioned next to each other in the Hebrew alphabet, while the letters of *emet* are the first, middle, and last letters of the alphabet. It's obvious which arrangement puts the word on a more solid footing.

8. Proverbs/*Mishlei* 12:19.

9. *Madregat ha'Adam,* 109.

10. Philosophers call this the "correspondence theory" of truth, considering truth as something that corresponds directly to a testable reality.

11. A rabbinic ordinance not found in the Torah: Rambam *Hilchot Avel* 14:1.

12. Here in *Ketubot* 16b–17a.

13. Exodus/*Sh'mot* 23:7.

14. "The world stands on three things: justice, truth and peace"—*Pirkei Avot* 1:18.

15. *The Path of the Just,* trans. Feldman, 94.

16. *Sotah* 42a.

17. Or *sh'mirat lashon*—literally, "guarding the tongue." How important is guarding the tongue? Rabbi Yisrael Salanter, founder of the Mussar movement, once said, "It is worthwhile for a person to learn *Mussar* throughout his life, even if its only benefit is to prevent him from uttering a remark of *lashon ha'ra.*" *Sparks of Mussar,* 11–12.

18. *Yevamot* 65b.

19. *Eruvin* 53b.

20. Zechariah 8:16.

21. Psalms/*Tehillim* 85:11.

22. *To Heal a Fractured World,* 156.

23. *Strive for Truth!,* vol. 1, p. 180.

CHAPTER 19

1. *B'rachot* 20b.

2. This is one of the sources for the tradition of breaking a glass at a Jewish wedding (*Tosafot* to *B'rachot* 21a).

3. The soul-trait of *miyut ta'anug*: "moderation of worldly pleasure.".

4. Genesis/*Bereshit* 28:20.

5. "I place before you life and death, blessing and curse. Choose life, that you may live" (Deuteronomy/*Devarim* 30:19).

6. Amos Oz, *Panther in the Basement,* trans. Nicholas de Lange (New York: Harvest, 1995), 100.

7. *The Path of the Just,* trans. Feldman, 119.

8. Israel Meir ha'Cohen, *Kuntras Sefat Tamim* (Jerusalem: Agudat Notsre Lashon, 2001), 5. This source is available in English in Rabbi Shimon Finkelman, *Chofetz Chaim: Lessons in Truth* (New York: Mesorah Publications, 2001).

9. Rosh Yeshiva of the Slabodka Yeshiva (1875–1952); in his foreword to *Cheshbon ha'Nefesh,* trans. Silverstein.

10. *Yoma* 76b.

11. Ascetic voices can be found in the Jewish tradition. *Pirkei Avot* 6:4, for example, says: "This is the way of the Torah: you shall eat bread with salt, drink a measurement of water, sleep on the ground, and live a life of pain." The mainstream has developed a virtual consensus, however, and is not in favor.

12. Numbers/*Bamidbar* 6:11.

13. Ibid.; "soul" here is the translation of the Hebrew *nefesh*.

14. *Nedarim* 10a.

15. *Ta'anit* 11a.

16. *Nedarim* 9:1.

17. This is the trait of "abstinence," or *p'rishut* in Hebrew. See chapters 13–15 of *The Path of the Just.*

18. *Shevil ha'zahav* in Hebrew.

19. *Hilchot De'ot* 3:1, 2.

20. Ibid.

21. *Kedushin* 66b.

22. *Ohr Yisrael,* 354.

CHAPTER 20

1. The phrase is from Micah 6:8.

2. The Alter of Slabodka.

3. Psalms/*Tehillim* 23:6.

4. *Pirkei Avot* 2:1.

5. Psalms/*Tehillim* 136.

6. Exodus/*Sh'mot* 34:6.

7. Jeremiah/*Yirmiyahu* 9:24.

8. Psalms/*Tehillim* 89:2.

9. The Chafetz Chaim wrote an entire book called *Ahavat Chesed* that focused mostly on the giving of money as an act of *chesed*.

10. As explained in his *Discourse on Lovingkindness* (*Kuntras ha'Chesed*), "Seventeen Chapters on Giving and Taking" in *Strive for Truth!*, vol. 1.

11. *Shabbat* 104a.

12. Genesis/*Bereshit* 18:6–7.

13. 1872–1970.

14. Deuteronomy/*Devarim* 13:5.

15. *Sotah* 14a.

16. Commentators understand God's appearance to Abraham at Mamre to be an example of visiting the sick, since in the previous verses, in Genesis/*Bereshit* 17, we read of Abraham's circumcision.

17. Mussar *va'ad* of June 25, 2003.

18. From *Me-Or Enayim*, trans. Rahel Halabe and Rabbi Arthur Green (Jerusalem: Me'ar Ha'sefarim, 1999). A commentary on Parshat Yitro.

19. The transcendent divine beyond form, known as *Ain Sof,* literally, "without end."

20. Exodus/*Sh'mot* 34:6–7.

21. *Rav chesed.*

22. Chapter 6.

23. "*Ki chafetz chesed hu,*" Micah 7:18.

24. *Chevrah kaddisha.*

25. *Pirkei Avot* 1:14.

CHAPTER 21

1. The phrase for this chapter is based on the Talmud, *Shevuot* 39a, where we read: "All Israel are guarantors one for the other."

2. In the same vein, some say: *acharit*—"end."

3. The words for "after" and "other" are identical in Hebrew, being spelled *aleph-chet-resh*. The only difference is the vowels, which are dots under the letters that are often omitted in written form.

4. *Pirkei Avot* 2:13.

5. *Bava Kamma* 26a.

6. That is, *olam ha'zeh* and *olam ha'ba* in Hebrew.

7. *Bava Kamma* 30a.

8. The principle known as *bein adam l'chavero.*

9. *Strive for Truth!*, vol. 2, p. 58.

10. *Gehinnom* (Gehenna).

11. *Eruvin* 19a.

12. "Letter 6" in *Ohr Yisrael.*

13. 1864–1935; first Ashkenazi Chief Rabbi of Israel.

14. *Ayn Aya,* vol. 3 (Jerusalem: Machon A. S. HaRav Tzvi Yehudah Kook, 1987), 157.

15. "Building Your Interior World," a talk delivered in the Bet Mussar, Jerusalem, May 9, 2001.

16. All quotes from *Chochmah u'Mussar* are from the translation by Rabbi Ira Stone in his forthcoming book, *A Responsible Life.*

17. Genesis/*Bereshit* 4:9.

18. Deuteronomy/*Devarim* 22:1–3.

19. Michael J. Broyde and Michael Hecht, *The Return of Lost Property According to Jewish and Common Law: A Comparison,* in *Jewish Law Articles,* www.jlaw.com.

20. Elie Wiesel, *Sages and Dreamers* (New York: Summit Books, 1991), 184.

21. 1885–1969.

22. *Musar for Moderns,* 34.

CHAPTER 22

1. Called *bitachon* in Hebrew.

2. 1194–c.1270. Also known as Nachmanides and Moshe ben Nahman Gerondi.

3. Quoted in Rabbi Sh'muel Houminer, *Faith and Trust* (Jerusalem: Quantum Press, 1994), 31.

4. From Shakespeare's *Hamlet.*

5. Psalms/*Tehillim* 2:12.

6. *The Duties of the Heart,* 178–79.

7. From Meir Levin, "The Paths of Bitachon," in *Novarodok: A Movement That Lived in Struggle and Its Unique Approach to the Problems of Man* (Northvale, N.J.: Jason Aronson, Inc., 1996), 83.

8. *The Path of the Just,* chapter 9, trans. Feldman.

9. Rabbi Avrahom Yeshaya Karelitz, the "Chazon Ish" (1878–1953), held no official positions and yet became known as a worldwide authority on all matters relating to Jewish law and life.

10. *Sefer Emunah u'Bitachon* (Book of Faith and Trust) (Tel Aviv: Gitler Brothers, 1944), 17.

11. Based on *Pele Yoetz* (entry on *De'aga*—worry). The *Pele Yoetz* is a classic Mussar text written by Rabbi Eliezer Papo (1785–1826).

12. See chapter 10 for the story to which this refers.

13. The Hebrew word for effort is *hishtadlut* or *hishtadlus.*

14. *The Mashgiach,* 191.

CHAPTER 23

1. The phrase is based on the Talmud, *Makkot* 24a.

2. Rav Abraham Isaac Kook, *Orot ha'Emunah* (Jerusalem: Mosad Harav Kook, 1985), 25.

3. *Sefer ha'Mitzvoth.*

4. If it didn't need footnote after footnote to explain almost every word, I could live with Rabbi Wolbe's definition: "Faith means a conviction of the heart that G-d is immediately present and that we are under His constant care" (ibid.).

5. *Pesachim* 118b.

6. Based on *Ohr Yisrael.*

7. Exodus/*Sh'mot* 14:30–15:19.

8. *V'ya'aminu.*

9. *Alei Shur,* vol. 2, 348.

10. In his discussion of the thirteen principles of faith, the first five deal with knowledge of God. Similarly, in *Hilchot Yesodei ha'Torah,* he describes the mitzvah of faith as knowledge and understanding.

11. Quoted in Rabbi Tzvi Freeman, *Bringing Heaven Down to Earth* (Avon, Mass.: Adams Media, 1999), 205.

12. This sort of anthropomorphic vision of God has its roots in the Torah, of course, which describes attributes of God like "face," "hand," "finger," etc. The Rambam wrote his entire *Guide for the Perplexed* to show that these anthropomorphic references have to be understood only as metaphors and nothing else.

13. *Lev Eliyahu,* 301.

14. From Rabbi Abraham Isaac Kook, "The Pangs of Cleansing," in *Abraham Isaac Kook,* trans. Ben Zion Bokser (New York: Paulist Press, 1978), 261–62.

15. *Lev Eliyahu,* 6.

16. Ibid., pp. 188–89.

17. Quoted in *Musar for Moderns,* 90.

18. *Ohr Yisrael,* 392, note 6.

19. Genesis/*Bereshit* 2:4.

20. Exodus/*Sh'mot* 31:17.

21. Psalms/*Tehillim* 27:8.

22. Deuteronomy/*Devarim* 4:29.

23. "*Haya lo ha'ratzon l'hitkarev l'emunah*"—Rabbi Dov Katz, *Tenuat ha'Mussar* (The Mussar Movement), vol. 2 (Tel Aviv: Avraham Tsiyoni, 1967), 106.

24. *Lev Eliyahu,* 3.

CHAPTER 24

1. Cited in Rabbi Yitzchak Blazer, "The Gates of Light," in *Ohr Yisrael,* 63.

2. Though the Rambam does a good job of mingling fear and awe, see *Mishneh Torah, Hilchot Yesod ha'Torah* 2:2.

3. Deuteronomy/*Devarim* 10:12.

4. *Orchot Tzaddikim*, 17. The translation uses the word *fear*. I have reverted to the Hebrew *yirah* in my quotation.

5. Rabbi Yisrael Salanter, *Iggeret ha'Mussar* (The Mussar Letter), in *Ohr Yisrael*, 393.

6. "The Gates of Light," 66.

7. *B'rachot* 33b.

8. *Shem Olam*, chap. 2 (Jerusalem: Ha'Mesorah, 1987).

9. "The Gates of Light," 64.

10. In his commentary on Parshat Yitro; quoted in "The Gates of Light," 64.

11. Personal communication.

12. *The Path of the Just*, trans. Feldman, 211.

13. Abraham Joshua Heschel, *God in Search of Man* (Northvale, N.J.: Jason Aronson, Inc., 1987), 74. Here and following I cite Rabbi Heschel, although I recognize that he is neither a teacher in the Mussar tradition nor universally embraced in the Jewish world. He does, however, write exceedingly movingly on the experiences of awe as the underpinning to faith, and so I quote him with just that in mind.

14. Psalms/*Tehillim* 111:10; Proverbs/*Mishlei* 9:10; see Proverbs/*Mishlei* 1:7 and 15:33; Ecclesiastes/*Kohelet* 12:13; *Sirach* 25:12–13; and *Pirkei Avot* 3:21:

> Where there is no wisdom, there is no awe;
> Where there is no awe, there is no wisdom.

15. Job/*Iyov* 28:28.

16. *Ayeh mekom kevodo?* (Where is the place of His glory?)

17. In the *kedusha* section of the Amidah for Shabbat *mussaf* prayers.

18. *Kevodo maley olam.*

19. Isaiah 6:3; incorporated into the morning liturgy just before the Sh'ma, again in the repetition of the Amidah, and again toward the end of the morning service.

20. *Kadosh, kadosh, kadosh, Adonai tzeva'ot; melo khol ha'aretz kevodo.*

21. Psalms/*Tehillim* 16:8: *shiviti Adonai l'negdi tamid.*

22. *Sanhedrin* 22a.

23. *Shiviti* paintings often also include Psalm 67 (*Lamenatzeach bin'ginot mizmor shir*—"For the director of music. With stringed instruments. A psalm. A song.") in the design of a menorah, along with the holy names of God.

24. *Duties of the Heart*, vol. 1, trans. David Haberman, 65.

25. *Shem Olam*, chapter 10.

26. *Shabbat* 15b.

27. Lived in Palestine in the fourth century C.E.

28. *Hilchot Berachot* 1:3.

29. *Ata Adonai.*

30. Ecclesiastes/*Kohelet* 12:13.
31. 1740–1810.

CHAPTER 26

1. *Or Yechezkel: Kovetz Inyanim, Elul* (Jerusalem: [publisher unknown], 1993), 26.
2. *Sanhedrin* 93b.
3. In his foreword to *Cheshbon ha'Nefesh,* trans. Silverstein, 5–6.
4. Proverbs/*Mishlei* 15:32.
5. Rabbi Yisrael Salanter variously called this stage *kevishah, kevishat ha'yetzer,* or *kevishat ha'middot.*
6. Proverbs/*Mishlei* 10:19.
7. Chapter 7.
8. Rabbi Luzzatto does use the word *nefesh* here. Rabbi Feldman translates as "incandescence" the Hebrew *telahet nafsho*—literally, "his glowing soul."
9. *Ohr Yisrael,* 232–33.
10. Rabbi M. M. Leffin, cited in Immanuel Etkes, *Rabbi Israel Salanter and the Mussar Movement* (Philadelphia and Jerusalem: Jewish Publication Society, 1993), 132.

CHAPTER 27

1. Newsletter of the Bais HaMussar, January 11, 2006 (no. 6).
2. *Cheshbon ha'nefesh* in Hebrew, the same phrase that gave the name to the book by Rabbi M. M. Leffin that I have quoted repeatedly.
3. 1898–1989; a scion of the Slabodka school of Mussar and Mussar supervisor of several yeshivas in Israel.
4. *The Mashgiach.*
5. Ibid., 628.
6. Rabbi Yerucham Levovitz, *mashgiach* of Mir, provides another model of how working on one trait can impact another one. He said that every person possesses one underlying trait that is perfect, and if you would be cognizant of your perfect trait and utilize it to its fullest, then that would be a great tool to employ on your journey toward wholeness. He uses truth as his example. If a child has done something wrong but has the strength of truth, then he or she will confess and start the process of rectification. Faced with a situation where laziness is hindering someone's work, this same trait of truth will compel that person to continue as best he can. A person who is not fond of doing acts of kindness will be prodded to help others by this quality of truth. "Over the course of time he will be able to rectify each and every one of his negative character traits" by calling on the strength of his master-trait. Imagine a person who is loose with truth but is ironclad-strong in his or her respect for other people's property.

In the Talmud, Shmuel says, "It is forbidden to deceive people." That's the conventional translation, which is accurate but which interprets away a useful teaching. His phrase—*asur lignov da'at ha'briyot*—literally translates as "to steal people's minds." It is forbidden to steal people's minds. "Stealing the mind" refers to the things we do to create a false impression with the intention of gaining some favor or benefit. It's a beautiful and powerful image that provides a very helpful slant on falsehood. Deceit is not just a distortion of the facts; it is actually a *theft*.

You may be quite used to being loose with truth, but how do you feel about stealing? If this teaching helps you to take a new look at falsehood as *theft*, and you have a strong, maybe unassailable, value of respect for property, then you can invoke your aversion to theft to restrain your tendency to lie. This text is based on the newsletter of the Bais HaMussar, January 11, 2006 (no. 6).

CHAPTER 28

1. These include books on the lives of Rabbi Yisrael Salanter, Rabbi Moshe Chaim Luzzatto, Rabbi Elyah Lopian, Rabbi Meir Chodosh, and others.

CHAPTER 29

1. Whom I will not identify to spare him embarrassment, but to whom I express my gratitude, as I do to the other learning partners whom I have studied with who have so enriched my life.

2. *Ohr Yisrael*, 183.

3. *Chitzonit mi'orrer pinimiut.*

4. From the same root that has given us the name Kabbalah, which refers to a Jewish mystical discipline. There is no connection between Mussar *kabbalot* and *Kabbalah* except that they share a linguistic root.

5. See chapter 17.

6. *Michtav mi'Eliyahu*, vol. 3, 127.

7. *Alei Shur*, vol. 2, chapter 5.

CONCLUSION

1. *Tam v'nishlam—Shevach l'El Borei Olam.*

2. Rabbi Judah Loew (1525-1609), *Tiferet Yisrael* [Israel's Glory] (New York: Talpiyot, 1953).

3. Of *teshuvah*.

4. Deuteronomy/*Devarim* 10:16, 30:6; Jeremiah 4:3-4.

5. *Shabbat* 104a.

6. *Lev Eliyahu*, 14.

7. *The Jewish Poets of Spain*, trans. David Goldstein (New York: Penguin, 1965), 173.

Index

desire. *See under* moderation; needing
Dessler, Eliyahu, 300n6
  on *bechirah*-points, 22–24, 263
  on giving and generosity, 157–58,
    188–89, 279
  on "giving and taking," 277
  humility, 51
  on material simplicity, 121
  on material world, 117–18
  order and, 87–89
  on positive and negative traits, 265
  on responsibility, 200
  on truth and one's heart, 163, 171
  visualizations, 33, 34
diary practices, 30, 31
disasters that are "blessings in disguise,"
  69–71
disorder. *See also* order
  image of, 91–92
  undermining, 94–96
distancing oneself from negative
  emotions, 104–5
Duties of the Heart (Pakuda), 29, 34, 46,
  67, 112, 224, 233, 242
dying, 217

ego, 17, 50, 83, 110, 111, 154, 205, 206. *See
  also* arrogance; honor; humility;
  pride
  role of, 17
  well-situated, 53–54
Egypt, Jewish slavery in, 83. *See also*
  Moses
Elazar, Shimon ben, 95–96
Eliezer of Dzikov, 27, 114
Elijah, 71, 148–49
Elijah of Vilna. *See* Vilna Ga'on
Elyah, Reb. *See* Lopian, Eliyahu
emotions, 32. *See also* negative emo-

tions; *specific* emotions
empathy, 76, 77, 81. *See also* identity with
  the other
enthusiasm, 125–28, 256
  aspects of, 128
  how to cultivate, 135–38
  laziness subverts, 129–30
  worrying vs., 133–35
equanimity, 98–99, 274–75
  beckoning by the light and, 105–6
  calmness of the soul, 100–101, 103–4,
    274
  distancing oneself and, 104–5
  human nature and, 99–100
  independent soul and, 103–4
  tests of, 101–3
eternity, 33. *See also* World-to-Come
eved HaShem. See God, being a servant
  of
evil. *See also* sin
  inclination to, 176, 181–83 (*see also*
    yetzer ha'ra)
Ezekiel, 85
Ezra, Moshe ibn, 18, 289

faith, 220–22
  belief and, 222–23
  defining, 221
  experience and, 227–28
  growing in, 228–31
  trust and, 210
fast of silence, 145–46
fear. *See* anxiety; punishment,
  fear/threat of; trust; *yirah*
Finkel, Noson Tzvi (Alter of Slabodka),
  9, 18, 84
forgiveness, 42
Frand, Yissocher, 200
free will, 23, 60, 291. *See also* choice

About the Author

ALAN MORINIS is an anthropologist, filmmaker, writer, and student of spiritual traditions. Born and raised in a culturally Jewish but nonobservant home, he trained as an anthropologist at Oxford University, where, on a Rhodes scholarship, he completed his doctorate on the Hindu tradition of pilgrimage. This work was published by Oxford University Press as *Pilgrimage in the Hindu Tradition.* It was followed by three edited volumes on pilgrimages and, in 1998, by a television documentary on the Hardwar Kumbh Mela in India that attracted ten million people to bathe in the Ganges River. He has also produced many other films, including feature films, television dramas, and documentaries. He has taught at several universities, including the University of British Columbia and Simon Fraser University.

His book *Climbing Jacob's Ladder,* which *Spirituality & Health* voted book of the year, tells the inward story of his discovery of Mussar and the way it transformed his life. He is now one of the foremost contemporary interpreters of the teachings and practices of the Mussar tradition for the general public, to whom he regularly gives lectures and workshops. He has founded the Mussar Institute (www.mussarinstitute.org), which offers courses and programs of many kinds.

Alan Morinis is married to Dr. Beverly Spring, with whom he has two daughters, Julia and Leora.